Reign In Hope

*An inspirational story of a lost girl who falls into the
arms of Hope in the midst of heartbreak.*

Lee Ann Monty

DEDICATION

This book is lovingly dedicated to…

My Lord and Savior Jesus Christ~my Redeemer

Max, Zachariah, Joshua, Micah, and Tylee~my Loves

ISBN: 978-1-949513-16-5

Email- info@leeannmonty.com
Website- www.leeannmonty.com

Front Cover image by Andrey_l

This is a work of creative nonfiction. The events are portrayed
to the best of my memory. While all stories in this book are true,
some names and identifying details have been changed to protect
the privacy of the people involved. The conversations in the book
all come from my recollections, though they are not written to
represent word-for-word transcripts.

Table Of Contents

ACKNOWLEDGEMENTS

The words 'thank-you' cannot adequately convey my deep love, respect and admiration for the following special people who have played an instrumental role in my life. You have each touched a place in my heart where your fingerprints are indelible.

To my Jesus: my redeemer, my savior, my Lord, and my comforter-in you I have everything. You paid a debt you did not owe. I owed a debt I could never pay. Thank you for your ever-lasting love that anchors my soul. I hear the voice of my Shepherd. I will follow you all the days of my life.

To my beloved Max: I love you with my whole heart. Thank you that your love never runs out on me. You are my courage when I'm afraid, my strength when I can't hold on and the one who holds my heart forever and for always.

To my children Zach, Josh, Micah and Tylee: you are the only four to ever call me mommy. You have each changed me for the better and taught me more about love than I could ever teach you. No matter how vast the distance of separation between us (how far away is heaven?) we will ALWAYS be a party of six. I love you, my precious ones.

To my dad: did you ever know that you're my hero? Your love was unconditional. Thank you for saying 'yes' to being my father. You taught me what to look for in a husband but I will always be daddy's girl. I miss your wisdom and your music. I miss you...

To my beautiful mom: when you get the choice to sit it out or dance...I hope you dance. You have walked with me through every season. Thank you for never giving up on me. Your love and prayers have always covered me. Thank you for allowing me to freely share this book with the world. I love you.

To my sisters: God has given me a beautiful gift of three sisters, and I'm thankful for each one of you. Our lives have been knit together by our Heavenly Father. I love you all. Thank you for releasing me to write my story.

To Dan: our childhood years have linked us for always; our shared laughter will echo for all eternity. When God blessed me with you, he gave me a best friend for life.

To Jamie: thank you for helping me tell my story to the world. Your encouragement and reassurance is a gift I shall never forget.

To Divya: you made me believe I could write a book and helped me bring it to fruition. This simply would not have happened without your loving guidance, wisdom and support. Thank you from the bottom of my heart.

A WORD FROM THE AUTHOR

This book has been written from my heart to yours. While all the incidents are true, some of the particular details, dates, conversations, and situations have been slightly altered for legal and safety concerns. Some individual's names and identifying characteristics have been changed to protect their privacy. All events are portrayed with brutal honesty to the best of my recollection.

To all my friends and family that I hold so dear: many of you will be learning of the dysfunction and complexity of my past for the very first time. I pray that you would read these words through the lens of love without judgement or condemnation. If you ever feel lost or alone like I have at times, please reach out to someone you trust. I believe that life is meant to be shared.

INTRODUCTION

No one wants to write a book about loss, brokenness, hardship, and the emotional baggage associated with them. My guess is no one wants a reason to read a book about those circumstances, either. But sooner or later, we all find ourselves touched by the cruel fingers of despair, no matter the cause. Ominously, hopelessness creeps up while we are making our best attempts at traveling this road called life.

I have not been spared from hardship. I have met up with grief uninvited. Challenging is the word to describe parts of my life, some of which I will share on the pages of this book. I've found that although we all go through difficulties and experience similar trials, no two stories are alike. There is something to be learned from one another. Every story matters: if we are willing to share our struggles and invite others to really see us up close. If we allow ourselves to be vulnerable and transparent in our pain, we can be a light in someone else's darkness. Many burdens are too heavy for us to carry alone. Life is meant to be shared.

I implore you to open your heart to those around you, no matter the season and whether times are good or bad. We must love, encourage, and support those whom God has placed in our path. My sincere prayer is that, as you read parts of my story, you will feel me leaning into your pain. You are not alone, as I am writing these words, especially for you.

There is so much to tell about my journey and how I ended up where I am today. I will freely share as much as I can on these pages. Will you come with me as I take you on a journey of tragedy and triumph, sadness and happiness, grief and joy, and loss and life? Are you willing to look at my pain up close and see if there are parts of my story that feel familiar to you?

When I was muddling through the dark and living out the details that have made up my life, I did not have the knowledge and experience I do today. Back then, I simply didn't know what I didn't know. And no one could have prepared me for both the unfathomable joy and the unimaginable pain that would make up the story of my life, which I have tried to live bravely thus far.

Today, I open my heart, bear my soul, and fearlessly put the most vulnerable parts of me on display for you to read. Tears of joy and pain intermingled with HOPE will tell the stories of faith and love. Take my hand and walk with me through the valleys of my deepest sorrows and unthinkable brokenness.

PART 1

FALL FROM GRACE

"When one's lost, I suppose it's good advice to stay where you are, until someone finds you. But who'd ever think to look for me here?"- Lewis Carroll~"Alice" in Alice in Wonderland

Seeds of doubt, fear, and despair grow best in the fertile ground of our most significant trials and tribulations. Once planted, the root system is quickly established, thus anchoring our hurting souls to hopelessness and grief. These unwanted seeds multiply effortlessly and thrive in the murky shadows void of light. Only direct exposure to "The Son," along with diligence in prayer, will choke out the tightly bound roots, freeing our hearts to soar and enabling us to *reign in hope*.

Chapter 1

MY SECRET GARDEN

In my dreams, I could be a Princess, and that's
what I was… ~Loretta Young

Max and I were newlyweds when we made the long trek across the miles back to our home state of Oklahoma from the sunny California coast. Our young marriage had already traveled across rocky terrain. It survived, but there existed some dirty little secrets buried beneath the proliferous soil which held our future. If these secrets ever surfaced if they were ever exposed our marriage may not survive.

I was not a skilled gardener, but the expertise would not be in the nurturing or growing; the mastery would be in hiding, keeping the deceit and lies from rearing their ugliness for my husband and the world to see. I must keep the seedlings of betrayal hidden and buried; I must keep them from finding the light and revealing the truth.

The youthful twenty-year-old girl who arrived in Oceanside, California, two years earlier, was not the same girl who was leaving this beachfront city. I was wounded before, but now I was broken. I was struck down before, but now I was nearly destroyed. I learned truths I could never unlearn and saw things I could never unsee.

Unfortunately, there is no way back to innocence. I was no longer naïve; I was now jaded and tainted as darkness settled even deeper into my soul. Life had already taught me some unbearably, cruel lessons.

That day, the goodbyes were bitter and sweet. My close friend, Jennifer, hugged me tightly as salty tears streamed down our faces. We met a few months after I moved to Oceanside. The two of us had been through so much together, and I loved her like a sister. Our friendship ran as deep as the sapphire ocean, where we had spent so much time together.

Jennifer knew the secrets I would be taking with me, and she was harboring the same ones. I could scarcely bear the thought of leaving her there, next to her little girl, knowing she was trapped in a lifestyle I was fortunate enough to leave behind.

After Jennifer and I tearfully said goodbye, I wiped the tears from my eyes, took a deep breath, and looked around one last time at the small apartment Max, and I had called home…the place where we adjusted to married life, learned how to depend on one another, learned how to stay together when we wanted to give up and survived what most young couples wouldn't.

As we drove away, I noticed a queasiness in my stomach. I quickly dismissed the discomfort, thinking it was just sadness mixed with nerves and excitement. I desperately needed to leave California. Max and I were ready for a new beginning. His next duty station would be at the main Headquarters Marine Corps Recruiting Station. His office was going to be on the sixth floor of the Alfred P. Murrah Federal Building in downtown Oklahoma City. That building would no longer be standing nine months later.

Once we got settled in the car, Max reached over and gently curled his fingers around mine. Gazing out the window, lost somewhere deep in my own head, my thoughts drifted back to a time long ago.

Let me take you back. I was four years old. My dad had been overseeing the building of our new house for over a year. He couldn't wait to bring my mother, my sisters, and me to see the nearly ready house that would become our new home. The finishing touches were yet to be made, but the enormous house was brimming with possibilities! Everyone was so excited to see it for the very first time.

My dad held my small hand in his and led me from the car to the oversized, glass-plated front door. In my other hand, I kept my well-loved, favorite baby doll whom I had affectionately named Bananas. I called her Bananas because when she was brand new, she was wearing a sunshine-yellow dress. Bananas was my personal version of "The Velveteen Rabbit."

The house was huge and empty; the new furniture had yet to be delivered. For my room, my mother selected a beautiful antique-looking white canopy bed with a matching dresser and nightstand. My soon-to-be room had a built-in desk and bookshelves that would eventually hold all my childhood treasures. An exceptionally large second-story window overlooked the rectangular-shaped swimming pool in the backyard. My dad led us throughout the entire house, excitedly sharing the plans he and my mother had for every room.

After the tour, everyone went off to explore the house on their own. I wanted to spend more time in my new room. Holding tightly onto the polished wooden handrail, I cautiously climbed the newly carpeted stairs, counting each step. I was excited to have my very own room, which was situated nearest to my parent's bedroom at the very end of a long hallway. It was connected to one of my sister's bedrooms by a pink Jack-and-Jill bathroom, complete with pink toilet, pink tub, double pink sinks, and wallpaper adorned with pink roses.

Standing in my room while gazing up at the sparkling crystal-like beads dangling from the chandelier, I already felt like a princess. I squealed with delight as I excitedly held Bananas high in the air, twirling her around in circles, leaving my tiny footprints in the white shag carpet. In my new room that day, my imagination soared as I showed Bananas her cradle and told her how much she would love her new home.

Move-in day finally arrived! I was so happy to get all my "babies" settled into their cradles. Our new home had a large playroom that was set up to look like a real house. I spent countless hours playing house with my dolls, pretending to be their mother.

While my world of pretend and imaginary friends was perfect, the reality of my world was not.

My earliest memories were riddled with fear. I was so small sitting on his lap. He said we should play a game on the floor. I sat criss-cross applesauce on the floor between his legs, which were stretched out in a large V. I didn't know how to play this game, but he said he'd teach me. I hadn't yet gone to Kindergarten, so I didn't know much at all about life. I couldn't even read or write.

I can recall the aroma of fried okra cooking in the nearby kitchen. It was summer. I was wearing a lavender and yellow swing top with tulips on it; it was open in the back and tied around my neck, and it had bright yellow bloomers to match. His rough, calloused hands wrapped all the way around my waist. I didn't like how his scratchy hands felt on my skin. Then, his fingers found their way inside my sunshine-yellow bloomers.

A rapid, terror-filled reaction jolted me, and I jumped up and ran away. I didn't want to stay at their house for dinner. I couldn't find my doll…where was my doll? I frantically searched and finally found Bananas crumpled up where I left her. I picked her up and held her tight against my chest. She was flawed, ugly, and naked. I lost her clothes a long time ago. I tried to fix it by scribbling a new dress on her with my markers, and I had cut her hair. I loved this ugly doll, for she was my earliest companion. I felt ugly and dumb like her…we were best friends.

Chapter 2

DAYDREAMS AND NIGHTMARES

It's never too late to have a happy childhood~Tom Robbins

Not long after we moved into the new house, I started school. I didn't like going to school; I wanted to be home with Bananas and my mom. I felt insecure, inadequate, and vulnerable on my own, so school felt big and frightening. It was torture for me to leave my dolls and my mom. Fear gripped me, and I wondered what Mom did all day while I attended Kindergarten. What if something terrible happened to my parents while I was in school? What if I became an orphan? I thought about my dollies throughout the day and couldn't wait to get back home. After school, I rushed to my playroom, and exuberantly announced, "Mommy's home!" I spent every free moment in my pretend world, where everything was perfect for my dollies and me.

Each night, my mother called me out of my fantasy land playroom. I begged for more time, so I could rock each of my dollies to sleep. After I had tucked them all in for the night, I would take Bananas with me into my bedroom. Her pink and white cradle with tiny mauve roses sat right next to my bed, now adorned with a delicate pink-ruffled bedspread and matching canopy with sheer curtains tied back with soft satin bows.

While drifting off to sleep in my canopy bed, I imagined the day when I would be someone's bride. In my dream, I would hold on to my dad's arm and wear a stunning white wedding gown. My dress, embellished with lace and pearls, would have a long train that would go all the way down the aisle and reach to the back of the church. With "Here Comes the Bride" playing in the background, my daddy would proudly walk me down the aisle and give me to a loving husband who would cherish me forever. I could easily envision this moment because I had rehearsed it plenty of times in my mind, and I secretly practiced it on "Daddy Date Night."

Daddy Date Night was so special. This was the night every year when little girls in my town would don their most beautiful dresses and be escorted to a fairytale ball by their daddy or granddaddy. My dad put on his navy-blue suit and his brightly polished white loafers. We drove to the "ball," and he escorted me inside. I danced with my daddy for hours. I liked it even better than Christmas!

I rehearsed this dream of my wedding day so many times, and each time, it was the same way. I knew absolutely nothing about sex or how babies were made. Still, in my dream, shortly after the wedding, I imagined babies would start to arrive. I would then become the mother of real baby girls! Somehow it never occurred to me at this tender age that I may give birth to a boy.

When I wasn't playing with my dolls, I was at my mother's dressing table, pretending to be her. I spent hours with her in her oversized bathroom with a giant sunken tub and huge walk-in closets. Her mirrored vanity seemed to go on forever. In her bathroom, any A-list Hollywood movie star would feel right at home.

I studied my mother carefully while she performed her beauty routine--at least on the days, she wasn't too depressed to get up and face the world. I observed her carefully so I could learn how to make myself look beautiful. She and I would primp in the mirror for hours, and she would let me put on her eyeshadow, lipstick, rouge, and perfume. But when I looked in the mirror with way too much makeup and dark red lipstick, I felt ugly and stupid like my lifeless Raggedy Ann doll.

My mother and her beauty were alluring--she was gorgeous, and she knew it. She could transform herself into an exquisite enchantress in under an hour. Her brown eyes sparkled beneath frosty, baby blue eyeshadow. She wore lots of mascara, and her jet-black eyeliner was finished to perfection with an elegant upward curl. Then she would light a cigarette and seductively blow a steady stream of grey smoke from her pouty red lips, lightly glistening with shimmery gloss.

I emulated her every move. I "smoked" crayons, licorice, and candy cigarettes. When she wasn't looking, I tried to light and smoke the cigarette butts she had left in the ashtray. I pretended it was my red lipstick left behind on the filters. I played dress up in her gowns and lingerie. I tried to look and act sexy in the full-length mirror, but I quickly grew discouraged when my skinny legs wobbled on her high heels. To me, my mother was perfect. She was posh and pampered, just like I wanted to be.

My dad was my biggest hero, yet he was someone I feared. His temper was unpredictable, and we didn't know what may set him off or when he might explode. The enormity and unpredictability of his volatile outbursts kept the entire family on edge. I shook and trembled under the weight of his anger. Red-faced and screaming while cursing and spewing hurtful, harsh, and angry words, he raged until he was hoarse. Then he would retreat to the basement or his office, and we would not see him for several days. My mother would lock herself in her bedroom, take too much medication, and then sleep for days on end.

During these frequent episodes, I spent my time going back and forth between them, trying my hardest to take care of them. I lived with sickening fear of finding my mother overdosed or my father dead from one of the many guns in the house. I always checked to make sure they were both still alive. A subtle whisper deep inside told me that somehow their problems were my fault. I had an unrelenting feeling I did not belong... something was wrong with me.

I didn't understand any of it at the time. I was the youngest and always seemed to be front and center of it all. In fact, during one sudden, heated argument between my parents, I sat helplessly caught in the middle, not knowing whether to leave or stay. I was afraid to move, so I sat quietly, shivering, and crying on the hearth of the fireplace. My dad's angry gaze turned to me, and he yelled, "What do you think this is a god-damned sideshow?!" Terrified, I just sat frozen in place until he yelled, "Get the hell outta here!!" I ran from the room crying. When I could find no one in the house to comfort me, I ran from bathroom to bathroom, flushing toilets while crying and screaming, "Stop fighting!" My voice was completely drowned out by the anger raging through our home, ripping any peace, comfort, and security from my grasp.

Over the years, I witnessed the two people I loved most constantly inflicting pain upon pain and sorrow upon sorrow on one another. I saw it all, for my little eyes and ears could not hide from the chaos swirling fiercely throughout the walls of the mansion my family called home. What the innocence of childhood kept me from comprehending at the time, I now fully understand as an adult. What seemed to be unprovoked and sudden outbursts of rage against my unsuspecting mother was really not that at all. There was plenty of smoke, lots of mirrors, and total unfaithfulness covered by her beauty and tainted with her lies.

As you can see, my childhood was filled with the highest of highs and the very lowest of lows. When I spent time alone with either of my parents, it was beautiful. My dad was a loving, caring, and devoted father who would give me all the happiness in the world and bend over backward to do it. Residing under years of deep hurt going back to his childhood was a kind and generous yet profoundly wounded man. Hurting people hurt people--that's how it is, and that's how it was. Separately, both my mother and father were stable, but together, they were toxic.

I was raised inhaling the noxious fumes of volatile anger and ingesting a slow poison that steadily did its damage, eroding my emotional wellbeing, and draining all hope of normal existence.

Chapter 3

KINDRED SPIRIT

Friendship is born at that moment when one person says to another: 'What! You too? I thought I was the only one.'
~C.S. Lewis

As far back into my childhood as I can remember, anxiety and panic attacks plagued me. I was terrified of men, monsters, the devil, death, and storms. I was afraid of being alone, my parents fighting, the rapture coming (and me being left behind), someone hurting my family or me, and being kidnapped the list goes on and on. I had terrible nightmares and woke up frozen in fear more nights than I can count. I was afraid to move, but the thought of staying in my room alone forced me into swift action. I would cry out for my dad to come get me. Most of the time, he would hear my screams, come get me, and carry me into my parent's room.

On nights when my dad didn't respond to my cries, I would jump from the bed as far as I could and run into my parent's room. I remember thinking there were demons or monsters under my bed, and they would grab my legs if I got out of bed. I couldn't fall asleep alone, and I always begged to sleep with my parents or one of my older sisters. The nightmares continued for years. I don't remember when they stopped, but I know I was a seasoned adult when I finally overcame them.

In first grade, I became friends with Danika. I am so grateful we are still friends today. Both of our childhoods were dysfunctional, and we muddled through the chaos together. I remember the first time she spent the night at my house. I was so excited to have a friend sleepover, and I looked forward to having someone in my room with me that night. However, I dreaded the thought of my parents getting into a fight and ruining our sleepover because when my dad got angry, the entire house knew it.

Sure enough, my parents got into a huge argument. I tried to drown out the cursing and shouting by turning up the music on my light-up stereo, but it didn't help. Humiliated and scared, I sunk into my oversized bean-bag chair, put my face in my hands, and began to cry. Danika put down the doll she was playing with and sweetly scooted closer. She gently put her hand on my back and said, "Don't cry, Lee...the same thing happens at my house when my parents fight." I looked up at her, saw the kindness in her eyes, and recognized a kindred spirit.

From then on, I knew Danika understood. I wanted her to be my best friend forever. I was safe with her. Together, we learned to cope with our dysfunctional lives through creative play. She loved her dolls as much as I loved mine. Danika began to spend more and more time at my house. My sisters were all quite a bit older than me and were already dating and driving, so they were not much company to me.

My friendship with Danika blossomed, and I quickly became overly attached to her. I now recognize our friendship progressed into an unhealthy codependency. Though I didn't realize it until later, a propensity towards codependency developed, and patterns formed from early childhood that I would battle for years and years. I cried and panicked when she spent a few days at her own house. I missed her terribly when she was not with me, and I resented her having other friends. I selfishly wanted her all to myself. I needed her, for she was a companion and a comfort, and I was closer to her than my sisters.

Looking back, I see how God has always taken care of me. I believe Danika was one of the ways He provided what I needed to help soothe my insecurities. She needed me, too. Her stories are hers to tell, but I know she would agree we survived our childhoods and adolescent years hand in hand, depending on each other for love, laughter, and security.

As we grew in age, our friendship never wavered. Sure, we had arguments and fought like sisters through the years. Still, we always had unconditional love and forgiveness for one another. Together, we grew up way too fast and learned adult matters before we were mature enough to handle them. We started smoking cigarettes around nine years old and started sneaking the family cars out to go for quick joy rides when we could get away with it.

Danika and I were already wild, bold, and daring, but together, we became braver. We were both the youngest in our families and had older siblings, who we watched and imitated. Soon, our innocence began to slip away. At only twelve or thirteen years old, we started "dating" high school boys. You may be thinking...*What in the world would high school boys want with little girls*? That's the same question I would pose now, but at that age, we thought we were grown. We wanted to prove we could run with the high school crowd, so we started drinking, dressing inappropriately, and cussing to sound cool.

Our parents loved us and did the best they could, but there were issues in both of our families, and they had their battles to fight. Danika and I were on our own to figure life out. And no doubt there were plenty of older "teachers" willing to school us on "all things adult." We began experimenting with all kinds of alcohol. I smoked my first marijuana joint the summer between sixth and seventh grade.

From Kindergarten through grade school, I felt very awkward and insecure. I desperately wanted to be liked and noticed. I was boy crazy and curious. I had kissed four boys by the end of sixth grade and had only gone steady once. By the end of seventh grade, I had done a lot more than kiss.

Danika and I behaved and dressed more mature than we were mentally or physically ready for. Still, physically, we looked older than we were. As young girls commonly do, we misunderstood the attention we received from older guys. To them, we were something to take advantage of, which to us looked like affection and maybe even the love and acceptance we both desperately craved.

Chapter 4

INNOCENCE LOST

My words lose their voice when innocence is lost
~Deepa Julian

Summer was my favorite time of the year. As a young teenager, I looked forward to the hot, sunny days. Lazily hanging out by the pool with my besties was a daily occurrence. We slathered our slender, shapely bodies with massive amounts of baby oil and sipped on cold sodas, sometimes spiked with Jack Daniels, or homemade Jungle Juice, also called Cowboy Kool-Aid and made with Everclear. We could easily get by with drinking Everclear a 190 proof alcoholic drink because Everclear is colorless and virtually tasteless. Even when mixed with grape Kool-Aid, it just looks like Kool-Aid, a harmless kid's beverage. We roasted ourselves to a golden tan under the hot Oklahoma sun. We talked about boys, shared who had done what with whom, and dreamed of a life of bliss where nothing was wrong, and everything was right.

After a long day of sunbathing and drinking, we would shower, tease our hair, and put on tons of makeup, hairspray, and too much perfume. We slipped into the shortest shorts and half-shirts we could find. Showing off our curvy figures and suntans were priority number one. It was always easy to find older guys to supply plenty of beer, cigarettes, and drugs if we wanted. It was not uncommon to be spending those endless summer nights in the company of much older males.

My first real boyfriend happened when I was thirteen—and he was eighteen, a senior in high school. When you're young and naive, you believe anything a cute older guy tells you. When you have little experience in life and very little parental supervision, you get into situations way over your head, and you find yourself in trouble.

Before too long that eighteen-year old boy broke my tender, junior-high heart...but not before teaching me way more than I wanted to know. Today I know it was sexual abuse, but at my tender age, it looked and felt like love. It wasn't long until I was dating the next boy, with each guy along the way taking advantage and taking another tiny piece of me. My innocence slipped away, leaving me even more broken and disillusioned.

Even though some of my friends were "going all the way," *I was not.* My sister became pregnant at the age of fifteen when I was only ten years old. I remember my parents yelling at her and trying to force her to get an abortion, which is how I found out about her predicament. I spent most of that night sitting on the basement stairs, crying for my poor sister who was trying to defend herself and her unborn baby.

My sister's pregnancy made a vast and unforgettable impact on me. I vowed that night I would not be "going all the way," and there was no way I was getting pregnant! I didn't really understand it all at the time. Though when I started messing around sexually a few years later and ended up naked in the swimming pool with a sexually-excited eighteen-year-old, I put two and two together and quickly figured it out.

When I arrived at school the next morning with eyes swollen from tears and no sleep, I pulled Danika into the restroom. I carefully checked under the stalls to make sure no one was there who could hear this horrible secret that soon the entire town would be gossiping about.

Once I understood where babies come from, it started making sense. I remembered learning in Sunday School about the Virgin Mary and that girls should keep their virginity until marriage. I then realized why I had been told as a little girl to "keep my legs closed" and "protect" my virginity. It now made sense...it wasn't because God might choose me for the next immaculate conception, but because sex makes babies.

For whatever reason, even in all my dysfunction, it was imperative for me to keep my virginity intact, officially keeping myself sexually pure. Looking back, I realize now I was not actually keeping myself *pure*, but at that time, I thought if I didn't let a boy down my pants, then I believed I was still sexually pure.

I didn't learn until much later that sex is a beautiful union between a man and a woman when covered under the sanctity of marriage.

In my early teens, I had been on the verge of intercourse many times and had been educated about all the other ways you can have sex without *officially* having sex. The confusing part at the time was figuring out what "counts" and what doesn't. My girlfriends and I would have many discussions about what activities were okay to do and which ones would make you a slut.

I did *not* want to be a slut, but I did want to have a boyfriend, and it just had to be an older guy to be cool. But older guys expected stuff. When you are inexperienced, and you don't know what is even happening until it is happening, it's hard to decide when it's too far—especially when you have a horny, hormone-raging boy trying to go down your pants.

So, after the first two or three "relationships," I considered myself experienced and made some decisions about what was too far. I figured out quickly that a hand in my pants was beyond my comfort zone. I can't remember what all the official "bases" meant back then, but I think a boy going down your pants was considered third base. I was NOT into baseball!

I decided never to let myself get in that situation again. I had been lucky so far and had been able to keep my virginity by avoiding intercourse officially.. It worked fine with the younger high school guys because they were mostly inexperienced and respectful when my limits were reached. It was the older high school guys and men beyond high school who presented bigger challenges.

After the second boy broke my heart, the girl he left me for became pregnant at fourteen. After that, even though I had many boyfriends, I never had the desire to give myself completely to anyone. I still believed in my childhood dream. I was waiting for Mr. Right and wanted to give my virginity to him.

Unfortunately, there was a twenty-four-year-old predator who moved to town. I quickly became the object of his obsession. I can't stand to speak his name, so I'll call him JB.

Chapter 5

BROKEN WINGS

S he made broken look beautiful and strong look invincible. She walked with the Universe on her shoulders and made it look like a pair of wings~Ariana

JB's family was financially well-off, and they had recently purchased a business in my hometown. JB was friendly, outgoing, impeccably dressed, and good-looking. There were several houses for rent on my dad's property, and JB made a great first impression with my dad when they met to discuss the possibility of him renting the house. Not realizing JB had designs on his Freshman daughter, my dad went ahead and rented to JB. I liked JB at first, but there was just something about him that made me feel slightly uncomfortable. He had a beautiful smile and always smelled good, but I wasn't really romantically interested in him.

Shortly before JB moved to town, I had been messing around (unknown to my parents) with a man who was thirty-four years old, more than twice my age. Brett's wife had recently passed away in a car crash, leaving him grief-stricken and raising their young daughter alone. Brett was handsome and had plenty of oil money, and he had a nice house in the country with a hot tub and lots of alcohol readily available in his fully stocked bar. I had known him most of my life. My parents and Brett's parents had been friends for years. It was obvious he was interested in me.

I knew this because Brett looked at me the same way his father always looked at my mother. One day, when I was about seven or eight years old, I walked in to find Brett's dad on top of my mother. I had observed men's attraction to my mother all my life. I knew "that look," the way a man behaves when he is sexually attracted to a woman.

My friends, though, talked me into acting interested in Brett so he would buy us alcohol and let us party at his house. I wanted to party as much as they did, so I agreed to take one for the team and put up with his overly-handsy, horny behavior for a few months. A few of my friends would sneak out of town to Brett's house in the country for all-night parties. However, after several months, I was over it and ready to be free of him. The parties were not fun for me because he was always trying to get me to have sex with him.

Brett was attractive in a Tom Selleck kind of way, but I was not about to lose my virginity to a man in his thirties sporting a mustache! Every single time we were in the hot tub, my bikini top would mysteriously come untied. I didn't notice it right away because the bubbles were vigorous, and I always had a few too many. Soon, Brett was not satisfied with my boundaries; he was used to mature sexual relationships. He was a grown man--an adult. But I wasn't.

I grew very tired of defending my virginity with Brett, so when JB asked me out, I gladly accepted. It was a win-win; I could ditch the hot tub guy without losing the benefits of getting free alcohol, cigs, and drugs for my friends and me! JB gladly met my every request. He became friendly with my dad, and he would come over and have a drink or two and talk about the oil and gas business with my parents. He offered to help me with Algebra because I was failing, and he was good at math. JB easily earned the freedom to stop by whenever. He was welcome to come over to my house with my parent's approval because he was my "tutor," and they thought he was an alright guy.

I trusted JB, but I do remember having an uneasy feeling when he was around. It was like an instinctual warning light would blink when he got close. The way his eyes undressed me was creepy. The way he leaned in unnecessarily close to help me solve an equation. The way I frequently caught him looking down my shirt. The way he touched my thighs underneath the kitchen table. He had not attempted to kiss me, but there was never any doubt he wanted to.

I started to notice him watching me frequently--and with a new intensity. He lived next door, so whenever I went outside, he would come out. I remember one day I was laying out suntanning by myself, and no one else was home. I had a feeling like someone was there, and when I opened my eyes, he was standing over me just looking at me. He said some words about how sexy I looked laying there and how he imagined I would look without my bathing suit. Honestly, it bothered me, but I was used to the opposite sex, even much older men, saying sexually suggestive and inappropriate words to me. It happened all the time, as even some of my dad's friends would stare at me, looking me over with a hungry, longing gaze.

Something I had learned from my mother at a young age was to use my beauty to my advantage. So, I brushed JB's advances off as he handed me a cold beer and pulled up a chair. He scooted closer and offered to put suntan lotion on my back. I rolled over and let him rub my back, the whole time wondering why I let him when it felt so uncomfortable.

Incidents like this happened frequently. But I was naïve, so I did not tell my parents or anyone else how uneasy he made me feel. Because he lived right next door, there were a lot of perfectly timed "coincidences." I never knew when I would turn around and he would be there.

Chapter 6

TAKEN

The trust of the innocent is the liar's most useful tool
~Stephen King

One day, he came over and asked my parents if he could take me out to dinner and a movie in a nearby town with a movie theater, about forty miles away. He told them how well I was doing in Algebra and that he would like to celebrate my progress. He promised to have me home by midnight, and since my parents felt comfortable with him, they said yes. I remember not wanting to go but feeling obligated because he had been helpful around the property, he had helped me with my homework, and most importantly, I was passing algebra...so what would it hurt?

However, an uneasy feeling crept up, refusing to be ignored as I was getting ready. I brushed it off, thinking it was just my anxiety rearing up. I thought I would just drink a few beers, and it would go away (of course, my parents did not know JB ever gave me alcohol or pot). The night of the "date," he walked up to our front door like a gentleman to pick me up.

I noticed as soon as I got into his brand-new Chevy pick-up that he had too much cologne on, but otherwise, he looked nice and seemed relaxed and in an excellent mood. I had been alone with him before when he was helping me with homework or when we were sitting outside, but I had never been in his vehicle. As soon as we got to the end of my driveway, he reached behind the seat and pulled out a six-pack of Coors Light. "Texas beer, stronger alcohol content," he said and winked as he cracked one open and handed it to me. I took the ice-cold beer from his hand as we pulled onto the road.

A few minutes later, I noticed he turned in the opposite direction from the town with the movie theater it was the other way. I felt uncomfortable, but again just thought it was my usual anxiety. I tipped the can up and took a few big swigs of the icy beer. I asked why we were going the wrong way, and he said there was something he had wanted to show me. He said he was thinking of purchasing some land and wanted to get my opinion.

I was flattered and thought that was a kind of grown-up thing to say, but after all, he was an adult and could afford to buy whatever he wanted. He was always flashing $100 bills and talking about all the trips we could take. I was thinking *"Like yeah, man, when I grow up, that would be great, but I can't even LEGALLY drive yet!"* Except I *had* been driving since I was nine years old. My dad had already purchased a brand new, fully loaded Nissan 300ZX Turbo sports car for me. My dad loved blessing his girls; he claimed he couldn't resist buying it for me even though I was only fifteen.

I soon finished the beer and rolled down the window to toss the can out. JB opened the next one and handed it to me. "Why aren't you drinking?" I asked. He turned his head and said, "I want to be sober for this." Confused, I replied, "okay." I thought it was admirable of him not to drink and drive, but I wondered what he meant by "this." I didn't ask.

We drove for a while. As I finished the second beer, JB was already cracking open a third. He handed it to me and flashed a smile, saying, "Drink up, pretty girl." At this point, I was getting very tipsy, followed by bored and sleepy. I don't know when I realized the road was no longer paved. *Where the heck were we?* The sun was starting to set, and I remember starting to feel fidgety. I was drowsy and drunk, but I was certainly not relaxed.

That internal warning was getting stronger. I spoke up and asked where we were; he flashed another smile and told me we were almost there. I did not recognize any of my surroundings. I grew up in this area but had never been on that road or this far out into the country. Nothing looked familiar.

My dad had taught me always to pay attention to my surroundings and look for landmarks so I could orient myself. I looked everywhere and could not find any clue about where we were. *Why would he want to buy land way out here*, I thought to myself?

JB finally pulled off the dirt road and drove over some bumpy pasture. Beer sloshed out of the can onto my lap. I started to get anxious. I reached into the floorboard for my purse and cigarettes, but I couldn't find my lighter. I popped the cigarette in my mouth and held it between my lips while I fumbled around for a lighter. JB stopped the vehicle on a small hill. Still fumbling, I looked up from my purse and noticed the sun was almost down--it was getting dark out. JB shut the vehicle off and turned slightly sideways in the seat.

As he did, he put his right arm across the back of the seat and smiled. He brushed his hand through his hair and tilted his head. Then he motioned his head, signaling me to move closer. I ignored his request and flipped on the interior light so I could find my lighter. I was getting nervous, causing the buzz to wear off, and I really wanted that cigarette. I found the lighter and was about to light up when he spoke.

JB said, "Don't light that cigarette if you plan to kiss me." I didn't plan to kiss him, so I lit the cigarette. I took a long drag--just like my mother did when I was a little girl--then slowly and methodically blew the smoke towards him. I put the cigarette between my lips to take another drag. He reached up and took the cigarette from my mouth. He leaned over, dropped it on the floorboard, and stepped on it with his Tony Lama boot.

"Take me home," I retorted. He reached behind the seat and grabbed two more beers. He casually said, "Naw, I don't have to have you home until midnight. We got plenty of time...relax." He opened both beers and handed me one, and then he took a long swig of the other one.

Again, he said, "Drink up, pretty girl. Just relax. I'm not gonna hurt ya." I tried to relax; it was true he had never hurt me before. Yes, he had made me feel uncomfortable plenty of times by the way he looked at me or put his hand on my leg when he was helping me with math equations, but he would never take advantage of me out here in the middle of nowhere. *Would he?*

He motioned for me to slide over and sit closer to him. This time I complied. I reasoned if I did what he wanted and acted like I was having a good time, we would make out a little, and then he would take me back to town. I scooted closer and drank more of my beer. He offered a "little something" to help me relax more, but I refused. I did not want to relax more--I wanted to get the hell out of there and go back to town. He didn't do anything for a while, which was alarming. He just had his arm around me, caressing my shoulder and drinking his beer.

We looked up at the stars and talked about his family. He told me I would just love his mother and sister and how he couldn't wait for me to meet them. I thought this was strange. I stopped drinking the beer. "This one's getting warm," I said. I used that excuse to scoot back over to the passenger side door so I could pour it out. I opened the door and intentionally spilled the cold beer onto the earthy ground. At ease, he finished his beer then reached behind me and pulled out another beer for him and a peach wine cooler for me. I wondered why he hadn't offered me the wine cooler before, but I didn't ask. I just shrugged it off.

I drank the wine cooler and felt a buzz coming back while we continued to talk about subjects, I considered way over my head. I welcomed the buzz, anything to get rid of that creepy feeling and underlying anxiety. I started to feel warmly calm. It didn't take much to get me tipsy since I only weighed about 110 pounds soaking wet, so after the second wine cooler, I was fairly at ease. JB reached for my hand, and I scooted back across the seat close to him. He pulled me in for a kiss, and I didn't resist him. We kissed for a few minutes, and he began to rub his hands all over me. I had kissed a lot of guys, but something felt different about this.

JB's kisses went from gentle at first to more intense. He untucked and unbuttoned his shirt, then unbuttoned his pants and put my hand on his crotch inside his jeans. He wasn't wearing any underwear. Trying to stay calm, while still kissing him, I slid my hand back up to his chest, but again he put my hand there. I moved away slightly and looked up at the night sky while he kissed my neck and chest. *No reason to panic,* I told myself. I had no cause to believe he wouldn't stop at my boundaries. His kissing on my neck and chest became more intense, and then he put his hands inside the back of my shirt to unhook my bra. I asked him to slow down.

He didn't.

In fact, he became even more intense with his kisses and rough with his touch. After a few minutes, he pulled away from me. I thought, *It's okay, it's over. Thank God. He is finished.*

He wasn't.

He ripped his shirt off and threw it on the dash. He started the truck; I'm assuming because the music had gone off at some point, and the lights on the dashboard went dark. He put his hands around my tiny waist and pulled me to a lying position across the seat. Still setting up, he started to unbutton my shorts. I firmly put my hand over the button and said, "No!" My pre-determined boundary had been reached, and I was ready for this--whatever it was--to end. He moved my hand and tried again at the top button of my jean shorts. Again, I pushed his hand and said, "NO!" He leaned down, kissed me hard, and pulled my shirt and bra up around my neck. I was hoping he had gotten the point after my second firm NO.

He hadn't.

He was grinding and pressing against me; it was hard to breathe. Again, trying to push him off of me, I said: "STOP!" He paused long enough to pull his jeans down. He tried again for my pants; then we began struggling. He forcefully unbuttoned and unzipped my shorts. Still firmly saying NO, I put my fingers through my belt loops and held tightly to the top of my shorts making it as difficult as possible for him to pull them down. He was much bigger and stronger than I was; I was a petite, young teen.

He was determined.

There was no one there on that dark road to hear my pleas for help--no one there to make him stop. With his arm pressing hard across my throat making it impossible to breathe, I instinctively let go of my shorts and moved my hands up to pry his arm off my neck. He moved his arm and pulled my shorts off. Then he laid down on top of me. My head was bent uncomfortably backwards, pressed hard against the driver's side door. I turned my head to avoid him kissing me, and tears were falling from my eyes as he thrust against me. I resisted the best I could, but he was relentless.

I felt a cold wetness as he slowly poured the rest of my wine cooler between my legs and proceeded to rape me.

I scratched at his face and chest as I begged and pleaded with him to stop. Intense pain ripped me physically and robbed me emotionally. Thankfully, it didn't take long for him to get off, and he ejaculated all over my stomach. I didn't know about ejaculation. Disgusted, I put my hands on my stomach and felt the wetness indicating what he had done. Screaming at him, I angrily wiped his semen all over his face, trying to claw at his eyes. I was so enraged--I wanted to kill him! He had taken my virginity, and at that moment, I just wanted to die. I was in shock and disbelief.

Afterward, I cried all the way back to town, contemplating

jumping out of the vehicle. I do not remember any conversation during the drive. When we got into town, he pulled into a convenience store called Love's Country Store. The lights from the store beamed into the cab of the pick-up, and he reached his hand over to wipe the smudged mascara from my cheeks. I slapped his hand away. In a sinister yet caring way, he said: "Baby, go in and get yourself cleaned up before I take you home."

Umm...what the hell? Is he joking right now? I sat there in disbelief for a few minutes crying. He then said in that same tone of voice, "Go on in and get cleaned up...you don't want your parents to know we had sex, do you?"

Seriously? I screamed back at him, "YOU RAPED ME! WE did not have sex! YOU DID!!" Again, he reached his hand over to calm me. I shoved it away and said: "DON'T TOUCH ME. DON'T YOU EVER TOUCH ME AGAIN! YOU SICK BASTARD."

I got out of the truck and slammed the door as hard as I could. Looking down not to make eye contact with anyone inside the store, I quickly walked straight into the bathroom. With the door closed and locked behind me, I glanced into the dirty mirror at my tear-streaked face before leaning back and sliding helplessly down to the cold, filthy floor.

My thoughts swirled as a sick feeling overcame me. I attempted to mentally process what I had experienced. There I was sobbing, lying in the fetal position on a grimy convenience store bathroom floor, having been sexually violated and my boundaries grossly transgressed. Feeling physically torn, emotionally-shattered, and irreversibly ruined, I screamed into my hands, "Who cares? I'm dirty now just like this filthy bathroom floor!" I laid on bare cement and wept until I had no more strength.

I don't know how long I was there. It must have been a while because JB came inside the store and knocked on the door. He said in a sickeningly sweet tone, "Hurry up in there, pretty girl! I have to have you home by midnight."

Is he kidding right now? He's concerned about my curfew?!? He just raped me an hour ago, and now he's "'worried" about getting me home on time? The audacity of this jerk!

I don't know how I mustered the strength to dry my tears, clean myself up, and walk calmly out of the store.

I don't know why I didn't call my parents or someone else to come pick me up.

I don't know why I didn't tell the lady working there that night what had happened and ask her to call the police.

I don't know why I walked out of that store and got back into his truck, allowing him to drive me home as if nothing out of the ordinary had happened.

I don't know why I didn't run screaming into the safety of my home and tell my parents how he had violated me.

I don't know why I didn't tell a single soul for as long as I could keep the disgusting, dirty secret.

Looking back as I write this, I know why I kept silent. I didn't know then, but I understand now it was guilt, shame, and fear, which prevented me from breathing a word about that night. I believed the lies playing in my own mind and the deception JB used to imprison me. These lies made me believe it was my fault.

If I wasn't "wild," this wouldn't have happened. If I had dressed differently, I would have been less desirable to him. If I had been smarter in school and didn't need help with Algebra, this wouldn't have happened. I realize today this irrational thinking caused me to keep the nasty secret quiet.

Chapter 7

TORMENT

Remove your torment from me; I fade away because of the force of your hand~Psalm 39:10

JB continued to harass me for months after the rape. The stalking became even worse and more terrifying. In one instance, my family had gone out of town for a few days, and we got home late one evening. My dad asked me to go to the post office and get the mail. The post office was kept unlocked during non-business hours for the townspeople to have access to their P.O. boxes. I had become much more cautious about my surroundings after the rape, but I had no concern about going to the post office alone. When I parked in front, I did not notice any other vehicles there. I walked in, found our mailbox, inserted the key, and reached in to take the thick stack of mail out of the box. Holding the mail between my forearm and my chest, I shut and locked the tiny door with the number 130 etched on the glass.

While still looking down browsing through the mail, I took a couple of steps and bumped into someone...it was JB. How was he standing that close to me?! I hadn't heard anyone come in, yet there he stood right in front of me! Startled, I dropped the stack and ran out to my car, leaving my dad's mail scattered all over the floor.

JB also harassed me over the phone. Long before caller ID made its debut, my parents had a phone line, and I had my own private number in my room. JB would call my private line frequently. Of course, I didn't know who was calling until I answered. The phone would ring, and when I answered, I heard "Hey, pretty girl" on the other end. Quickly I would hang up, then leave the receiver off the hook for hours so he couldn't call back.

However, my tactic didn't work because he would simply call my parent's line and ask to talk to me. Not realizing I was avoiding him, either my mom or dad would holler at me to come to the phone. I had to pretend nothing was wrong and talk to him for a couple of minutes.

I was constantly lying to my parents, even more than usual, and it wasn't even so I could get away with something fun. It was to hide a shameful secret that was poisoning me inside. I was covering up and lying to protect an awful truth, which was tearing me apart.

A few weeks after the rape, I came home one evening and walked into the kitchen. I almost passed out when I turned the corner to see JB sitting at the kitchen table, drinking a glass of iced tea with my parents! I stormed through the kitchen, and my dad reprimanded me for being rude and not saying hello to our guest. This asshole dared to come into my home, sit at my kitchen table, and ask my parent's permission to take me on vacation with him and his family.

JB's family was planning an island trip coming up in a few weeks. JB told my parents he really liked me and would like his family to meet me and for me to meet them. He said if I went, I would be sharing a room with his sister. He told my dad he knew there was quite an age difference between us and promised he would take really good care of me if I was allowed to go.

Feeling dizzy and sick to my stomach, I asked to be excused so I could go to my room. I ran to my room, slammed the door, and fell onto my bed screaming and crying into my pillow. I thought, *I'll never be free of him.*

JB had told me several times on the phone when he called that "nothing bad had happened" between us. He claimed I was overreacting and making a big deal out of nothing. He even said he thought I was "more mature than this." I told him I thought he was a complete psycho and I wanted nothing to do with him! I would tell him if he ever called me or came over to my house again, I was going to tell my dad what he had done.

JB would just laugh and say, "It's my word against yours, pretty girl. No one will believe you." He told me, "The first time is always uncomfortable, and it wouldn't have hurt if you would have just relaxed and let nature take its course." Screaming as hatefully as possible into the phone, I called him names and assured him I would never ever agree to go on a trip or anywhere else with him! I absolutely hated him!

Every time I threatened to tell, JB turned it around and made it seem like it was my fault. He said several times if I told anyone, he wouldn't get into trouble because my parents permitted him to take me out of town. JB also said his family had very high-powered attorneys on retainer, and they could easily get him off from any charges. Then he would say I would cause my dad to spend a bunch of money on lawyers for nothing. Eventually I ran out of things to say in my defense. I couldn't believe what was happening. I had sunk deeper into despair and finally thought he was right.

Another thing he told me was no one would listen to me since I didn't tell anyone, including the police, that night. Something about a "limitation of statues" or something along those lines. I understand now he was referring to the "statute of limitations," which would have still held up even years after the rape. I had no idea what those words even meant, but they sounded important, so I believed him. Now, of course, I understand he was using fear tactics and concepts beyond my understanding to manipulate me into staying quiet. If I had only known...I wish I had dared to tell someone.

Chapter 8

UNRAVELED

*We try to hide our feelings, but we forget that our
eyes speak~Unknown*

After the rape, I did not go to school for several weeks. I was terrified I was going crazy, and I might blurt out my secret right in the middle of class. I had irrational thoughts, and the anxiety attacks started getting worse. I mostly stayed home in my room and cried. I told my parents I didn't feel well and to please just let me rest.

After a few days, my parents started to worry and ask questions. I assured them it was probably just the flu. My dad noticed I wasn't eating, and this concerned him. I was small and definitely did not need to lose weight. He said if I didn't "perk up" soon, he was taking me in for a check-up. I was horrified at the thought! What if my doctor-- the same one who had treated me for asthma attacks all my life--could somehow tell just by looking at me I was no longer a virgin? What if I suddenly lost my mind and told what happened to the nurse and she didn't believe me?

I was keenly aware that pregnancy was the result of intercourse, which was one of the reasons why I didn't want to go all the way. The other reason, of course, was I wanted to save myself for "the one." My sister told me she had gotten pregnant the very first time she had sex just before her sixteenth birthday. I was fifteen, the same age she was...what if that's a very fertile age or something? I was sick with fear. I had heard other stories of girls getting pregnant their first time. I knew from hearing people talk I was not as likely to get pregnant if the guy pulls out, which JB did, but I was still so scared. *What if I was pregnant?*

The fear of a doctor visit and the weight of keeping this secret from everyone, including my best friend, began to feel too heavy. Since the first grade, I had not kept a single secret from Danika. Who was I becoming in all this hiding? I was hiding from everyone now-- I was different, and no one knows why. Danika and I made a pact in the first grade to tell each other *everything*, no matter how big or small. Now I was keeping the most terrible, awful secret from her. The worst thing that has ever happened in my whole life and I was too afraid to tell.

I knew for sure I couldn't tell my parents, although they would move heaven and earth to help me if they knew. This would absolutely devastate them. I could imagine my dad stomping over to JB's house in the middle of broad daylight with his 44 Magnum pistol. The one he kept loaded in the top drawer of his nightstand. The same heavy black pistol I had seen hundreds of times. The same gun he warned me never to touch, saying it was so powerful it could knock an elephant down.

My dad would be furious once he knew what JB did to me, but he would keep his cool while he made the short trek over to JB's house--the house my dad owned! My dad wouldn't even knock; he would just barge in and blast the unsuspecting bastard to smithereens. Then he would just calmly turn around and leave knowing that SOB would never hurt another little girl, especially not his daughter!

But there was no way could I let that happen; not because I didn't want JB dead, because believe me, I did. I wanted him dead so badly that I even thought of taking the same gun out of the top drawer of the nightstand, walking over to JB's house, and blowing him away myself! But the thought of my sweet daddy spending the rest of his life in prison because of me was too upsetting to think about. I just *had* to keep this hidden from my parents. After all, I reasoned, this was all my fault. I should have listened to my gut and never agreed to go in the first place.

After all, this is the sort of thing that happens to girls like me; flirty girls who tease guys with their short skirts and too much makeup. Yes, this was all my fault. I deserved what happened, and I would not let my parents find out. I knew I needed to snap out of this depression because everyone was expressing concern, and I was falling apart. I decided telling Danika what happened would help. Maybe once I told someone, I could forget it ever happened. Another reason I wanted to tell Danika was because she had more experience and knowledge about sex. I figured she could tell me if I should worry about the possibility of pregnancy.

At this time, Danika and I would talk on the phone every day when she got home from school. She filled me in on everything I was missing. Another friend, Maria, brought my homework every day after school. She stayed for several hours helping me get all the missed assignments done so I wouldn't end up failing my whole Freshman year (although ironically, I did end up failing Algebra.) During the third week after the rape, I could not stand the pressure anymore. I decided it was time to share the terrible secret with Danika and why I had been missing school.

That Friday night there was an "away" basketball game, and I still did not have my driver's license. My parents would allow me to drive in town, but I was not allowed to drive out of the city limits. Several of my friends were going with older kids who had driver's licenses, but my parents wouldn't allow me to ride with them. My mom didn't even want me to go at all since I had only been back in school for a couple of days and was just getting over "my illness." I asked my dad to take me. I remember our 45-minute drive to the game. I hardly spoke to my dad. I just looked out the window into the darkness and silently cried. I wanted to tell him how my virginity had been stolen, but I didn't dare say a word.

When we arrived at the game, I quickly found Danika and told her I desperately needed to talk with her. We found the nearest girl's restroom and did our routine check under the stalls to make sure we were alone. We weren't. After a few minutes and several toilet flushes later, I finally told my horrible secret. I shared it all: the hurt, the pain, the shame, and the feeling of something lost. I confided in my truest, trusted friend, and she cried with me. Danika knew more than anyone on the planet how much I cherished my virginity. She now understood why I had been so "sick" the past few weeks.

We discussed and then dismissed the idea I could be pregnant. She felt sure I was safe because JB "pulled out," and this meant I wasn't pregnant. But we would have to wait for my period to be certain, she said. My period did come, and thankfully, I was not pregnant.

It did help that at least one other person knew my secret, but the shame, guilt, fear, and pain were mine alone to carry. I took it with me everywhere. No matter how much I tried to forget, I would never be the same girl I was before. What remained of my childhood innocence was gone. I was only fifteen and already drowning in a sea of regret. I was sinking fast.

I really believed I would never be free of JB, and even if he went away, the memories of that night would not. I did not want to live with such mental torment. I couldn't eat or sleep, and I was afraid to go anywhere. The anxiety I had dealt with all my life was even worse now. I did not enjoy school, my friends, or even parties. I began to drink more and experiment with new drugs. I still smoked pot, but I began mixing it with speed. I also smoked "laced" pot. I tried anything to not feel so worthless.

My dad was still on my case about losing too much weight and my grades dropping. He was threatening to take me to a doctor or a psychiatrist to figure out what was wrong. This was clearly something more than the flu. I suggested to my parents maybe I had mononucleosis. When I was about nine years old, one of my sisters got mono, and she was extremely sick for at least a month. I thought mono was a better sickness to claim because it lasted longer, and I could miss more school.

It worked for a while, but eventually the suspected "mono" went away, and I tried my hardest to find myself again. I did not want to burden my parents and cause them more stress. They were fighting all the time anyway, and financially, they were struggling. The pressure from all fronts was building. My dad's business was suffering, and my mom was using prescription drugs to hide from the world and to cope with my dad's temper and her own inner turmoil. My dad was dealing with the brunt of the mounting pressure alone, so he was irritable and had no patience with anyone.

My mother was never good at coping, even in the less stressful times. She mentally checked out and was ultimately withdrawn from everyone. She would rarely come out of her room. Their arguing terrified me, even when I became a teenager. I was so afraid I would come home and find one of them dead. I somehow believed it was my responsibility to keep them together and safe.

Chapter 9

RIPPLE EFFECTS

"I'm just tired of everything...even of the echoes. There is nothing in my life but echoes...echoes of lost hopes and dreams and joys." — L.M. Montgomery, Anne of Avonlea

Now my anxiety and depression were at an all-time high, and sadness began to take root in my heart. I fought it the best I knew how. One day I didn't think I could stand it any longer. I decided I was going to end the pain and take my own life.

I considered several options and narrowed it down to two: either an overdose or a car wreck. I had access to plenty of pills and could easily make it look "accidental." But for some reason, I thought this method would be too embarrassing for my family. I didn't want to cause them embarrassment, so I eliminated that idea. The car wreck made more sense anyway, and it would avoid ruining their reputation. I decided it was the best way to end it.

The day I chose was absolutely gorgeous. It was a warm and sunny afternoon, with only fluffy clouds that looked like snowy mountains in the sky. Nothing like the ominous gray ones that threaten to bring a storm...just inviting, cotton-candy clouds. The sky certainly did not reflect the storms raging inside me. I wanted to make sure my attempt was successful because I couldn't bear the thought of leaving my parents to care for an invalid. That would push them over the edge for sure.

I had heard head-on collisions in a fiberglass sports car like mine were nearly always fatal, but I didn't want to collide with another car. I didn't want to harm anyone else, so I planned a collision with a brick wall. I knew of an abandoned brick building with a long, paved road leading up to it. My little black sports car with a twin-turbo engine could get to a high rate of speed very quickly.

I flashed back to the day my dad proudly gave me this car. He had me drive outside of town on the highway. He looked over and said, "Ok Lee...open her up! Floor it!" Confused as to why my responsible parent would direct me to speed down the highway, I reluctantly gripped the steering wheel and pushed on the gas pedal. We sped up slightly, and then he repeated with a louder voice, "FLOOR IT!" I shrugged, "Okay then." I stomped on the gas pedal and immediately felt the G-force push me back into my seat. It sounded like an airplane taking off when the turbo power kicked in! After a couple of terrifying seconds, my dad said, "Alright Lee, slow it back down."

My dad then explained his purpose behind this exercise. "I just want you to know what kind of power this little car has hidden under the hood," he said. My dad then lovingly cautioned me to always use good judgement and never get too confident. "Always drive safely," he said, "keeping yourself and others in mind."

It killed me to remember that day. How could I do this to my parents? My dad was so excited to bless me with that car! This would devastate him and my mom. I went back and forth in my mind about it. It worried me this might not look like an accident and may still ruin my family's reputation, but at least it wouldn't be a drug overdose.

That afternoon, I sat on the end of what I had determined would be my "runway" to heaven, looking up into the sky through my open T-tops. I pictured Jesus just on the other side of those fluffy clouds. Crying and gazing upward, I asked Jesus where He was when I was raped. *Why hadn't He rescued me that night? Did He even care about me?* I had invited Jesus in my heart at an early age, so I knew I was "saved." If I went through with my plan, I knew I would go to heaven. I wasn't afraid.

But looking up at the beautiful sky, I cried out to Jesus to help me. I didn't hear an audible voice. I didn't officially see Jesus, but I felt Him gently speak to my broken heart. I *felt* His unconditional love for me coming straight down from the heavens and going right into my heart.

That day instead of dying, LIFE sprung up within me. The very thing Satan wanted to use to kill me, God used to begin my restoration! I don't know how long I sat there, just me and Jesus, but I knew the healing had begun. Jesus introduced me to HOPE that afternoon.

At that moment, I was still staring at the brick wall, but I knew I wasn't alone anymore. I knew deep in my heart. Jesus was always with me and always would be...even when I didn't understand. I dried my tears, slowly put my car in reverse, and backed away, realizing I had made a *choice.* I had chosen LIFE. Everything around me was still the same yet vastly different at the same time. For the first time in my life, I felt like I had finally made a *good* choice.

Chapter 10

HE LOVES ME

"I got lost in him, and it was the kind of lost that's exactly like being found." ~Claire LaZebnik, Epic Fail

Not long after that day, God brought someone new into my life. God would use this person as a healing balm for my soul. Not only was I introduced to HOPE, but soon I would meet a new unconditional LOVE demonstrated through a young man named Max.

One day at school, Danika returned to class from taking the lunch count to the secretary in the office and saw Max sitting there. "Hey, there's a new kid in the office! He's cute!" she excitedly told me.

When the bell rang signaling the end of the class period, she grabbed my jacket and playfully pulled me to the window of the principal's office. We peered into the glass and giggled. There he sat, my future husband.

Max was wearing a striped Polo shirt, Guess jeans, and Michael Jordan Nikes. His brown wavy hair was casually swept to the side. As he looked up, our eyes met. His kind azure eyes, his handsome chiseled features, and that sheepish grin showing off his silver braces...I was immediately a smitten kitten!

Our relationship initially began as a friendship. In my short fifteen years, I had already made some terrible choices. As you've seen, I put myself in some situations which I did not have the maturity to handle. My parents loved me and provided a wonderful home, but they had their own battles. This became more and more apparent the older I became. They truly did the best they could, but I was a handful, and having raised my older sisters, they were getting tired.

At first, it felt like Max and I were opposites. I was the wild and drunk party girl, and he was the sober and responsible designated driver. I was constantly pushing the limits while he was content to follow the rules and stay in bounds. I smoked, drank, and did drugs, but he never touched them.

I did wonder what he saw in me. Max was such a sweet caring guy, but I was jaded.

It wasn't long before the more I was around Max, the more I *wanted* to be around him. He made me feel safe, loved, and cared for. I didn't have to put on an act; I was free just to be myself.. Max was never pushy or overly flirty. He was *always* a gentleman. As we began to hang out more, I slowly opened up to him. He was easy going and so much fun to be around, and our conversations flowed effortlessly.

We would ride around town and listen to music. Terrance Trent D'Arby's song, "Wishing Well," was one of our favorites. We also wore the heck out of George Michael's album *Faith*. Max loved The Beastie Boys and The Pet Shop Boys, so we listened to his cassette tapes of those groups often. We drove around and talked for hours. Once my curfew rolled around, we sat on my front porch and talked late into the night.

I soon lost interest in every guy except for Max. He loved me without ever asking for anything in return. I had been through a very rough season, and he was there for me emotionally. The more time I spent with him, my desire to drink alcohol and do drugs faded.

Looking back, I know God graciously sent Max to my rescue. I loved him, and he loved me, even before our very first kiss on my front porch. We didn't rush into our first kiss; by the time it occurred, a sound friendship was solidly in place. From the day we shared our first kiss, we were inseparable.

Somewhere between the leaves turning golden brown in the fall to the chilly nights of winter, we had fallen deeply in love. At the young age of only fifteen, I knew he was "the one." But it would be five years later and many more heartaches before my dad would proudly walk me down the aisle, giving me to the man of my dreams.

One evening, Max and I were sitting on a blanket in my front yard under a big tree where my swing set used to be when I was a little girl. While gently holding my hand, he told me he thought I was beautiful. He told me that the day he was in the principal's office enrolling in school was not the first time he had ever seen me. He saw me for the first time on the evening his family rolled into town with their moving truck. He then told me the story.

Max's family had been unloading for several hours and getting settled into their new home when Max and his older brother decided to take a break and go get something to eat. They went to the only place open that time of night, a convenience store called Love's Country Store. Max said he saw a very beautiful--but highly intoxicated--young woman. A tender sadness filled his eyes as he recounted this part of the story. He told me he wondered who I was and hoped I would make it home safely. Unfortunately, I was too inebriated to even notice him. I have no memory of that night. I have no idea who I was with, what we were doing, or what happened after I left Love's. The first impression had unknowingly been made. Thankfully, Max did not judge me, not on that night or ever. Instead he gave many more opportunities for me to show him my heart.

I believe God put a special love in Max's heart for me that night--an unconditional, non-judgmental, pure, honest, and time-tested love. Max had seen firsthand what kind of girl I was without ever having met me.

Max and I spent every waking moment possible together, and before we knew it, the school year ended. One day early in the summer, Max told me his family was moving. His parents had been transferred back to the town three hours away where they had moved from just nine months before. *What? Why?* I was so upset. Life was finally going well. I felt happy and safe and loved. I was doing so much better. I hardly even drank anymore, and I had not smoked pot since right after we met. I needed him! Why was God letting Max leave? I didn't see the blessing in Max's coming anymore because I was only focused on his leaving.

As their moving van and all his family's belongings drove out of town, the all-too-familiar panic-evoking feelings rose up within me once again. I cracked open a bottle of cheap Boone's Farm strawberry wine and lit a joint. Inhaling deeply, I held the bitter-tasting smoke, allowing it to burn my lungs for as long as I could. I leaned back in the seat and slowly exhaled, watching the intoxicating smoke fill the inside of my tiny car.

Chapter 11

BITTERSWEET

Let me take you by the hand because nothing in this twisted world is harder than facing your demons by yourself~E.MO

M ax and I continued to date despite several hundred miles separating us, seeing each other as often as we could over the rest of the summer. Both sets of parents were as accommodating as possible. We took turns driving to the other's house for a few days. I would pack my little black 300ZX and fly down the highway, counting every mile until I was in his arms again. The days together would quickly pass, and before I knew it, we were saying our goodbyes, holding onto each other for as long as we could. I would immediately start counting the days until Max would make the three-hour drive to my house.

Back and forth we traveled, sharing the highs and lows and the steady rhythm of emotion. I was elated when I was with him and depressed when I wasn't. We ran up hundreds of dollars in long-distance phone bills in-between visits—there were no free minutes back then. Our parents were understanding, saying little about it. They just paid the bills to foster our young love.

Our summer flew by. Max's Senior year and my Junior year started. I was not coping well. I felt sad most of the time. I was anxious, and my old habits soon returned, except now they were even worse. My dad had taken a job requiring him to be gone the majority of the time. Danika moved in with me and my mom, so during the week it would just be us girls. My mother was not a strong disciplinarian, so Danika and I frequently skipped school and did pretty much whatever we wanted.

Danika and I regularly partied, even on school nights. We were exceptionally good at hiding what we were really up to. At times, we partied right in my house! Friends would sneak alcohol in, hidden under their letter jackets or in their backpacks. Soon, we started getting high at lunch. We would leave school when the bell rang and go somewhere and smoke. One of our friends could get these small bottles that she called "locker room." Whatever was inside smelled horrible. But we would sniff the contents, getting high as a kite.

Some days--and more nights than I can count—Danika and I drank 190-proof Everclear mixed in either Hawaiian Punch, grape Kool-Aid, or peach sweet tea. The only problem, which we didn't see as a problem then, was it would get us wasted so fast. We quickly got what we referred to as "shitfaced" before we even realized what happened. Years later, I read an article which stated Everclear inebriates one faster than they can feel it. So, you down a few glasses of great-tasting "Kool-Aid," and you're flat on your ass before you know what hit you. It really "snuck up on you," so we tried to be careful.

That fall, Danika and I narrowly escaped an arrest when we were pulled over by the police. We thought we were cool, but the officer thought otherwise. Red and blue lights flashing in the rear view indicated we were in for it. The officer confiscated our 12-pack of Coors Light and half a bottle of Everclear we hadn't gotten to yet. We later found out it was considered a felony for minors to be in possession of Everclear. We also found out Everclear is so dangerous that it is illegal to sell or possess by legal adults in some states!

My dad happened to be home from working out of town that weekend when we got hauled in. He made a quick call to the District Attorney. A few hours of interrogation at the police station forced us to tell who had purchased the alcohol for us, and then we were let go. I was grounded for two weeks. No problem, though--I had plenty of "stash" in my bedroom to last for at least a month-long grounding.

On the weekends I went to visit Max, I did not party. He didn't party ever, so when I was with him, I didn't either. When he came to see me on Friday afternoons, I would usually still be high from lunch or just coming down. He could always tell and made it clear he didn't approve, but he never got angry or tried to shame me into good behavior. Max had a special way; he would just love me.

May rolled around and brought with it some major changes. My dad had accepted a job where he could be home, but it meant we had to move away from the only place I knew. I'd had the same friends since kindergarten, and now I was leaving just before my Senior year. My emotions were a jumbled mess.

Anxiety rose as I thought of starting over in a much larger town. My little hometown didn't even have a single stoplight. This new town had hundreds of them. My old class had thirty-four kids, but my new class would have almost four hundred. I didn't know a single person there. And it was a three-hour drive away, so seeing my old friends would be difficult.

For me, the hardest person to leave behind would be Danika. She had lived with my family off and on since grade school. She knew everything about me, and we had spent almost every day of our lives together up to that point. I was even closer to her than my blood sisters. How could I leave my childhood home, my friends, and even the teachers who always went the extra mile to help me pass my classes? I knew this move would either make or break me. I was afraid it would break me.

Chapter 12

ONE THOUSAND MILES APART

I'll save a seat for you just in case you want to be a part of my journey.

That May, Max graduated high school and joined the United States Marines. He wanted to serve his country without burdening his parents with the expense of college. My parents and I now had the move behind us, and we were getting settled into our new house. Max and I were still very much in love, and we wanted to spend every possible moment together before he left for boot camp. My parents allowed Max to move in with us until he had to leave. We hung out by the pool during the day and spent the evenings talking and making love. We made the most of every day we had together, soaking up every second of the five and a half months before he left.

In August 1989, I started my Senior year of high school. It wasn't as bad as I thought it would be. I made new friends quickly and easily. The best part was I only had to go for three hours in the morning. I was surprised to learn I only lacked three credits to graduate. I could get those classes done in the morning and have the rest of the day to spend with Max. Although I made friends, they were not a priority. I only wanted to rush home to be with Max. At the time, I could not be bothered with high school folly.

The sad day arrived in November when my young boyfriend tearfully embraced his mother and me before boarding an airplane. He reluctantly left me standing there with tears flowing, and he flew off to California where he would become a proud United States Marine. My heart felt so empty when he left; it was the same lost, lonely feeling I had before we met three years earlier and the same feeling I had the day I watched his family's moving van drive away. The airplane had not even left the tarmac, yet the dreaded and familiar underlying loneliness and depression began to creep back in. I went looking for the nearest bottle or joint, whatever I could find first.

After Max's departure, I tried to stay positive and make the remainder of my Senior year the best it could possibly be. I was popular and had many friends. But while Max was away at boot camp, I missed him terribly. We wrote each other a letter every single day, and I really did try to stay out of trouble. However, it wasn't long before the suppressed party girl would return and take over.

Max graduated with honors from Marine Corps Recruit Depot (MCRD) in San Diego, California. My parents allowed me to fly out for his graduation. I sat proudly in the audience next to his mother, father, and sister. We applauded with happy tears streaming as his name was announced and he became "official." Then we flew back to Oklahoma together, wishing we never had to leave each other again.

Max and I had a few short weeks of loving bliss before he left again for three more months of specialized training. The emotional roller coaster was exhausting. I would almost acclimate to his absence, and then he would come back, and I would get attached again. But this time, we then had only a few days together before he was sent overseas for his first duty assignment. We would be separated by thousands of miles spread over a vast, salty ocean for well over a year's time.

After Max's departure, I managed to stay out of trouble mostly, but I frequently partied with my high school friends and overindulged on marijuana, speed, and alcohol. I also ran around with older girls who were dating pilots, so I went to the Air Force base and hung out in the O Club--don't ask me how I got served because I honestly don't know. I didn't manage to just get served but to get way overserved.

In May of 1990, I graduated high school and headed off to college at a university about a two-hour drive from my parents' home. As soon as I left home, the depression and anxiety I so easily hid from the world started to haunt me. I turned to drugs and alcohol once again to ease the pain.

College life for me was not at all academic; in fact, I hardly ever went to class and did not crack open a single textbook. It was a constant party. I slept through most of my classes, too tired and hungover from the night before to function the next day. Staying out of trouble seemed impossible, so I decided not to try anymore. I missed Max so much. The party girl in me ran wild, and I just sat back and let her self-destruct.

The next time I saw Max about fifteen months later, I would be even more deeply wounded than before. Although much healing and forgiveness has taken place over the years, I still carry the scars that were written across my heart during this tumultuous time while Max was a world away.

Chapter 13

BOOZED AND CONFUSED

The best way to get confused is to try convincing your heart of something your head knows is a lie~Unknown

Shortly after arriving at college and settling into the dorms, I was introduced to Kenny. My roommate, Tracy, and I became close friends with the two girls who lived directly across the hall from us, and Kenny was a friend of theirs. He would come to the dorms with his friends who were dating girls on my floor.

Kenny was tall with a muscular build, dark-skinned, and very handsome. He was six years older than me and had already spent four years in the Navy. I had never dated anyone like him. The initial attraction wasn't strong, but it wasn't very before I found myself falling for him.

Kenny would conveniently show up at every party and club I was at. None of us girls were even old enough to get into bars and clubs in the first place, but that didn't stop us. We quickly made friends with the guys at the door, the bouncers, and the club managers. We *always* got in, and I don't remember ever once paying a cover charge--or for drinks.

From the beginning, it was clear Kenny had a strong attraction to me. And I was vulnerable, carrying an unfulfilled longing for closeness. Because I missed Max, I let my guard down over time. I allowed my heart to drift further from Max and closer to Kenny. The attraction became mutual, and we began to spend more time together. Kenny was a major "player" who had dated many other girls and usually several at a time. But somehow, Kenny made me feel special even though I knew he was dating other girls, too.

At first, I denied any feelings for Kenny and resisted getting romantically involved because I deeply loved Max and missed him terribly. I would go out and get so drunk that I couldn't get back to my dorm room alone. My girlfriends would be drunk, too, but I was always the drunkest. We would all stumble in at the wee hours of the morning, laughing and talking so loudly that we would get in trouble from the senior resident in charge.

On those late nights in my drunken stupor, I would clumsily dial the overseas number to call Max. I remember getting the number wrong many times because my eyes would be blurry from crying, and I was so intoxicated or high I could not think straight. I don't remember much of these conversations, but I know he was terribly worried about me. After about a month or two of these very long-distance late night/early morning calls I was charging to my parent's home phone, they got the bill. It was over $1000, and those calls were quickly put to a halt by my dad.

Again, I felt very alone. Without being able to talk to Max very often, I began to turn my attention to Kenny for comfort. He gladly obliged. We would take walks around the campus, go eat, or just drive around and talk. Kenny quickly became very possessive over me and started insisting on spending every day together. It didn't bother me because at the time, it felt like love, and he made me feel safe.

It was not at all what I was used to; Max was never pushy and possessive, but somehow, I just let Kenny consume my world. I would still go out with my girlfriends and party, but he was always there and didn't allow me to dance or talk with other men. It would be a fight every time if he thought I was even remotely interested in someone else. Looking back, I see major red flags, but at the time, I thought he was just being protective.

One night, my roommate wanted us to go out. She was sick of Kenny always being around and didn't want him to go with us. She said there was a party and we should go. I remember asking her if any white people would be there because she mostly dated black guys, and I knew her kind of parties. I also knew if Kenny found out I went; he would go ballistic. She assured me there would be a mix of both girls and guys and not just one race. Don't get me wrong--I was now completely out of my small-town girl comfort zone and dating a black man, but I was uncomfortable in a big, loud, drunk crowd of black guys.

Ignoring the internal warning signals that night and against better judgment, I snuck to the party in an apartment just off campus. Not wanting Kenny to know I was going, I pretended to be sick and told him I was staying in and going to bed early. He believed my lie. We got all dolled up, and then Tracy and I drove the short distance to the party. We had to park about a block away because of all the cars already there.

As we began to walk to the apartment, something just didn't feel right. The loud, vulgar rap music could be heard a block away. I knew I should have turned around and got back in the car. But I didn't. Thank God I was completely sober, or I very well could be telling you a different story.

We reached the front door, and it was so crowded we could barely get in. My heartbeat wildly in my chest as my eyes adjusted to the dim lighting. The marijuana and cigarette smoke was thick, making it hard to breathe. Normally, that would have been my kind of place, but something was different, and I could feel it. What I didn't know then, but I do know now is the Holy Spirit was with me, and by the grace of God, I was spared that night.

I desperately scanned the room to find a familiar face, but I saw no one I knew. Large, black hands began to grope me, and I started to panic. I grabbed Tracy and forcefully turned her to face me and screamed, "Let's get the hell outta here" above the music. I later learned while I was in the shower and getting ready, she was getting high. By the time we got there, she was overly relaxed, so she did not see a problem whatsoever.

Soon, we were surrounded by college football players and other rambunctious men who thought we must have come for their pleasure. Tracy began to dance around provocatively as I hopelessly looked around for a way to escape. As eyes and hands were all over me, I surveyed the room. Handsy men blocked the front door, and the sliding door straight ahead of me only led to a balcony crowded with drunks. I pushed my way through the rowdy crowd, planning to go hide in the bathroom and see if there was a window I could crawl out of.

Of course, the bathroom door was locked. There was a bedroom next to the bathroom with the door open. I didn't see anyone in there and quickly decided to duck in there and look for a phone or window. This was before cell phones, so there were only landlines, and I didn't know if whoever lived here had one or not. But there was a phone sitting on a small table next to a rumpled unmade bed. I ran towards it, picked up the receiver, and dialed the dorms for someone to come get me.

Thankfully, a friend named Kelsey answered on the first ring. She knew where the party was because she almost came with us, but she decided to wait for a few others and come later. I screamed into the phone to come get me NOW! I barely got the words out when the overhead light came on.

Startled, I turned around and there stood four huge black men staring hungrily at me. One of them shut the door and started moving towards me unbuttoning his jeans. Another one said, "Oh hell no, man! I get her first!" The two of them started to banter back and forth, and I dropped to my knees sobbing and pleading for them not to hurt me. I knew exactly what their intent was, so all I could do was pray. I felt paralyzed. Without divine intervention, a gang rape was inevitable.

For some reason, while I was weeping and begging on the floor, one of the four had a change of heart. When I briefly looked up, I noticed his facial expression was different. His hungry eyes turned soft, and his intensity disappeared. With authority no one argued with, he said, "No one gets her! We are letting her go."

Still on my knees and sobbing, I looked at him with disbelief. He nodded his head towards the door where two of the guys stood in a bodyguard-type stance. "MOVE!" he commanded. The one who had started unbuttoning his pants glared at him, then walked toward me with a look of disgust and spat in my direction. Trembling, I got up off the floor, feeling as though I would collapse. The one who so graciously spared me walked to the door and parted the two guarding it, while the fourth guy stood off to the side drinking a beer.

Cautiously, I moved toward the door; still shaking, I reached for the door. As soon as I put my hand on the doorknob, a green beer bottle smashed against the wall just inches from my head. The guy who had just spat at me and missed had thrown an almost full bottle of beer at my head. Praise God he missed again!

I'll never forget the image of shattered glass and beer running down the wall as I bolted out of that bedroom. I quickly found Tracy, and with a strength I didn't know I had, I grabbed a hold of her arm and jerked her through the crowd. With adrenaline coursing through my veins, I shoved my way past everyone and got us the hell out of there! Once in the safety of her car, I started vomiting and crying. It is incredibly scary to think of what could have happened if God had not intervened. That is the only possible explanation of why I escaped unharmed.

Reluctantly, I told Kenny about it only because everyone in the dorms was talking about it. I knew he would hear about it, so it better come from me. He was so angry. He told me it was my fault for thinking I could go anywhere without his protection. After that, he started staying all night with me in the dorms. It was a huge risk because, of course, it was against the rules. I was still so shaken up and became afraid of seeing any of those guys around campus. My anxiety worsened, and I started skipping class even more, drinking during the day, and smoking pot frequently.

Chapter 14

PIT OF DESTRUCTION

Ask me no questions and I'll tell you no lies~Lynyrd Skynyrd

Part of me wanted Kenny to stay around and "protect" me, and part of me wanted him to leave me alone. He was adamant and insisted he needed to make sure I was back in the dorms safely every night. Most of the time, I would be too drunk to fight with him about it. Not too long after he started spending the night, I did what I never thought I would ever do. I gave into his desires and surrendered my body and my heart to him. I had sworn Max would be my one and only; I had failed yet again.

I felt like the biggest asshole for cheating on Max, but he was so far away. I still loved him and never had for one second stopped loving him, but I allowed someone else to have what should have only ever been his. Consumed with guilt, I would push Kenny away.

Kenny would tell me he knew how guys in the military were. He said none of them could be faithful, but I thought he just didn't know Max. He said I was crazy if I thought Max wasn't sleeping with other girls. Besides, he would say, "Max will never know, so what's the big deal?" Over time, I started believing it and convinced myself Max probably wasn't being faithful to me anyway, so why should I care? I took some Ecstasy, let my guard down, believed the lies, and fell in love.

I fell further into a pit of destruction. I was still officially enrolled in college, but I wasn't even going to class. I was going to a LOT of clubs, though, and life was a party. Three to four nights per week, I was drinking and dancing until wee hours of the morning. Once a club closed for the night, there was always an after party…and that was dangerous for us as underage girls.

For one thing, the men outnumbered the women every time. Another issue was we would all be stumbling drunk once we got there. Several of my girlfriends told me they felt pressured into sex at these parties. Many of them were sexually assaulted, and I was, too... multiple times. My friends told me they felt like they couldn't say no, and even if they did, it wouldn't matter. Usually they were so drunk or drugged that they didn't even realize what was happening.

Of course, I had to sneak to a party or club in the first place because I wasn't "allowed" to go anywhere without Kenny. I never told him about any of this. I don't know what he would have done if he found out. Sex, drugs, and alcohol were always present...the perfect life-wrecking trio disguised as a really good time. There are always consequences for our choices.

Mostly, in the beginning, the consequences of this lifestyle are just vaguely uncomfortable like nursing a hangover. But over time, the consequences get gradually worse, and soon, they become too expensive. The cost of the aftermath is always more than you can afford to pay. And I was running out of funds.

I missed Danika. Since our family had moved for my Senior year, there was a strain on our friendship. She had also decided on a different college. We still loved each other like sisters, but we just weren't as close. Our lives had always been intricately linked, but now it was different.

But when Danika had a free weekend coming up, we made plans for her to come with her boyfriend, Todd. I hadn't told Danika about

Kenny. I knew she would be upset I was involved with someone besides Max...and the fact Kenny was black might bother her. She knew how much Max and I loved each other, but I believed she would understand my need to fill the void. I just wanted to tell her in person, not over the phone. Since she was coming for a visit, I knew I couldn't hide Kenny from her much longer.

When she and Todd arrived, it was just like old times. And like old times, it didn't take long for the party to start. We rented a hotel room and fired up the first dooby. We soon ran out and wanted more. I casually told Danika that my friend, Kenny, would be over shortly, and he would know where to get what we wanted.

Once Kenny arrived, the four of us ventured down to the "bad" part of the city where he knew of people who dealt drugs, even though Kenny never did drugs. Before long, we found what we were looking for and went back to the hotel to restart the party.

By this time, it was screamingly obvious to Danika that Kenny and I were more than friends. Her reaction was what I expected. She didn't like me dating a "black guy" and said she thought he was too old for me. *Ummm. Hello!* Danika and I had always dated older guys, but I soon realized it wasn't his age that bothered her. It was his skin color.

After several hours of tweaking, we got hungry. Since Kenny drank very little that night, he offered to go grab food for us. Danika saw Kenny rummaging through my purse to find his wallet and keys, and it freaked her out. Some heated words were exchanged between Danika and me.

The next day Danika called my parents and told them she was worried about me. She told them I was dating an older black man who was stealing money out of my purse and I was on drugs. All of it was mostly true, except the stealing part. Kenny never stole from me or anyone else that I know of. Also, he did not condone me doing drugs. In fact, he tried to talk me out of getting high with Danika that night and didn't want to take us to buy more. Although he went along with it, he spoke his mind, which made Danika think he was too controlling over me. She also told my dad she was worried Kenny was possessive. Of course, none of this settled well with my parents.

Later that same day, I was back in the dorm room with a few other girls. One girl named Jamie, looked out from the second story window and asked, "Hey Lee, isn't that your dad?" I scurried to the window to see my dad backing up his pickup to the loading doors. Within a few minutes, a loud knock on our door announced the presence of my angry father. I opened the door, and without a single word, he stormed into the room and started throwing my belongings around. I was too afraid to say anything. Neither me nor my sisters would ever argue with my dad. Not very many people were brave enough to go up against him, and I wasn't one of them.

After a few minutes of hastily packing leaving the majority of my stuff behind I climbed into the passenger side of the pickup, and we drove two hours home. Later that week, we came back for my car and a few boxes my roommate had packed up for me. That was the end of my college career for many years to come.

And it was not the last time my dad would separate me from Kenny.

Chapter 15

WEB OF LIES

Who needs enemies when you've got yourself?

Once we got home, my parents said I was *not* too old to ground. They officially grounded me, and I was required to live at home unless I could find a job making enough money to support myself. The only experience I had was a part-time job at the mall, so I certainly wasn't highly qualified for much of anything. I found a job at a beauty supply company, which paid fairly well and left plenty of time for my party-style social life.

At this time, Max was still overseas, and we were not able to talk often. No doubt I still loved him, but I had also fallen for Kenny. However, my parents made it clear they did not approve of my relationship with him. They made it as difficult as possible for us to see each other.

One of my sisters, though, lived in a college town, Stillwater, situated halfway between where I lived and Oklahoma City, where Kenny lived. Kenn and I decided it would be our meet-up place. My parents allowed it because they thought I was just visiting my sister. Kenny and I met there several times a week. More lies.

By the fall of the next school year, I talked my parents into letting me take a few classes at a Vo-Tech school, and I moved in with my sister. I got a job at a daycare center as a preschool teacher, which I loved as much as I loved the kids. Kenny and I were going back and forth to see each other, and we were fighting all the time. He was convinced I was cheating on him. And he was right--I was.

One night when driving home from a frat party while highly intoxicated, I was pulled over by an attractive officer named Brent. He said he had seen me around and had been wanting to ask me out. He said he would follow me home to make sure I got there safe. He did, and one thing led to another. This night began a casual dating relationship between Brent and me.

Still, I was going out to parties and clubs almost every night and frequently had parties at my sister's house. I had several high school friends who were attending college in Stillwater. I wasn't attending the college, but that didn't stop me from attending the college parties.

As for Kenny, I didn't trust him any more than he trusted me. I heard he was seeing other girls, and he was hearing the same about me being unfaithful. The fact we couldn't trust each other should have been a red flag that this was not going to work. On top of that, I had such guilt and anxiety about the relationship anyway because I did still love Max. However, now I loved Kenny, and then there was Brent. My heart was torn.

After about a month of going back and forth, Kenny moved to Stillwater to "keep an eye on me," and we moved into an apartment together. I broke it off with Brent.

Fear and anxiety still plagued me, and I depended on medication and alcohol or illegal drugs to cope. I knew everything about how I was living my life was wrong. I was deceiving Max, I was deceiving my parents, and I was making my sister lie for me. I was living a lie. My whole life was a lie. I was trying to justify my choice to live with Kenny. I knew it was morally wrong, but most everything about my life was morally wrong.

What bothered me the most was I knew even dating Kenny was a complete betrayal of Max, not to mention *living* with Kenny. To try and make myself feel better, I would tell myself Max was cheating, too. Plus, wasn't our relationship just high school love anyway? The guilt was destroying me.

I was stuck. I was a nineteen-year-old mess living with a twenty-six-year-old man. I decided if I ended it with Kenny, then maybe I could finally get my act together. When Max came home, I could tell him face to face how much I had screwed up and beg for his forgiveness. So, I decided it was time; I knew in my heart Kenny was not my forever.

However, every time I tried to put an end to my relationship with Kenny, it ended in a huge fight. Kenny began to threaten me. At times, I was afraid of him because he could be very scary when he was angry. Most of the time, he was sweet and gentle, but if provoked, he could turn on you quickly. When he was mad, everyone anywhere around knew it.

During a heated argument, if I would try to leave, Kenny would refuse to let me go. Raging, he would bring his fist back like he was going to punch me. Thankfully, he never did, but I was always fearful. I was afraid to tell anyone because I was embarrassed, I had made another series of bad choices which led me to this place. I didn't dare tell my parents.

Several more months passed, and my plan to break it off with Kenny wasn't working. He and I had settled into a routine. Life was the most "normal" it had been in a while. I was drugging and drinking way less often--only on the weekends or when Kenny and I fought. We both worked during the week and then spent the evenings together at home. We were usually in bed by 10:00 p.m. My parents were still disappointed and worried, but for the most part, they were leaving me alone to figure out my screwed-up mess.

But just as it always does, life was about to take another unexpected turn.

Late one night, the phone rang. Kenny and I were already asleep. I groggily answered the phone, and on the other end was Max. We'd had enough overseas calls that I could immediately tell this was *not* an international call. My heart sank in my chest. I was elated but fearful at the same time. *Was he back in the States?* Shaking so much I could barely hold the phone, I asked him where he was. He told me he was about three hours away, and he was headed to my apartment.

Chapter 16

WHEN HEARTS COLLIDE

Darling, forever is a long, long time, and time has a way of changing things. ~The Fox and the Hound

This was the day I had been waiting for, but I was unprepared at the same time. How had it snuck up on me like this? It had been close to a year and a half since Max and I had seen each other. I wanted to see him, but I was a different person now someone he didn't know. I was in another relationship, and Max was about to step right in the middle of it.

What should have been the most joyous reunion of my life would instead be heartbreaking. What Max would soon find out would wound his heart deeply, and I knew there was no softening the blow. As much as I wanted to keep it from happening, there was no way I could stop it. Two worlds were about to collide.

My web of deceit was unraveling around me. After a short, awkward conversation with Max, I hung up the phone. My thoughts swirled as I tried to quickly devise a plan to get Kenny out of the apartment and hide all evidence I was living with another man. I knew I had to act quickly because Max was only a few hours from arriving at my front door.

I shook Kenny. I begged, "Kenny, wake up! Max will be here soon! You have to get your stuff and get out of here right now. Tonight!" I was surprised when Kenny sat up in bed and calmly stated, "I'm not going anywhere. We share a life together, and I'm not leaving." I pleaded with him to get up, pack what he could, and get out so I could think how to handle this.

Kenny and I both knew we would have to face this someday, but I didn't expect it to be in a state of panic in the middle of the night. I thought I had more time, like another month or so or at least another few weeks, not just a few hours. I had planned to break up with Kenny before Max returned, but now Max was on his way.

Again, I pleaded with Kenny to get his stuff and leave. Anxiety and panic were coursing through me like a turbulent river. I cried, "You CANNOT be here when Max arrives. PLEASE just leave! We can figure this out later." I knew how irrational this plan was, but it was the only thing I could come up with.

Kenny began to get angry and more adamant that he would not be going anywhere. I started throwing his clothes, shoes, and whatever else he had lying around in a large leather duffle bag. "Please just go somewhere tonight, and we can talk tomorrow. I promise I'll tell Max about us when he gets here," I begged. After an hour or so of me insisting Kenny leave and promising I would tell Max the truth, Kenny agreed to go for a few days so I could sort all this out. He was not happy about it and assured me he may pop in unannounced at the apartment.

Once Kenny finally left, I scurried around the apartment to clean up. There were traces of Kenny everywhere after all, this was the place he ate, showered, shaved, and slept every day. It was a big undertaking to clear all traces of him, and I didn't have much time. In the bathroom, I removed every tiny, curly black hair from the tub and sink. I washed our bedding, hid his belongings, and rearranged to cover all traces of Kenny. When I was done, I had just enough time for a shower. I tried to pull myself together. I had to calm down because Max knew me too well, and he would notice if I was an emotional wreck.

It felt like only a few minutes before I heard a soft knock at my front door. My heart danced joyously, knowing my first love was finally home and standing on the other side of the door. But the joy was weighed down by a heavy shame and sadness. I felt like a failure and a tramp. Tears rose up so suddenly I could do nothing but let them fall. I felt like a worthless, messed-up girl.

I took a deep breath. I knew Max did nothing to deserve the heartbreak he was about to walk into. I wanted to just disappear into thin air but instead, I opened the door. There Max stood in the dim lighting on my porch with a bouquet of fresh flowers in his hand. His handsome face was tanned from the Okinawa sun, and his smile was more beautiful than ever.

Thankfully, I was somehow able to make it look as though I had been expecting his very unexpected homecoming. Max and I clung to each other for a long-awaited, much-needed embrace. He gently held my face, and with his thumbs, he wiped my tears. Then he leaned down and sweetly kissed my lips. For a moment, my world was right. I was in the arms of the only man who had and always would hold my heart. I wanted this feeling--this kiss, this embrace to last forever.

It didn't.

I was jolted back to reality when I opened my eyes. While still in Max's embrace, I saw Kenny sitting in his vehicle a short distance away. He was watching my every move.

That first night, I could not bring myself to tell Max the truth, nor could I tell him the next day or the day after that. Although I didn't say it, Max knew something was wrong because I was anxious, distraught, and distracted. I was on edge that Kenny would come barging in at any moment and tell Max everything. Kenny had threatened plenty of times to answer the phone when Max called and tell Max everything, and I knew Kenny would spare no details if given a chance.

And Kenny was true to his word. He was in and out of the apartment over the next few days--even when Max and I were there! Kenny pretended to be a maintenance man needing to "check on things" inside the apartment. I almost passed out when Kenny introduced himself to Max during one of his random "checks," and they shook hands.

Since Max came straight to my apartment when he got back to the United States, I suggested he go see his family after a few days. I knew he missed his parents and the rest of his family, and he also had several close friends he wanted to see. I was both devastated and relieved when Max left early the next morning. I hugged him goodbye knowing there was a strong chance this may be the last time he ever allowed me this close to his heart.

But before he left, I did tell him parts of the truth. I told Max I had known Kenny for almost the entire time Max had been overseas. I told him we were friends and that Kenny was protective over me. I confessed to allowing Kenny to stay over sometimes so I didn't have to be alone. These were all facts, but I minimized the situation and kept Max in the dark, protecting him from the ugly truth. But you know what? Max is a smart guy. He knew there was much more to the story.

As promised, Kenny came back to the apartment after work later that day. He asked lots of questions, and I led him to believe I had ended it with Max, but my intent really was to end it with Kenny. Seeing Max again was all it took to convince me he was all I needed. I knew Kenny was not right for me, even though I loved him. The thought of losing Max forever, though, made me heartsick.

As a result, I started to pull away from Kenny. Because our relationship was very sexual, he noticed when I began to distance myself emotionally and physically from him. He knew I was not over Max when I started dismissing his advances. My rejection angered him immensely. We began to argue every day. Kenny started showing up at my job just to "talk" and work out our issues, but I knew my heart belonged to Max.

The holiday season was fast approaching. Max had been reassigned to a duty station in California, and he headed there after his visit with his family in Oklahoma. Again, we were miles apart, and I thought about him every single day. We still talked occasionally, but there was an emotional gulf between us. I still had not told him everything. My dishonesty drove us further apart. I was the common denominator of two broken relationships, and my poor choices led me there. I thought I had lost Max and didn't deserve him anyway. I really didn't deserve either of them.

I didn't know what to do.

Chapter 17

UNPLANNED

"Paralized by fear of an unknown future, we rushed blindly to do that which was an immediate remedy."~ Pam Koerbel

As a child, my favorite month of the year was December. Something about December seemed magical. I anticipated that feeling of happiness and wonder every year. None of the other holidays could stir the same depth of emotion in my heart. I wished it could be December all the time...always December and always Christmas. I loved everything about it--the chilly air, my beloved rabbit fur coats, snow days, baking with Grandma, Christmas shopping, and the break from school.

My birthday is also in December, which added to the splendor. I would start planning my birthday party the minute the scrumptious Thanksgiving meal was cleared from the dining room table. A slumber party was at the top of my birthday plan list. What fond memories I have of all my little girlfriends gathering at my house for an all-night giggle fest; but something felt different, less magical about December once I left home as a young adult. This one especially.

Kenny and I were still living together, and I had not been feeling "myself" for several months. Our relationship was strained. I was an emotional wreck already, but now something odd was going on. I suddenly wanted to sleep all the time and had no desire to eat. I was well-acquainted with the heaviness of anxiety and depression, but something else was weighing me down. I had gained several pounds, which began to show on my small frame even though I wasn't eating much of anything. And I was nauseated all the time. Kenny noticed the difference in my weight and commented several times I was getting a little "tummy."

Suddenly one day at work, it hit me. *What if I'm pregnant?* I was on birth control pills, so until that day, it never occurred to me pregnancy was even a possibility. Yes, I was sometimes forgetful about taking them, but I would always double up the next day or when I remembered, so surely, I was safe--*wasn't I?* I couldn't even remember my last period. I immediately felt sick as I pondered the possibility.

I don't remember getting a pregnancy test or even "officially" finding out. I basically spent four months in denial. Although I had not officially confirmed my suspicion, Kenny, and I both knew I was pregnant.

About ten days before Christmas, I decided to go home to my parent's house. I wanted to get away from the apartment and sit in my bedroom at home, pretending I was a little girl again and that none of this was happening. Kenny didn't want me to go because he was not allowed anywhere near my parents' home, and if he called, they would not even tell me. I reasoned that at home I would have time to think and maybe all my problems would just go away...the same way Christmas joy did every year.

My birthday and Christmas came and went, yet I didn't smile for either occasion. My parents noticed my depression and despondency while I was home. Where was their lively little girl?

During the holidays that year, I slept more than I was awake. I wore borrowed sweats and baggy clothes to hide my swollen tummy. My wardrobe was overflowing with adorable, fashionable clothes, but they were beginning not to fit. I did not own sweatpants or baggy clothing--I had always taken pride in my appearance, refusing ever to look sloppy. So, when I wore oversized clothing and a worn-out bomber jacket for more than a week straight during the "most wonderful time of the year," my parents took immediate notice.

When they approached me, I brushed off their concerns by telling them I just wanted to be comfortable at home and there was no one around I needed to impress. They didn't buy it, but to keep the peace and keep me around longer, they let it go. I found out later they believed I was strung out on drugs, and this terrified them.

When the holidays passed, I went back to work and back to our apartment. Kenny and I had missed each other, and we desperately needed to talk. Kenny asked me to marry him and assured me we would make it work. I knew better. We loved each other, but our relationship was not stable. I had always wanted to be a mom and now I was carrying a child, but this was nothing like I had imagined. I wanted to bring a child into a safe, loving, and happy home with parents who were committed and married; who were in love with each other and who were financially independent. I couldn't even make my own car payment! I loved Kenny, and I loved this baby, but I knew I could not marry him.

I told Kenny I needed some time to think about his proposal. Over and over, he tried to convince me that once we were married and our baby was born, our relationship would get better. He said he loved me, and nothing was going to change that. I didn't know what to do or what to think. I just wanted to go to sleep and not wake up. I was only nineteen and completely worn out.

Now the only thing to do was to tell my parents. I called my mom and told her I was not feeling well, and I asked her to come see me at my sister's house. My parents would not go to my apartment because they did not like Kenny, and they certainly did not approve of us living together. But my mom knew when she heard my voice something was terribly wrong. I asked her to come alone because I did not want to face my dad. She said she would be there the next morning and asked me to spend the night with my sister because she was worried about me. I packed an overnight bag and went to my sister's house. Kenny was angry but finally agreed to let me go.

My sister and I sat up most of the night while I cried. We discussed all the "options." We talked about adoption and abortion. But I knew in my heart what I wanted to do. I wanted to keep my baby. I could feel the flutters of this little one floating around. This baby depended on me for life, and that felt special. My small round tummy held someone I wanted to meet, someone I wanted to hold, and someone I already loved. I was getting attached to this tiny person, and this tiny person was attached to me. I told my sister I did not want to marry Kenny, but I did want our baby.

Early the next morning while I lay sobbing on my sister's couch, I heard the front door open. As I watched my mom walk in, my heart sank when I saw she was followed closely by my dad. My mom put her purse and a cup of hot coffee on the side table and sat on the edge of the couch where I was laying. My dad placed a box of warm donuts and a small carton of ice-cold milk on the coffee table in front of me and sat down in a chair close by. I couldn't look at him. I turned my face away--shame and fear covered my tear-stained cheeks.

The three of us sat in silence for a few moments before my dad spoke. He finally said, "Tell us what is going on with you. Your mother and I have known something is not right for several months now. What is going on?" I could not look up, and every time I tried to speak, my voice would fail me. I could only quietly sob.

Then my dad said, "Well, it's one of two things...you're either on drugs, or you're pregnant." Without looking up, I quietly said, "Well, I'm not on drugs."

Chapter 18

I WILL CARRY YOU

So I will carry you while your heart beats here~long beyond the empty cradle, through the coming years. I will carry you all your life~and I will praise the One who's chosen me to carry you. ~ Selah You Deliver Me 2009

At this confirmation, the three of us sat in awkward silence for a few minutes, each absorbed in our own thoughts. I eventually looked up to see both my parent's eyes were brimming with tears. Their grief intensified the shame and guilt I was feeling. I sat motionless, staring down at the wadded-up pile of Kleenex in my lap.

At this moment, I felt completely worthless. I had again disappointed the two people who loved me unconditionally, not to mention how hurt Max would be. Oh, my heart, my beloved, precious Max. The thought of telling him I was pregnant with someone else's baby suddenly sent me running to the nearest bathroom so I could throw up. When I finished rinsing my face and mouth, I glanced at the unrecognizable young girl staring back at me in the water-spotted mirror. The once carefree, beautiful girl was now full of sorrow, shame, and pain. Who was she... this strange girl I didn't know?

I returned to the living room and sat back down on the couch. My dad asked me how far along I was, to which I answered, "I don't know." A few other questions were asked, and I didn't know the answers to those either. It was decided I needed to go to a doctor to determine how many weeks I had been carrying this baby. An appointment was scheduled for later that afternoon.

As I showered and readied myself for the appointment, I looked down at the "baby bump" protruding from my abdomen and felt its roundness. For the first time, I allowed myself to imagine this little person as my baby. I knew I had messed up, and I didn't know how all of this would play out, but I couldn't deny the baby's existence any longer. Although abortion had crossed my mind, I knew I wanted to carry this little one to term.

Once we arrived at the doctor and I gave a urine sample to the nurse, I entered an exam room with my parents. I climbed up on the small gray table and sat fully clothed, feeling like a helpless child with my feet dangling from the exam table. While we waited on the doctor, the silence was thick. My mom and dad sat in nearby chairs, nervously flipping through crinkled magazine pages. I sat nervously awaiting whatever was next.

Finally, the doctor breezed into the cold room, warming it up a bit with his kind eyes and smile. After a few brief words were exchanged, the doctor could easily see this was an unplanned pregnancy and not a happy occasion. Undeterred, he said, "The test is positive, so let's take a look and listen." He helped me to lay back before he pulled my shirt up and had me scrunch my pants just below my pelvic bone to reveal my secret.

How embarrassing it was to have my parents see my exposed and visibly pregnant tummy. I wanted to die. I could hear my tears landing on the paper pillow my head was resting on. I tried to focus on the tiny black dots in the tiles on the ceiling, squinting my eyes to block out the unrelenting fluorescent lights blaring down on my shame.

The doctor began pressing and feeling around on my swollen belly before he squeezed some cold gel on my tummy. Holding a small radio-looking device, he began moving a wand slowly around on my abdomen. I heard what sounded like static waves for a few seconds, and then I listened to a steady swish-swish-swish sound. A knowing and affirming nod of the doctor's head told me he found my secret. "Do you hear?" he said. "That's a strong steady heartbeat you're hearing."

A few seconds later, the doctor turned off the Doppler, wiped the gel off my belly, and helped me into a sitting position. "What questions do you have?" the doctor asked. My dad immediately spoke, asking, "How far along is she?" The doctor said he believed close to four months.

Then my dad asked the next question which sent me into a silent panic. "It's not too late for an abortion, is it?" *Ummm...what? What was happening?* Suddenly, lightheaded, and dizzy, I laid back and rolled over on my side. I bit my bottom lip, trying not to cry and wishing to die.

The ride home was achingly silent. I stared out my window in the backseat, quietly wiping the tears with the back of my sleeve while my parents sat in the front seat, chain-smoking with the windows up.

My dad pulled the car into one of the empty parking spaces in front of my apartment building, and without saying a word, he got out of the car and opened the door for me to get out. We all walked numbly to my apartment. Once inside, my dad told me to get a phone book. I stood there looking around like I was lost, as if I had never been in the apartment before. I forced myself into the kitchen to get the phone book. I handed it to him and went to my bedroom to lay down.

A few minutes later, my dad walked into my bedroom. He handed me a cordless phone and put the opened phone book beside me. At the top of the bright yellow page, I saw the word "Abortion." I thought to myself *Wait...what! He can't make me!* But as quickly as the thought occurred, I questioned it--*Can he?* I just looked up at him and started to cry. "No, Dad," was all I could say. Without a pause, he sat down next to me on the bed and tenderly spoke. "Honey, I know this is hard, but you must trust me. You cannot have this baby. It will ruin your life."

I pleaded, "But Dad, it's too late now. I've already ruined my life, and I want this baby...please, Dad!"

Now with both of us crying, my dad said, "I know you are worried about your baby, but I am worried about mine. I have to do what is best for you." He pushed the phone book closer and pointed to the number he wanted me to call. "Please, honey. It's for the best. I'll give you a few minutes to make the call. Then gather your clothes and pack a bag because you are coming home with us."

Shaking and crying, I sat in paralyzed disbelief, trying to figure out what to do. I did not want to have an abortion. I knew my parents would not give up easily, but I thought if I was persistent enough, they would eventually back down. I could hear them in the other room rummaging through my closet, looking for a suitcase.

What if Kenny comes home in the middle of this? The thought of it made me shudder. I could imagine Kenny and my dad getting into a fight. I did not trust either one of them to stay calm. I knew Kenny would tell my parents to get the F-K out! Who knows what could happen? I had to get my parents out of the apartment.

I begged my mom and dad to leave so I could at least tell Kenny. I could not just leave without a word. Plus, was not this a decision for Kenny and me to make? My dad became more agitated the more I protested, so he went outside to smoke a cigarette. I sat at the kitchen table with my mom and begged her to talk my dad into leaving. I promised I would tell Kenny and then drive myself to their house the next day.

My dad soon finished his cigarette, walked back into the apartment straight past us, and went into the bedroom to retrieve the phone and phone book. Without a smile, he put them both down in front of me. Standing over me, he spoke with the same authoritative tone in his voice that had scared me my whole life. He said, "Make the appointment. Now!"

I stalled, but again he said, "Now!" Hands trembling, I picked up the phone, dialed the number, and scheduled an appointment for the following Saturday to kill my unborn baby.

Panic swirled throughout my body. My dad said I had an hour to get packed and then he would load my stuff. I wanted to argue and stand up to him, but I felt weak and defeated. The only thing I knew for certain was I did not want Kenny to walk into the middle of it, so I obeyed my father. I hastily packed, wrote a note to Kenny telling him I had gone with my parents, and said I would call him when I could. I put the note under a vase of flowers on the kitchen table and walked out of my apartment for the last time. Later, my sister went over and took the rest of my furniture and belongings to her house for us to get some other time.

My parents would not even let me drive my own car. I handed my keys over to my mom and got into the car with my dad. I could not make myself look at either one of them. When we got to my parent's house, I stormed into the house and slammed my bedroom door like an angry child.

I screamed and cried until I was hoarse. I refused food, and I would not talk to either of them. They would not let me leave the house, and they took out the phones except for one, which they kept with them at all times. My parents--my protectors and providers--had become cruel and complete strangers.

At night, my mother insisted she sleep in my bed with me so I would not "escape." I threatened to kill myself, so they watched me constantly for the entire week. I never got to call Kenny.

The night before the appointment, I lay in my bed on my side. I turned away from my mother and held my tummy. I cried all night. I wanted to pray, but I thought God was mad at me, too. I wanted to ask Him to save my baby, but I didn't think He would answer me since I was "living in sin." My parents had tried to convince me that biracial relationships were not God's will, so I was not even sure how God felt about my baby. One sin had led to another and another, and now an innocent child would have to be sacrificed to hide my biracial "sin" from the world.

I was worthless.

Chapter 19

EMPTY

Definition of empty~containing nothing; not filled or occupied...then why does it feel so heavy?

All night, I begged the sun not to come up I pleaded with the darkness of night to stay so my baby could, too. I wanted that night to last forever so I would not have to give my child over to death before he or she ever took a breath. Despite my pleas, the moon and stars relented to the rising morning sun. I reluctantly climbed into the backseat of my parent's car. I refused breakfast and sat motionless in a tearful daze as we drove, each mile bringing me closer to the place that would separate my baby's tiny body from mine.

I did not want to do this. Where was God? I had learned about Him as a child, and I had even asked Him into my heart. Why was He so far away when I needed Him? *God, please stop this!*

We arrived a half-hour early because there was no way my dad was taking a chance on missing this appointment. If it did not happen today, it couldn't happen. It would be too late because I would be too far along.

We arrived and walked into the drab and lifeless clinic. Most of the chairs in the large waiting room were vacant, but they did not stay empty for long. The longer we sat there, the more people began filing in the doors. No one smiled. I saw young girls like me with what looked like parents. I saw young couples, and I saw duos with one girl there to support another girl. What we all had in common was an unplanned pregnancy.

Maybe not all the babies tucked safely away in their mother's womb that day were unwanted.

Maybe some of the girls were experiencing the same inner grief and torment I was, as I sat there trying to ignore my baby wiggling around in my womb.

Maybe...hopefully...some of these girls would change their minds before it was too late.

Maybe they were convinced this horrible place was their only option.

But I was not convinced. I had a plan. I just hoped it would work.

I planned to tell the truth during counseling, which is a time the girl must go through before the abortion procedure to make an informed decision. I thought that, upon hearing my confession, they would tear up the paperwork and refund my dad's money, and we could all go home. However, unbeknownst to me, my parents had arranged for my mother to be with me the entire time--right up to the point of no return.

So, when they called my name, my mother stood up and held onto my arm and walked me to the back office. My file was reviewed, and a few quick questions asked. I numbly nodded my head yes or no to answer the routine questions. No, I did not know when my last period was, nor did I know exactly how far along I was. It was recommended for me to say the least instead of the most far along I could be that way, there would be no delays in getting the procedure done. "Most likely you will be able to have the one-day procedure," the lady told us, "but if it doesn't work, then they will have to finish it the next day after giving some medications."

Then I was required to sign papers giving them permission to invade my body and kill my child.

The only question I answered audibly with a definite yes was if I have to do this, I wanted to be put under...completely unconscious. I didn't care if I ever woke up. I didn't want to be awake, which I made clear. When the nurse asked me if I had questions, I said, "No questions, but I don't want to do it." My mom nudged me and frowned before she brushed it off and sternly told the lady the decision had already been made-- I was just scared and it was for the best, so we just needed to go ahead and move forward.

With that, the hefty lady shut the folder containing my paperwork, put what looked like a time and date stamp in red ink, and then escorted us back out to the waiting room. Now almost all the chairs were occupied, yet no one was talking. I began to wonder about each of the young women I saw there that day. I wondered why they would voluntarily come to a grim place like this. Were they being forced like I was? Were they scared? Did they feel as sick about this as I did?

The moment I had been dreading for more than a week arrived. The door opened, and a different lady holding my folder glanced at it and then called my name. This time when my mom tried to go with me, the lady would not let her come. The door closed behind us, and I solemnly followed her down a long, stark hallway. There were numbered doors on each side of the hall. She stopped at a door at the end of the hall and opened it. Inside was a large room with a bunch of small changing rooms. She instructed me to go into one of the changing rooms, take off all my clothes, and put on a gown that was folded on a small bench.

Once I finished changing, I sat nervously on the edge of a small folding chair just outside the dressing room to wait for her. The walls were adorned with the most distasteful artwork I have ever seen. There were large framed pencil-type drawings of various women's genitalia. These were not the medical type posters one often sees in OB/GYN offices. These were actual drawings; I am still disturbed by these images more than twenty years after seeing them hanging on those walls.

After a few minutes, she returned for me. I felt dizzy as I stood to my feet to follow her. I wiped my sweaty palms on the front of my gown and then held onto the small mound that was my baby. My throat was parched, and it was difficult to swallow. I had not had anything to eat or drink since the day before. I was startled by my sudden raging hunger and thirst.

I felt like I was going to collapse before I could take another step. I wish I would have collapsed right there in the hallway. My vision blurred as I fought the raging anxiety and panic. The large woman stopped in front of one of the numbered doors, but I did not look at the number. I knew if I looked at it, I would hate that number for the rest of my life.

She opened the door and told me to sit on the exam table and wait. While I sat there naked and shivering under the thin, ugly gown, I rehearsed what I would say when the doctor came in the room. I was freezing cold yet sweating at the same time. I was so thirsty and lightheaded. I just wanted to go back to my apartment and crawl under my safe warm blankets and hide from the entire world.

I do not know how long I sat there when, without warning, the door abruptly swung open. Two large black women entered the room followed by a tall, wizard-looking, white-haired wrinkled man, minus the pointy hat. With no expression or compassion on their faces, they approached me, and I completely lost my composure. Coming towards me, the two women split, each walking to one side of the exam type table where I sat. The wizard-looking man wearing a duster-length white coat lab coat stood closely by, adjusting dials on a free-standing machine, and looking at my folder.

I knew this was my last chance. I had to tell them what I had been waiting to say this whole time. I blurted out, "I don't want to have an abortion." They looked at me like I had three heads. One of the women, cocking her nappy head to the side, said in a thick, ghetto-sounding accent, "Gurl, you crazy. It's too late now! Didn't you go to counseling?" I began to cry at their reaction. "Yes," I stammered through my tears, "but my mom was in there, and I couldn't say no in front of her. I needed to wait until I was alone, and now I finally am, so I'm saying I don't want an abortion."

The three of them looked at each other with an amused expression and then back at me. Then the other big lady spoke. "Look lil' gurl, you shoulda got all that straight b'fore you got back here. We ain't got time for shit like this." I looked at Dr. Wizard, thinking he would hear this unprofessional language and come to my rescue, firing both of them on the spot. Instead, much to my surprise, he snapped the folder shut and tossed it on a nearby counter. Then looking over his small round, glasses that sat low on his nose, he coldly spoke words I will never forget.

"Scoot your ass down to the end of the table. Let's get this over with."

Chapter 20

TORN

*Definition of torn~ To pull apart or in pieces by force; rend.
To pull or snatch violently; wrench away with force. To divide
or disrupt. To wound or injure by or as if by rending;
lacerate: grief that tears the heart. (Freedictionary.com)*

With his eyes showing zero emotion, he turned his gaze from me to the strange-looking machine looming beside us and turned it on. One of the women "clotheslined" me across the neck, abruptly forcing me to lay back. In a panic, I started kicking and screaming. One of them laid herself across the upper part of my body, covering my nose and mouth with her large hands. The other one told me, "Shut the hell up, and give me your arm." I begged and pleaded for them to stop, but they didn't.

My legs were forced apart and belted into cold, metal stirrups. I cried out in pain as I felt a steady, stabbing, excruciating pain and heard a vacuum-type suction noise. I screamed, "I wanted to be asleep!" One of the heavy women said, "Calm your crazy ass down and let me put this needle in your arm then!" I couldn't stand the immense pain or the sounds of the killing any longer.

"Dear God, please help me," I managed to utter before I fully submitted to the torture. I straightened out my arm, allowing a long needle to be inserted that would put me out of consciousness. "How long... please, how much longer? I'm dying."

Those were the last words I said before everything went black.

I groggily tried to open my eyes, which felt like they had been glued shut. One of those same women was slapping me on both sides of my face, harshly shaking me awake. "Gurl, you takin' way too long to wake up. This ain't the Shangri La!" I blinked a few times trying to remember where I was. I could not swallow, I was extremely disoriented, and I hurt badly. I instinctively rolled on my side to ease the cramping and closed my eyes. The woman said, "Oh naw you don't, cupcake. You gotsta get ur ass up. We need this room for the next 'un." It took only a few seconds for me to remember where I was and what had happened.

I was too hoarse from screaming to say much, but I tried anyway. I told her not to fucking touch me. I somehow made it to a semi-upright position and put on the thick pad and stretchy panties she left beside me. All I could think of was water at that moment. I focused my eyes and saw an unused IV pole nearby. I tried holding on to it to help me stand, but it rolled and tipped over, crashing to the floor. I could not stand up straight and should not have been attempting to walk. I tried yelling for someone to help me. I felt like I was going to pass out.

Someone else who worked there assisted me to the recovery room. This was a huge, open room filled with rolling, gurney-type beds like the ones on ambulances and many old, unsanitary-looking recliners. There were at least twenty beds. There was a nurse's station at the far end of the room, but there was only one "nurse," and she stayed seated the entire time I was there. I did not see her tend to a single girl while I was in recovery.

I needed to lay down. I was hurting more than I ever had in my life. The lady brought me some Tylenol and a paper cup with some water. Still disoriented and shaky, I accidentally dropped the red and white pills on the floor. My throat burned when I swallowed those first few sips of water, but I was so thirsty that I gladly drank all of the water in the small cup. I held it out and said, "More please."

She went to get more water. As she began to walk away, my body rejected the fluid. She looked over her shoulder but didn't turn around. She just kept walking in the opposite direction while nasty, green bile ran down my face and into my long, blonde hair.

When she returned with another cup of water, she asked who brought me. I said my parents had, and she asked if I wanted her to go get my mom. Weakly, I replied, "Yes." I don't know how long I laid there curled up in the fetal position with green vomit in my hair, rocking back and forth to ease the immense cramping. I could hardly stand to open my eyes and look around the room.

When I finally could look around, I saw almost every recliner or gurney held a young woman who had just undergone the same agonizing procedure I had. All of us were lying on our sides, writhing in pain--in the exact same position our babies had been in right before they were cruelly ripped from our wombs. Another girl was brought in every few minutes.

The "recovery" lasted as long as you needed. The only requirements to be met before being released were that you had to be able to hobble well enough to get yourself out and your bleeding had to be "under control," whatever that meant.

I noticed the "nurse" sat at her desk doing what looked like some sort of paperwork. As far as I could tell, her only job was to check the girl's pad to approve or deny her request to leave. She conducted her duty with the same uncaring demeanor as her coworkers did theirs. No compassion, no helpful words or actions--just cold eyes looking through each girl who hobbled to her desk to be cleared to leave or sent back to recover longer. As a result, my mother and one other girl's mother were the only two people paying attention to all the girls.

My attention shifted from the lifeless woman at the nurse's desk to a small-framed girl who had just rolled off her gurney and crashed onto the cold hard floor. A sickening thud was heard as she hit the floor. My mom and the other mom both quickly jumped up and ran over to help her. Seeing her crying and moaning in pain on the dirty floor made me physically ill.

Suddenly, bile rose up again. Still lying helplessly on my side, I felt the vomit trickle down the side of my face and into my hair again. The other mom saw me vomiting, and she kindly brought me some wet paper towels and wiped the green sickness from my face and hair. With tears and a visible sadness in her eyes, she said, "You are a beautiful girl. You are going to be okay."

To this very day, I still remember this woman and her words while she lovingly cleaned me up. She spoke HOPE to me that horrible day. She has most likely forgotten me, but I will not forget her. Kindness amid pure evil tends to become etched in the mind forever.

After I could no longer watch young women writhe in pain, hear their cries and moans, and smell putrid vomit and blood, I was determined to get up and walk out of there. My mom brought me my clothes and helped me put them on. I still could not stand up all the way, but I gathered enough strength to shuffle my way to the lifeless nurse and ask for her approval to leave.

This is exactly the way it happened.

Bent over almost in half, like an aged woman, I limped to the front of her station area and told her my name. She then told me to walk around to where she sat and to stand up straight. It took all the strength I had to put my left hand on her desk and push myself upwards. Next, she grabbed a hold of the waistband of my sweatpants and stretched them as far as they could go, almost pulling me forward onto her lap. She looked into my underwear at the bloody pad, then she nodded her head a few times in an affirmative way and said I could go.

I could not get out of there fast enough. My mom helped me put on my shoes and took hold of my arm for the second time that day. She helped me walk slowly down the long hallway and into the waiting area. My dad looked up at me and tried to smile. He stood up and put my arm across his shoulders and told me to put my other arm across my mom's shoulders. I did, and the three of us walked out, without my baby who was left torn and discarded into some waste receptacle with hundreds of others from that day.

Since that day, I never have been nor will I ever be the same.

In the parking lot, my dad helped me get settled in the back seat of the car and handed me a pillow and blanket he had put in the trunk that morning. He said he would get me whatever I wanted to eat. The thought of food repulsed me, but I was still very thirsty. I couldn't eat, but I was able to drink a milkshake and some water. Exhaustion superseded the physical pain, and I slept the rest of the way home.

Once home, my parents helped me into the house. All I wanted was a hot shower and some clean pajamas. After the shower, I took some pain medicine and crawled into my bed. It was the same bed, but I was not the same girl who used to sleep there. I was missing a part of myself--a part of my heart.

My baby, the innocent little one who had been with me just the night before, who rested safely beneath my heart, was gone. I would never hold this child or see its tiny face on this side of heaven. I wouldn't get to count fingers and toes; I would never hear the laughter or the cries.

My arms and heart were emptied when my womb was.

My mother did not sleep in bed with me that night. I was no longer a flight risk, for I was too weak. That night and many nights after, I grieved for a child I would never meet. I still do.

Chapter 21

LOVE HATES A SECRET

You only know a part of me, I am a universe full of secrets~Unknown

Never again did my parents speak of that day. My mom and dad both moved on like it never happened. I did not tell them of the traumatic experience I had behind closed doors. For some strange reason, I felt I needed to protect them from knowing the suffering and pain I experienced. My mom saw part of it in the recovery room, but she was spared from the sounds, the smells, the tearing, the ripping, the blood, and the murdering.

I slept most of that Sunday. I had not yet been able to talk to Kenny. He still had no idea what was going on or that our child was gone. My parents were watching me like a hawk, so I had to be careful. I found out my dad had officially moved Kenny and me out of the apartment we shared. My dad paid the remainder of the lease since my name was on it, and he asked my sister to tell Kenny to get his belongings out. Kenny did so without knowing why, when, or if I would be back.

After a few days, I snuck to a friend's house to call him. He was furious with me for leaving. I tried to explain, but he didn't understand. I did not tell him about the abortion; I just couldn't do it over the phone. I told my parents I needed to go back and officially end it with Kenny. I said it was completely unfair not to allow me to tell him in person.

I decided with or without my parent's permission, I was going to see Kenny. I drove to his Aunt's house to pick him up. I didn't get out of the car for two reasons. First, I didn't want to face his family, and secondly, I didn't want Kenny to see my flattened belly yet. When he got into my car, neither of us knew what to say. We drove to a nearby park to talk.

I didn't know how to tell him. I knew he was going to be angry, but I was totally unprepared for his reaction. Before I could say anything, Kenny put his large hand on my stomach where our baby had been. It was flat where there was a visible bump the last time, he saw me three weeks ago. The bump was gone. I started to cry.

Kenny opened the car door and stepped out visibly shaking. He screamed NO and fell to the ground weeping. I got out of the car and went to him. I tried to console him, but I was unsure of what to do. I had been grieving this loss for several weeks, but this was all new to him. I had never seen Kenny so upset or crying so audibly. I had seen him angry lots of times, and I had even seen him cry several times after a fight, but I had never seen him--or anyone, for that matter--as emotionally distraught as he was at that moment.

Kenny was the only person who loved our baby as much as I did, and this crushed him. I don't know how long he cried, but finally he calmed down enough for me to tell him the story of how our baby died.

We sat together in the park until well after dark. We talked and cried for hours. We agreed as much as we loved each other, it would never work between us. We were from two quite different sides of the track. My parents were never going to accept our relationship, and he would never forgive them for the loss of our baby. We both knew they would make it impossible for us to be happy. I was emotionally spent, and I had no more strength to fight them or him. We agreed to part as friends and try to move forward with our lives.

After taking Kenny back to his Aunt's house, I drove away feeling even more lost and empty than I ever had before. Our baby was gone. I knew I had to bury our relationship and leave it in the past. I loved Kenny and he loved me, but we both knew it needed to be over. I grieved for all that had been lost.

The only slight glimmer of hope was maybe I could still have a friendship with Max. He was my first love, and nothing could ever change that. I would always love him, but I feared I had lost him, even as a friend. And, if I had lost him, I wouldn't blame him one bit why would he possibly want anything to do with me now?

After my parents found out about the pregnancy and made me go to their house, the only person they said I could speak to was Max. They asked me if I had told him, and I admitted I hadn't yet, but I knew I had to. I reluctantly called Max and told him the whole ugly truth, including the scheduled abortion.

Max was calm, and he didn't accuse me of being a cheating tramp. He did nothing to deserve what I was putting him through. He had stayed faithful to our relationship, and here I was pregnant by another man. He didn't insult, yell, cuss, or call me names. He was tender, reassuring, and loving—never harsh. I was brutally honest with him for the first time in a very long time.

To this day, I don't understand how Max could love me despite all my dysfunction. Unfortunately, this would not be the last time I would put him through undeserved distress and turmoil. I was a wreck, and it would take the love of both Max and God to save me.

Years ago, I had given my heart to Max, and I had asked Jesus into my heart when I was a child, but I was still not whole. I would remain broken until I surrendered my whole heart back to its maker, allowing Him to transform me and put all the broken pieces back together again. Not until I fully surrendered my life to the Lord would I ever experience the healing and peace I had been chasing since I was a child.

Wholeness, peace, joy, fulfillment: for now, they eluded me. I was in hot pursuit, but I could never quite reach them. The further I fell from grace, the more I lost sight of the HOPE Jesus introduced me to on that day when I chose to stay in the race and continue the chase.

Chapter 22

BACK IN THE SACK

*Why do I keep looking for happiness in the same place I lost it? My search is futile~*Lee

On the afternoon of the abortion, Max called my parents to check on me. He did not want to speak to me that day, the next, or the day after that, but he checked with my parents just to make sure I was doing okay. Finally, on the fourth day, Max asked to talk to me.

When I heard his voice, I was comforted for the first time since the abortion. I had not told my parents any details of the experience, but I told Max every detail of the horror I experienced that day. I never wanted to keep another secret from him, as painful as it was for both of us. Just like after the rape, Max entered into the depths of my pain and sat right in the midst of it with me for as long as I needed. We talked a few more times after that, but they were short conversations. Max needed time to process everything, and so did I.

Several weeks later, Max called and told me he needed to end our relationship. His words were soft and gentle. He said he would always love me but did not see forever with me anymore. He wanted me to keep the promise ring he had given me before he left for boot camp, though. The ring represented his promise to come back for me, a promise he kept.

It was me who couldn't keep my promise, a promise to wait for him.

I had betrayed his trust and broken every promise along with his heart. I couldn't possibly blame him for breaking up with me. I couldn't be mad at him or hold any hard feelings. He had been more than kind to me. Standing with me through the absolute lowest times of my life, he had been exceedingly long-suffering and fair. I knew I would always love him, but I wanted him to find someone who would love him better than I could. I loved him enough to let him go.

After so much loss in such a short period of time, I lost all HOPE and sank even lower into self-loathing and depression. The chase began again. I chased loneliness with tequila, I chased emptiness with vodka, I chased anxiety with marijuana, and I chased depression with Xanax. I took Ecstasy hoping it would feel like love. I embraced Jim Beam and Jack Daniels like the old friends they were.

I was still living with my parents, and as usual, they were worried about me. Once again, I was staying out late into the night. There was an Air Force base where we lived, so there was no shortage of "flyboys." I started going to the base several nights a week, and it wasn't long before I was dating several of the pilots. I did not want anything serious, but I had never *not* had a boyfriend--or several at a time--so why start now?

I had just turned twenty. I wanted to get out of my own head because there was too much sadness and confusion in there. The only way I knew how to go on was to accept the next date or go to the next club. I was and always had been a tease; I was a pro at leading men exactly where I wanted them to go. I had been practicing since I was twelve years old.

Up to now, though, I had only given myself to two men, both emotionally and physically, and those relationships both ended. So, I reset my boundaries back to the ones I had when I was fifteen--before the rape. I did not intend to have sex with anyone again until marriage. The consequences were much too expensive, and my emotional bank account was empty.

I played by my rules for a few weeks--until one night, I let a situation go too far. Two of my girlfriends and I had gone out to the Air Force Base to party, and we had started drinking even before we got there. After several hours of flirting, dancing, and way too many drinks in the O Club, I ended up leaving with one of the pilots I had been dating.

I was hammered and just wanted to lay down and sleep it off for a little while. We went back to his barracks, but he was not in the mood for sleep. My defenses were down, and I was too drunk to care. I let him undress me; one thing led to another, and we had sex.

I woke up about the time I needed to be at work the next morning. I quietly gathered my clothes, found my keys, and left without saying good-bye. I was so mad at myself; I sped home and walked into the house half-dressed only to find my parents sitting at the kitchen table drinking coffee. They stared at me in disbelief. Then they started in on me about being out all night, at who knows where, doing who knows what, with who knows who, and it better NOT be Kenny!

I retorted that I could do whatever I wanted because "I'm not a teenager!" This didn't go over well at all. If I couldn't live by their rules, then they said I couldn't live there. "FINE!!" I shouted. "I'm moving out!"

And I did. I got an apartment with a girlfriend. Her brother owned some apartments, and he let us have one for super cheap. Now I didn't have to answer to *anyone*. Not my parents, not Kenny, not Max. I was on my own.

The Air Force guy I had slept with kept calling me, and I did my best to avoid him. I had no interest in ever sleeping with him again. I knew it would be difficult to say no to sex now, so the easiest thing to do was hook up with someone else. I did the next weekend. The relationship didn't last long with the new guy either. He was graduating with orders to fly A-10s at another base. So, I continued this behavior of flirting, hooking up, dating for a few weeks, teasing, dumping, and doing it all over again.

Before long, the base and the bars in town became boring, so my girlfriends and I started going to clubs in nearby Oklahoma City. Guess who I ran into? Kenny. When I saw him, he bought me a drink. Then he bought another, and we ended up leaving together. I had no problem falling back into bed with him--he was familiar, and I still loved him.

But true to Kenny's nature, it was not even a week before he started his possessive rages. We were just casually dating, so he had no right to be so jealous, at least in my mind. He demanded to know every guy I talked to. He threatened to kick everyone's ass who even looked at me. He threatened to kick my ass if he thought I had given him reason to.

After a few weeks, he started driving several hours to my apartment, showing up randomly to keep an eye on me. These unannounced visits turned into overnights together, and soon, he was staying several days at a time. I knew if my parents found out he was back in my life; they would kill him—and me.

The fighting with Kenny became more violent. He used to threaten to hit me, but he never had. Now I was terrified he would really do it. One night he showed up at my apartment. My roommate and I had several friends over drinking and hanging out, and most of them were guys. Kenny barged in unexpectedly, started knocking things over, and demanded everyone leave. I stood up to him, and he shoved me.

I landed on a cement block on the balcony and fractured my tailbone and scraped up my arms. He pulled me up by my hair and pushed me around, saying if he ever caught another guy anywhere near me, he would kick both our asses. Fighting like this went on for several months, and one of us was about to crack.

I didn't know how to end it with Kenny, but I knew I had to—and this time for good.

Chapter 23

WILL YOU MARRY ME?

*You will forever be my always~*Swapna Rajput

My parent's prayers were answered when HOPE found me once again. One day, my dad came by my work and asked me to come over for dinner. I had not seen them very often since I moved out. He told me they had been praying for me and how much they missed me. He also said they had something to tell me.

During our dinner conversation, my dad shared that Max had called a couple of times to check on me. I didn't have a phone at my new apartment (and cell phones didn't exist yet), so my dad told Max he'd give me the message. Later that evening, I called Max. His soothing voice on the other end of the phone line reduced me to tears; just the sound of his voice was all it took to reawaken the love I had buried deep in my heart. Oh, how I missed him, and now I knew he was missing me, too!

Max and I talked for over an hour, then arranged to talk again in a few days. These calls lasted for several weeks, and the more we talked, the more we both wanted to give our relationship another chance. Max told me he had dated a few girls since our official break-up, but none of them filled the empty place in his heart. He said the thought of spending forever without me left him undone. Even after all the heartache I had put him through, he told me he still loved me and always would. This was my chance at genuine love for a lifetime.

A lifeline was offered, and I intended to take it! HOPE had searched me out--HOPE had returned for me.

Soon, Max asked my dad if I could come out to California and spend a few months so we could work on our relationship. My dad said no; he could not condone it unless we were married. But my dad did agree to let me go to Oceanside for a two-week visit. He told us this should be enough time to decide our future. I couldn't wait to get on an airplane and fly off into the sunset, leaving my past behind.

But before I could go, I had to break it off with Kenny and make some excuse as to why I was leaving. He was more violent and possessive than ever, so I told him only part of the truth. I told Kenny that my parents wanted to do something nice for me, so they were sending me on a vacation to get away and heal emotionally. I said I would be gone for several weeks, but of course, I did not tell him I was going to visit Max. I was too afraid of his reaction.

Excitedly, I packed plenty of suntan lotion and headed west to sunny California to see my first love.

Max picked me up at the airport with a borrowed pick-up truck and a bouquet of flowers. He made arrangements for us to stay with another Marine and his wife. During the day, we drove around sightseeing, and at night, we sat on the beach listening to the waves roll in and talking late into the night. We had so much to work through. Less than six months ago, I had been pregnant with another man's child. A man I was still involved with. That's a lot to bounce back from.

While I knew without a doubt I wanted to be with Max, I lived in Oklahoma, and he lived in California. Long distance dating would never work--there was too much hurt and pain as well as the trust barrier being shattered long ago. I knew I could never be trusted.

As the date to depart California drew near, we still had not decided. Our hearts had been through so much, and while we were making progress, we needed more time. On the last night of my visit, we sat on the soft, golden sand cuddled up in a warm blanket to shield us from the cool Pacific breeze. Words were buried under all the emotion we felt, so we sat in silence for a long while just listening to the sound of our hearts beating together in a steady rhythm. As we listened, allowing our hearts to decide, we both knew our real love story was yet to be written.

That night under the stars, Max proposed to me. He asked me to be his forever as he slid a heart-shaped diamond ring on my left hand...and I said yes.

Chapter 24

TAINTED LOVE

Don't touch me please I cannot stand the way you tease
~Ed Cobb

A wedding date was set for just six short weeks away, and we tearfully said our goodbyes.

I returned to Oklahoma and went back to work the next day. I did not have an official plan for how to tell Kenny where I had been and what had happened. I didn't have long to think about it either. Someone told Kenny I was back. When I got off work that day, Kenny was waiting for me at my apartment. I hurriedly slipped the small gold band with the heart-shaped diamond from my finger and dropped it in my purse. I could not let him see the ring!

Kenny was excited to see me. He told me how beautiful, tanned, and rested I looked from my little getaway. I weakly smiled and told him we needed to talk. I wanted to wait until my roommate got home to tell him so if he got violent, she would be there. It was well past time for her to get home, and she still did not show up. Finally, I couldn't stall any longer. He knew something was going on.

Kenny and I sat down on the couch, and I began: "Kenny, while I was away, I did a lot of thinking. I realized this is never going to work between us. We have tried multiple times, and it just doesn't work. We are toxic together...so it's over. This time, it's really over."

Kenny tried to run the same lines he always did when we had a break-up conversation. At first, he was sugary sweet, saying, "Oh baby, you don't mean it. You know you love me." I insisted it was really different this time, but he was adamant it wasn't. He said we had tried multiple times to be apart and that never worked either.

After about fifteen minutes or so, he was done talking. He pulled me close, and while kissing me, he said, "Come on baby, I want you. Take off your clothes. I've missed you so much, baby girl." I tried to resist him, but the more I pushed him away, the more passionate he got. Within a few more minutes, he picked me up and carried me to the bedroom.

Before I knew it, Kenny and I were back in bed together. And I hated myself for it! *Why couldn't I stand up to him? Why was I so weak that he could melt me like butter? What was wrong with me? I had only been engaged for a couple of days! Could I not be faithful for at least a week??* I was so mad at myself! Guilt consumed me, and I couldn't even face my own reflection in the mirror.

I soon went into self-destruct overdrive. I drank excessively over the next few weeks and mixed several drugs, trying to drown the worthless and guilty feelings I battled inside. I was a hot mess. I knew I could never let Kenny into my bed again; I had to avoid him at all costs. I told him I had to go out of town for some training on a new cosmetic line. It was a total lie, but I did not want to see him. I started going out to the Air Force base again to party at night. It was the only place I could go where Kenny couldn't get to me...well, besides my parent's house, but I didn't want to go there.

Ironically, my mother and I planned my upcoming wedding during the day, but at night, I was in the O Club dancing, drinking, and messing around with Air Force pilots to avoid sleeping with Kenny.

And on the day, I picked out my wedding dress, I was hungover and guilt-ridden. I felt like a complete fraud standing there looking in the mirror, wearing a gorgeous white gown with the long train, just like I envisioned as a child. Except this was nothing like I envisioned--I was wrong on so many levels. I did not deserve to be anyone's bride...especially Max's.

Max deserved someone much better than me. What in the world did he see in me anyway?

The wedding arrangements were now complete: invitations had been stamped and mailed, cake and floral bouquets were ordered, and my dress and pew bows were all ready. But was I ready? I sat at my round glass-top kitchen table staring at the small, white cocktail-sized napkins. Each one was embossed in royal blue foil lettering with our names. I traced our names, "Max Tyler and Lee Ann," with my pointer finger while trying to make sense of everything in my head.

Could I possibly go through with getting married? Should I go through with it? Was it too late to back out and spare Max a lifetime of dysfunction with me? The invitations had been mailed, and the scheduled day was quickly approaching. And Max would be on a flight to me in less than a week.

To prepare, I had been packing my apartment and getting ready to leave my past in Oklahoma. I had never been away from my family and friends for more than a few weeks at a time. I was nervous and excited, ready but not ready, all at the same time. I got up to finish loading a few more boxes to take over to my parent's house. I put the boxes in the back of my car and was walking back up the stairs to my apartment to get my purse.

Kenny pulled up. I didn't expect him that day because I had been successfully avoiding him. I was still "supposed" to be out of town. I had not told him the whole truth. I was a pro at telling half-truths, but the whole truth I rarely ever told...not even to myself. I had told Kenny that I was moving out of my apartment, so the boxes were no surprise. I just had not told him where I was moving or why, but I was about to.

Kenny angrily followed me upstairs. He knew I had been avoiding him, and he was there to demand I tell him why. I tried to be as calm as possible, reminding him of all the break-up conversations we had. I told him I was avoiding him because staying away from him was the only way we would ever end it.

I started crying, and Kenny was trying to comfort me while not understanding the gravity of the situation. I pushed him away, crying even harder before I was able to say these words--just above a whisper--"Kenny, I love you, but this really HAS to be over." Then after a long pause, I continued. "I'm getting married to Max," I said softly.

I don't know if Kenny didn't hear me or maybe just didn't believe me. He just looked at me like my statement had not registered, so I repeated it, louder this time while looking him straight in the eyes. "Kenny, I'm getting married to Max. This is over. It HAS to be over!"

He started cussing me out and threatening me. He said he would not let me marry anyone else. "You're MINE!" he screamed and shoved me on the bed. Crying and trying to get away from him, I wildly kicked my legs and hit him in the chest while he just sat on me holding me down with his body weight. He finally laid down on top of me sobbing. I stopped fighting, and we cried together. We laid there for a few minutes without any words, both of us emotionally wrung out.

Then Kenny leaned down and softly kissed me. I didn't resist. I returned his affection and kissed him back. My body said *yes* while my heart screamed *no*. My sanity was temporarily swept away by the intense physical attraction between the two of us. We made love that afternoon and evening, both of us knowing it would be the last time.

It was extremely late when I tenderly said, "Kenny, you have to go now." Not knowing how he would react, I braced myself for his reply, but he surprised me. He sadly said, "I have always known how much you love Max. I just wish you could love me like that." He stood up and walked into the bathroom to get dressed, leaving me sobbing on the bed.

I only saw Kenny one more time before the wedding day. I had not seen or heard from him in almost a week. I had been out partying with my girlfriends all evening, and we had all gone back to my apartment to hang out. Max was arriving the next day. We just got settled in when I heard the familiar sound of Kenny's car. My heart started racing, and a cold chill went down my spine. I just knew something wasn't right.

Kenny stomped up the steps and banged on the door. I was terrified to open it, but I knew he wouldn't go away if I didn't. I opened the door partway, planning to go outside to talk with him. He was drunk and pushed his way past me. The more I tried to talk him down, the more upset he got. I went into the kitchen to get away from him, but he followed me in there. He shoved me into the counter and spun me around to face him. Angrily, he reared back his fist and said, "If I can't stop you from walking down the aisle, I can damn sure make sure you walk down it with a black eye!"

Kenny's fist was shaking, and he was trembling. I calmly reached my hands up, maintaining eye contact. I gently placed my hands on each side of his face like I had so many times before when he wasn't angry. I looked into his eyes and said, "I will always love you." He relaxed and put his fist down. He smoothed my hair back and said, "I love you, baby. I'm so sorry. For everything." We stood in the kitchen, crying, and hugging for a while.

When I looked up at him, he leaned down and kissed me one last time, and then he calmly walked out the door. It was finally over.

****

To say I was on an emotional rollercoaster would be a colossal understatement. My heart did not have room for two men, and I had to completely let go of one to give the other my whole heart forever.

I had finally closed the chapters that contained my love for Kenny, although it took longer than it should have. I loved both of them, but I could only marry one. I knew in my heart of hearts that Max was the one. I was ready to get married and start our life in California.

Chapter 25

MARITAL BLISS?

A successful marriage requires falling in love many times,
*always with the same person~*Mignon McLaughlin

Max was arriving several days before our wedding so we could have the required blood tests done and undergo the recommended pre-marital counseling sessions. I mean, we didn't even need premarital counseling. *Did we?* As I drove to the airport to pick Max up, I tried desperately to clear my head of what had happened the night before. I was thankful I did not have to explain a black eye, and I hoped Kenny would not show up again.

At the airport, I parked my car and then sat inside for a few minutes, primping, and pulling myself together before going inside to meet Max. When I saw him in the distance walking towards me, mixed emotions battled within my heart. He wrapped me in a warm hug, and then we strolled arm-in-arm as we made our way to the baggage claim area.

Immediately, though, I could tell Max was not his usual self. I sensed something was off. It bothered me, but I dismissed the thought, deciding it was *me* who was off, not him. We talked and held hands as we drove, but there was definitely a different vibe between us. It felt strange like he was hiding something from me. But I knew it was me who was harboring more secrets.

I kept telling myself it was just my imagination and my own guilt that I was projecting onto him. I wanted to blurt out how I had been unfaithful multiple times since we had been together in California. I wanted to tell him everything, but I didn't. I kept silent, allowing secrets and fears to slowly eat away at more of my soul.

During the drive from the airport, Max casually mentioned he had been to a party of some sort the night before he flew out. I thought it strange because Max didn't go to parties. He said he drank way too much and ended up staying the night where the party was. *Hmmm*, I thought. Max drinking too much? I had never known him to drink at all.

Then he tells me while he was "sleeping it off," he woke up to find his motorcycle had been stolen. Okay, so maybe that's what it was. He was upset about his stolen bike. But I wasn't buying it. I could tell there was more he wasn't telling me. *Maybe it wouldn't be a bad idea to add a few extra sessions of premarital counseling*, I thought.

Over the next couple of days, the phone rang a few times. It was a California number—a female asking to speak to Max. Who was I to question him? But I did it anyway. "Who's the girl who keeps calling?" I asked. Max told me the party was at her apartment, and he just ended up crashing there with several others so he wouldn't be driving while intoxicated. I thought it was very responsible of him and about how many times I had not made that choice. He said since it was her place the motorcycle was stolen from; she was handling the police reports and details while he was gone for a few weeks. Makes sense. But I still sensed there was more to the story.

Again, I put it out of my mind, thinking it was my own guilty conscience bothering me. Besides, I had no reason to distrust Max. He had never given me any reason to even be suspicious of him. Even so, he was somewhat distant and distracted. I wondered if he knew about Kenny and me. Maybe that was it.

The emotional distance was evident, even to my parents. My mom spoke up about it two days before the wedding. She and my dad sat us down and told us they could tell something wasn't right. They were used to my shenanigans, but to have Max acting strange worried them. The four of us sat down outside by the pool to talk.

"Kids," my mom said. "Listen. I know this is a big deal getting married and all, and if you guys are unsure and want to back out, it's okay." Then, my parents took turns telling us what a lifelong commitment marriage is and how they would rather us wait until we are sure than to make a mistake and end up getting a divorce down the road. They said we should really go talk about it, just the two of us, and decide one way or the other.

"Just let us know as soon as you can so we can cancel everything tomorrow and let everyone on the guest list know the wedding has been called off," my mom stated in a matter-of-fact tone. My dad ended the talk by saying, "We want you to get married, but we love you both too much to make you feel pressured if you're not ready. Do what you think is best for you."

Max and I drove to a Mexican restaurant and settled into a booth at the back of the restaurant to decide one way or the other. Nothing about that conversation stands out in my memory. It was more about what wasn't said than what was. It was about what we kept hidden when we had the opportunity, to be honest, that would haunt us later. We were both keeping secrets. So, with skeletons in the closet hanging right next to the tux and wedding gown, we agreed to walk down the aisle, for better or for worse.

At last, my wedding day arrived. My dad stood with me, arm-in-arm at the back of the church. He said, "Listen, honey. This is your last chance. See that door over there? We can walk out of it together and never look back. You don't have to do this. Are you sure?" I looked at the door and back at my dad several times before taking a deep breath, exhaling, and saying, "Yes, Dad. I'm sure."

On a hot day in the middle of August, I held my dad's arm for the last time as his little girl. With tears streaming down his softly wrinkled face, my dad proudly walked me down the aisle. Max and I said our vows in front of our closest family and friends. Songs played, rings were exchanged, cake was eaten, and photographs were taken.

With unrevealed secrets waiting in the wings and each of us temporarily ignoring our doubts, we became husband and wife.

Chapter 26

CALI

"Meant to be?' It's just something people say so that they don't have to look at all the things they did wrong and wish they could take back. Only by the time they figure that out, it's too late."~ Zoey Dean, California Dreaming

The goodbyes to my parents, family, and friends were tough. I wanted to go, but I wanted to stay. Max and I were practically strangers. We had spent only a few days together before the wedding and only a few short weeks when we got engaged. So much had happened, and we were no longer the two teenage love birds we had been before Max left to become a Marine. At only twenty years of age, we had already been through so much, yet our lives were really only just beginning.

What little we had was loaded into a rented moving truck and with only $1,500 to our names, gifted from my parents, we set out as husband and wife to conquer the world. We were newlyweds, but this was no honeymoon.

We barely spoke in the noisy moving truck, and I cried and smoked cheap cigarettes the entire way from Oklahoma to California. Leaving all that is familiar and stepping into the unknown is difficult under normal circumstances, but with the past events looming over us and unexposed secrets, I had a feeling we were headed for trouble.

Bouncing down the seemingly endless highway was wearisome. The unsightly torn fabric, held together with silver duct tape, covered the uncomfortable bucket seats in the cab of the truck and stuck to the back of my thighs. The air conditioner quit working after only about a hundred miles into the long haul. The hot Texas air blew in through the open windows. Even if we had wanted to talk, it would have been almost impossible to hear each other's words. The truck rattled noisily, but the silence between us was deafening. The distance between the seats in the cab was nothing compared to the distance of our hearts.

Did this marriage even stand a chance?

After a few miserable days, we finally pulled into Oceanside, California, the city we would call home for the next two years. Early the next morning, Max and I set out to find a place to live and sort out our lives. We settled on a one-bedroom apartment we really couldn't afford. As an enlisted Marine, Max's paycheck from the U.S. Government certainly did not reflect his worth. With no other option, we signed a lease and began to unpack our worldly goods and our lives.

Once we were unpacked and settled in, Max had to go back to work. It was so lonely sitting in the apartment all day by myself. I didn't know anyone, and we couldn't afford cable. We only had one vehicle, which Max drove to work. I was left cooped up all day with absolutely nothing to do. I sat alone with my thoughts day after day. I hated my new life.

When Max got his first paycheck after we got married, we finally got a telephone line activated in the apartment. The phone line became a lifeline for me. We could not afford a long-distance phone bill, so I collect-called my parents and friends. I missed them all terribly. I had never been isolated like this before. I'd always had lots of people around. After a few weeks, I was stir crazy.

A day or two after we got the phone put in, it rang, and when I picked up the receiver, I heard the vaguely familiar voice of the girl who had been calling my parent's house while we were still in Oklahoma. In a cheery voice, she asked, "Is Max there?" Surprised but not alarmed, I responded calmly telling her he was not home. The call ended, but she continued to call several times over the next few days. I told Max the same girl was calling for him and inquired what she was calling about. He said she was calling about the details of the night his motorcycle was stolen.

I had a very suspicious and unsettled feeling. I sensed there was more to the story.

During the next few days, Max was still acting strange like he had since he arrived in Oklahoma for our wedding. I knew he was hiding something. Stuck in the apartment all day, I had plenty of time to play out many different scenarios in my head, my own guilt contributing to the possibilities. I also had plenty of time on my hands to dig through Max's belongings.

When we arrived in California, Max went to his barracks and packed up all his stuff, but he had not yet had a chance to unpack everything once he brought it to our apartment. So, I decided to help him out while he was at work. I began to sort through boxes and bags. It didn't take long to discover Max's secret. I found a few cards, a few letters, and a few condoms!

My hands shook, and I was seething with anger as I read the words "she" had written to him. My anger raged as I began ripping and tearing through his bags. More incriminating evidence surfaced as I uncovered the details of his secret. This Julie girl was NOT a friend of a friend like Max had said, she was his girlfriend! Now all his edginess and uncharacteristic behavior made sense.

I screamed and cried into the emptiness of the apartment. I paced the tiny apartment all day, waiting to explode when Max got home from work. Somehow all the heartbreak I had put him through didn't matter to me. At that moment, all I could focus on was *his* betrayal.

How could he do this to me?

On a typical day, Max got home around 5:00 p.m. I intended to be ready! But around 3:00 p.m., the phone rang. I answered, and the same cheery female voice rang out on the other end of the line. Determined to be calm and rational, I asked her who she was to Max. She said with punctuated excitement, "I'm his girlfriend!" I took a deep breath to keep from losing my $h*t and replied nonchalantly, "I'm his wife."

Stuttering and stammering over her words, she stated she honestly didn't know. After I questioned her further, I knew she was telling the truth. Max told her he was going to Oklahoma for a wedding, but he said it was his sister's wedding. Julie thought she was calling his parent's house and that I was his SISTER!

Well played, Max...well played.

It all made sense now--why she felt at liberty to call my parent's home and our home and ask for Max. She had no idea what was going on and neither did I. She told me they met at a bar on the 4th of July. Max, who never went to bars and rarely drank alcohol, had gone out with some friends to celebrate the 4th. I'm not sure how everything went down that night or the following nights before he came to Oklahoma in August. But I do know he spent the night at her apartment the night before he came home to marry me, and that night, his motorcycle was indeed stolen. *Serves him right*, I seethed!

Once everything was out in the open, and before we hung up, we decided not to tell Max his gig was up. We wanted to see what he would do. *It's all over now*, I thought. I wanted so badly to jump on him like a wild animal, scratching and clawing at him when he got home. But instead, I cleaned up the mess I had made. I methodically gathered every shredded piece of evidence, carefully putting it back inside the large duffle bag where I found it. I even put the condoms back in the secret compartment of the bag where he had hidden them.

Then I cleaned my tear-stained face, reapplied my make-up, and positioned myself on the couch where I would be sipping lemon water through a straw while casually flipping through a *Cosmopolitan* magazine when he walked through the door.

It took everything I had to stay calm and act like my heart was not shredded into a million pieces just like the "love letters" I had ripped apart just hours before. But I was a good little actress. I had been performing as a lead actress for roles of my own making for most of my life. I had become skilled at the art of deception and quite seasoned at the masquerade of pretend.

A few minutes after 5:00 p.m., Max breezed through the front door and greeted me with a peck on the cheek. He sat down in the chair opposite the couch and began unlacing his combat boots. Looking up at me briefly while untying, he said he had something he needed to take care of. I breathed deeply through my nose to keep from flying into an accusing rage. He said he needed to "wrap up a few things" and pick up the insurance documents from a friend of a friend.

I said, "Oh yes, she called again today...Julie? Is that her name?" Max stood to his feet pulling off his camouflage jacket and pants. He answered, "Yeah, that's her name." I wanted to punch him!

I continued to sit on the couch, acting vaguely interested and pretending to be engrossed in reading a story about a love triangle from the magazine I held, wishing I wasn't experiencing a love triangle of my own. Did they even know each other long enough to call it love? What was it between them exactly? Why hadn't Max just told her the truth in the first place instead of fabricating a whopper like he did? I had good reason not to tell what I was hiding--or so I thought at the time. I wondered if now would be a good time to break his heart again, just like he had broken mine.

Casually I asked, "Do you want me to come with you?" I already knew the answer, but I wanted to ask the question just the same. "Naah, it won't take too long. I'll be home before nine," he said. "Okay, I'll just work on the laundry while you're gone then," I said, acting as normal as possible. I really wanted to scream "AND DON'T FORGET YOUR CONDOMS!!!" while throwing them at him, but I didn't. He showered, changed clothes, and fixed himself a pimento cheese sandwich. With a half-eaten sandwich in one hand, he leaned down and gave me a half-hearted kiss on my cheek, then pulled the door closed, leaving me sitting there alone again.

As soon as the door closed behind him, I ran to the window and looked down, watching him back out of the parking space. My tears ran in torrents. I couldn't believe this was my life! I knew my husband was driving to see another woman, and for the millionth time in my life, I didn't know what to do. I wanted to pack and leave before he got back. I wanted to call Kenny and tell him I made a huge mistake and was coming back to Oklahoma. But I knew better; even if my marriage to Max failed, I couldn't go back to Kenny.

But where could I go? I only knew a few people, including some of Max's co-workers, but I didn't know them well. I had no friends. I was alone all day with nothing to do. Max almost always drove the car to work making it nearly impossible for me to make any friends. He didn't do it to keep me isolated; it was just the only way he could get back and forth to the base while the insurance was working on the stolen motorcycle claim. I felt so utterly alone. I didn't want to keep calling my friends and family and having them pay for the call, so I just sat around, waiting for one of them to call me, which was never often enough.

After Max left to "wrap up a few things," I sadly realized I had no place to go and no money. I gathered up our dirty clothes and some loose change and descended the steps to the community laundry room. I spent the evening washing and folding the clothes of a man I wasn't even sure I loved anymore. We had been married less than one month, and it felt like the marriage had ended before it even began. I started planning to leave. If Max could get the insurance paperwork filed, he would be able to replace his motorcycle, and then I could take the car and leave.

I had to have a plan. I decided I would get a job and stay just long enough to save enough money to get back home. I was too prideful to ask my parents to help me. After all, they had given me plenty of chances to back out of the wedding, and now it was too late. I had cost them time and money in planning and paying for a wedding; and on top of that, they had given us $1,500 to get us started. That money was already spent on moving, deposits, rent, and groceries. We were flat-broke. Max did not bring home enough money to pay our rent, monthly bills, and car payment, so we started racking up credit cards to fill in the gaps. I knew it would be several months before we could actually split up. We would just have to co-exist as roommates until I could afford to leave. But at least I had a plan.

As I cried over dirty laundry that night, I wondered what he was telling Julie at that moment or what they were doing. I knew what he meant by his vague statement about needing to "wrap up a few things," but I wondered how he would tell her what she already knew. I also wondered what he would tell me or if he would ever tell me unless I forced him. I knew I didn't want to tell him about my unfaithfulness, so I could understand if he didn't want me to find out about his secret.

Max returned home before 9:00 p.m., just like he said he would. He didn't say much when he got back, but something in his countenance was different. I could tell a heavy weight had been lifted from his shoulders. The secret he had been hiding from me was now removed, and I got a glimpse of the old Max. The Max I loved a long time ago had just walked in the door. My heart softened as he quietly climbed into bed next to me. We did not talk, cuddle, or make love. We just lay there next to each other in the same bed but feeling worlds and worlds apart.

It's difficult to explain how it happened, but from that night on, we slowly got better. We sat down the following Saturday and had a much-needed heart-to-heart talk. We both admitted our failures. We each asked the other's forgiveness and tearfully committed to giving our marriage an honest effort. The underlying love we had known resurfaced as grace, and forgiveness flowed freely from our hearts.

A dying love and seemingly failed marriage was rekindled. What was once broken was now being restored, piece by tattered piece. We each allowed the other to hold the brokenness up to the light so the pieces could be mended, leaving a masterpiece of togetherness in place of a mangled rubble of regret.

Chapter 27

WHERE'S THE MONEY?

"I've never been poor, only broke. Being poor is a frame of mind. Being broke is only a temporary situation."~Mike Todd

Once the secrets and lies of the recent past were behind us, a new beginning promised much-needed healing. HOPE stood in front of us again, and we welcomed him like a long-lost friend. We spent our weekends making love and making up for lost time. The pain of infidelity faded into the sunset as we sat on the beach cuddled in a blanket, surrounded by the warmth of rebirthed love. We fell head over heels in love with each other all over again. During the remainder of that year and the next, we learned how to transition from two individuals into one couple, united for life.

We were happy and in love, but we were broker-than-a-joke. Paycheck to paycheck would have been nice, but we struggled to make it that far. While money can't buy happiness, it sure can buy groceries and pay bills. With constant financial strain looming over us, it was a challenge to enjoy life. We couldn't go anywhere if it wasn't free. I tried to find a job close by so we could share the vehicle, but the hours never worked out. Almost as soon as Max's motorcycle was recovered, he sold it so we could pay rent and bills. I ended up babysitting for some of Max's co-workers, but they couldn't afford to pay much, so that didn't really help.

One evening just before Christmas, we sat on the floor behind a broken hand-me-down coffee table to share a .99 cent TV dinner. The groceries had run out a week before payday. We would be sharing a .99 cent TV dinner every night until Max got paid and we could buy a small amount of groceries. I called my parents one day and told my dad how desperate our situation was. Within a few days of that phone conversation, boxes of food started showing up at our front door. My parents would go shopping and lovingly pack up our favorite non-perishables in a large box and send it to us every few weeks. I'm so grateful for their generosity during that time.

Our first Christmas together as a married couple was unlike any other Christmas I had ever experienced. Our tree was small and sparsely decorated. We splurged on a package of red and gold velvet bows and a small box of miniature candy canes. We bought the least expensive bag of popcorn kernels we could find. The entire "Operation Christmas Tree Decoration" cost less than five dollars. We were content with our purchases and drove to our apartment to make the best of the situation. We were together and we were in love, so it was enough.

On Christmas Eve, we cooked the kernels into fluffy white popcorn. We snuggled tightly on the couch and listened to the radio while we sewed the butterless popcorn with a needle and thread, making two long strands to adorn our tree. We ate the leftovers and an apple for dinner that night. Then we climbed into bed to give each other the gift of young married love.

On Christmas morning, I woke to the smell of sizzling bacon and the welcome sight of warm syrup drizzled over pancakes. I exclaimed, "Where did you get all of this? And when? We can't afford this?!" Max was determined to have a real breakfast on Christmas morning. He smiled and said, "Just enjoy it!"

After breakfast, he pulled out a red stocking with thick, white trim. He handed me the stocking. "But we can't afford presents. I didn't get you anything," I murmured softly with my head lowered. "It's okay," Max said. "There's something in there for both of us."

Tears filled my eyes as I looked into the stocking. It held two pretty pairs of skimpy panties and an orange. "We will both enjoy it when you wear those panties," he said with a grin. What a sweet gesture of unselfish love! I decided right then and there our next Christmas would be better.

I turned twenty-one exactly a week before Christmas. Like anyone else, I had always looked forward to this birthday. But Max and I had no money. We sat in our apartment and shared a .99 cent TV dinner just like we would on Christmas. Dessert was a package of Twizzlers my parents had sent in one of the care packages. I hated being broke.

Max's birthday was coming up, and I wanted it to be special. Also, I desperately missed my family and wanted to fly home to visit in the spring, which cost money. Anxiety and depression, my old companions, started dominating my thoughts. I had never been this poor in my entire life. Four months of not enough was *enough*.

So, I sat down with a borrowed Sunday newspaper and began reading the want-ads. I circled a few job possibilities to check into, but one ad in particular caught my attention. In bold letters, it read, "EARN WHILE YOU LEARN." It was an advertisement for a massage parlor looking for girls.

The part that interested me the most was I could start working while I was going to massage school. I thought, "Now that's a great idea!" Looking back on it now, I realize it was a horrible idea. Who would want to pay for a massage from a young girl who hadn't even learned the proper techniques?

Believe me when I tell you *lots* of men will.

I kept going back to the ad I had circled with a hot pink highlighter. My mind considered the possibilities. *It has to be a safe, professional, and legitimate business to advertise in the newspaper...right?* I looked at the address listed under the words "Apply in person." I read the address out loud trying to figure out if I knew where it was. Then it dawned on me that I had heard of the street many times in conversations.

The street was a pretty drive along the beach lined with palm trees and home to many businesses and shops. During the day, it looked like a great area, but at night, it transformed into a place most respectable people would want to avoid. Prostitutes walked freely up and down the street. There were transvestites, homeless people, drug dealers, pimps, and prostitutes all over the area. Once night fell, the place transformed into something virtually unrecognizable.

I decided to show the ad to Max. He was not too comfortable with the idea but agreed it wouldn't hurt to at least check it out. I got up early that morning to drive Max to work so I could have the car. I had an uneasy feeling in the pit of my stomach the whole time I was getting ready and during the drive there. I knew this feeling well; it was the same uneasiness I had felt other times before I made a bad decision, but I ignored it.

I had no idea what to wear so I dressed in my usual way. I had a darling figure and was never afraid to show it off or use it to my advantage. I decided on a white off-shoulder flowy half-shirt that exposed my flat, golden-tanned stomach and tiny cut-off jean shorts with a hint of sexy. I accidentally spilled bleach on the shorts a few weeks earlier, which added to the distressed look, making them original. I wore wedge slides with royal blue and turquoise accent straps. I finished out the outfit with big hoop earrings.

I slipped a steak knife into my matching royal blue clutch, just in case I needed to defend myself, and I headed out the door. The cool ocean breeze blew into the open windows and sunroof, tousling my wavy blonde hair. The song, "Enjoy The Silence" by Depeche Mode blared in my ears as I sang along to the familiar lyrics. I was trying to drown out the uneasiness and anxiety I was fighting.

Once I found the address, I drove around the block several times trying to conjure up enough nerve to park and go inside. Fearful, anxious thoughts gave way to factual thoughts. It was a fact we were broke. It was a fact we had racked up credit cards to the maximum limit. It was a fact we were too proud to ask for help. It was a fact I was parked out front and determined to go in.

One last time, I pulled the visor down to reapply my lip gloss and adjust my hair. "Be brave," I told myself out loud. I took a deep breath. My hands shook as I opened the car door and stepped out onto the busy street. I walked up to a small three-bedroom house, which had been turned into a massage parlor. I climbed the steps onto the front porch and carefully turned the doorknob to enter, not sure if I should knock first.

Chapter 28

NAIVE

"Maybe it's because I'm a little naïve, but I do like to think that there aren't really very many truly bad people in the world. I think that everybody has their reasons for what they do, and if you really look in their eyes, you could probably understand them." ~Stephenie Meyer

It felt like I had walked into an Austin Powers rendition of a 70's living room. Colorful beads were hanging in the windows and doorways. Old 70's-looking furniture, shaggy carpet, mirrors, and black lights completed the look. Inside, about five feet in front of the door, there was a small reception desk, and above that, a "Massage Menu" sign with prices.

Bells jingling above the door announced my arrival. A gorgeous woman sat behind the desk on a swivel-type stool, looking down at a magazine. When she looked up, the most unusual eyes I had ever seen looked straight into mine. Her smile put me at ease. "Can I help you?" she asked. I stammered a bit while trying to take in my surroundings. I replied, "Yeah, I came to apply for a job. The ad said to apply in person." I could tell she was older than I was, but her demeanor was not suggestive of her age.

"What's your name?" she asked. "I'm Jennifer. I'll let Mike know you're here." She stood and disappeared behind a beaded doorway. After a few minutes, she came back and told me Mike would be here shortly. She invited me to take a seat. I didn't want to take a seat. I wanted to look around and ask her a million questions about this place. Instead, I sat.

I kept a close eye on the hanging beads, wondering what went on behind them. Mike did not enter through the colorful beads; instead, he came in through the same door I had entered. I wasn't the least bit impressed with his appearance. His sandy brown hair was disheveled and greasy, and he desperately needed a shower and a shave. His tan shorts were dirty, and he wore a blue shirt two sizes too small. A lit cigarette hung from his lips. When he reached his hand forward to shake mine, I noticed he had dirt caked under his nails. I clutched my purse tighter and subtly felt around to make sure I could get to my knife if needed. Nothing about him seemed dangerous, really, but I still felt nervous and uncomfortable.

Mike gave me a tour of the place and told me the other girls would train me. He said he was usually outside working in the yard or next door. He also owned several other businesses, including an all-nude strip club and the property next door. He told me he was always close by to keep an eye on the girls. Then he said, "You'll do great here. Can you work tonight?" Taken back, I said, "Don't I have to go to school or something? I've never given a massage."

Without missing a beat, Mike took the cigarette out of his mouth and told me yes, technically I would need to enroll in a massage school at some point, but I could work there without school for as long as I needed to.

Mike went on to explain that when a man pays for a massage, he pays "the house." The fee is $60 for an hour and $40 for a half-hour. He said a ticket is written with the guy's first name and signed by the girl who gives the massage. The money is paper clipped to the ticket and dropped into the slot in a locked box. Mike then said every two weeks, he adds the tickets up and writes the girls a check for their part. He said it's a 60/40 split: the house gets 60%, and the girls get 40%.

I did the math quickly in my head--$24 an hour! Oh my gosh, I could get us out of debt making $24 an hour. The only catch was it was not $24 an hour—it was only $24 for the hours you actually had a customer to massage. So, if you only did two or three massages a day, you made much less. Mike finished by saying, "You get to keep any tips you make." I told him I would talk it over with my husband, but if Max had no objections, I could start right away.

Max reluctantly agreed to let me work there. The idea of it did not settle any better with him than it did with me initially, but the thought of additional income made us both willing to give it a try. I had absolutely no idea what I was stepping into. This naive Oklahoma girl was about to be introduced to a whole other world. I never even knew such places existed.

The massage parlor was open from 10:oo a.m. to 2:oo a.m. The hours were divided into two eight-hour shifts. The day shift was 10:00 a.m. to 6:00 p.m., and the night shift was 6:00 p.m. to 2:00 a.m. Mike required all new girls to work some night shifts when they first started. Once girls built up a clientele, they had more say in the preferred shift. The first few months, I was stuck with the night shift. It was scary down there after dark. Anyone could just walk in.

One night, shortly before I started working there, a girl was forced into the shower area and raped. After that, for "safety" reasons, there were always two girls--and sometimes three--scheduled at night on the weekends. We usually had at least one male customer there all the time. Our customers were always male. I never had a female customer--ever.

Mike was in and out all night, but we knew he was next door if we needed him. Unless we were actually with a paying customer, we were not paid, but we were required to stay the whole eight hours in case of a walk-in. Ten girls worked there during the time I did, and all but two were married to Marines. They were working for the same reason I did--they needed the money.

Once a girl had been there awhile, she would usually start to get "regulars." This was what we called a customer who came in at predicted times and would mostly request the same girl. With no formal massage training, I was clueless as to what actually went on. Once I got enrolled in massage school, I did start to learn how to give a professional massage, but very few customers ever wanted a professional massage.

My first week, I was "trained" mostly by Jennifer and an older lady named Deb. The training consisted of helping give a massage. The customer loved these training sessions because he got the attention of two girls while only paying for one.

The small massage rooms were decorated similar to the living room area. At least one of the walls in every room was mirrored. The other walls had random psychedelic posters that seemed to come alive in the room. The rooms were kept very dark, even during the daytime. The only lighting was black lighting, making the sheets and towels glow vividly. Everything else had a purple/blueish tint. Tanned skin looked amazing with this lighting. We all had gorgeous tans.

On the massage tables, there were no top sheets provided to cover the customer, but there was a bottom sheet. There were hand towels and washcloths folded neatly on a small table in the corner. There was a radio, a plastic squeeze bottle with mineral oil, a plastic squeeze bottle with pink liquid soap, a medium-sized container of baby powder, a large plastic bowl, and a medium-sized plastic pitcher.

A typical massage went like this: the customer selects a girl and pays the house fee. Next, he is required to take a shower before the massage. He leaves his clothing in the shower area and walks to the massage room, wearing a white towel wrapped around his waist. The towel would be discarded, and he would get on the massage table and wait.

Usually the man would lay face down with his rear-end exposed.

Sometimes he would be lying down face up with his genitals exposed, and other times, he would be sitting on the edge of the table with his legs dangling over. A hand towel was provided for him to cover his private parts, but it was extremely rare for a customer to do so. If he was face up or sitting up, I would ask him to roll over on his stomach. I would then take the hand towel and lay it across his butt. I did not want to look at it the whole time.

The first half-hour would be spent rubbing his neck, shoulders, back, arms, legs, and feet with warm oil. At the halfway point, he would turn over to have his chest, arms, legs, neck, and face done. The hour massage would finish with a body shampoo, which would get most of the oil off of him. The body shampoo was followed up by a "light touch" with baby powder.

I was told by my trainers most men want a "happy ending." It was up to me if I wanted to do that. "What's a happy ending?" I asked. I had never heard of a happy ending. I soon found out what it was, and that there were several options.

My first reaction was to gasp! No way was I going to do any of those options! I asked Jennifer if she did them, and she said casually, "Always." I went through the list of all the girls, asking her if so-and-so did happy endings. She said everyone did except one lady who was much older than the rest of us.

Now it made perfect sense why the older lady was never requested by any customers. If she happened to get a walk-in, you could see a scowl on the customer's face when the massage was over. He would then pay again and go behind the beaded curtains with another girl. The next time, he would emerge with a much more relaxed look.

For a couple of very frustrating months, I did my best to provide the most relaxing "straight" massages possible to every customer. But both the customer and I would walk away disappointed for different reasons. I was disappointed because the highest tip I would get was $20. The customer was disappointed because he was refused a happy ending. I would get request after request, so that was never the problem. I would just finish one massage and walk out to several more lined up. The problem was having to deal with handsy, horny men for an hour and making less than $50 when it was over. I had put up with handsy and horny behavior since I was a 12-year-old girl, but I now had an opportunity to be paid for it.

Before long, Mike told me I could have my choice of shifts. I chose the day shift so I could be home with Max at night. The day shift had its advantages. I worked with Jennifer every day. We enjoyed each other's company and became close friends.

Both our husbands were in the Marine Corps. She had a little girl I adored. Jennifer was the same age as one of my older sisters, and she took care of me like an older sister would. We soon discovered we lived in the same apartment complex. She and her husband each had their own vehicle, but Max and I still only had one car. She offered to let me ride to work with her, and since we both worked the day shift Monday-Friday, it was perfect.

As I got to know Jennifer more, I discovered we had a lot more in common than our jobs. We started to spend time together on weekends and some evenings. She filled such a void in my life. I missed my girlfriends and sisters back home. Jennifer and I were both wild, crazy girls who liked the same movies, music, and shopping! Jennifer always had more money than I did, and I knew why. She never hid the fact she happily gave happy endings to all her clients.

One day on the way to work, I asked her, "How do you make yourself touch IT? Doesn't that just completely gross you out!?" She giggled and turned down one of our favorite songs by Ace of Base. "Yes, it does! I hate it actually, but I guess you get used to it. And I need the money, so I just do it," she said. I replied, "I just don't think I could do it. I get grossed out just SEEING it! I always throw a hand towel over it and try to ignore it standing up like a glowing white ghost!"

We laughed and talked more about it. Then she offered a suggestion. She said, "If you want, we could start off with 'a two-girl thing.' That way, you get used to it, and you're not alone at first." My brows furrowed as I asked, "What's a two-girl thing?" Jennifer explained it's where there are two girls instead of one. She said it's kind of like training, but I would stay with her the whole time instead of leaving at the end. "Does the customer have to pay for a massage from both of us?" I asked. "Only if Mike is around, but if he's not there, then the guy would just pay for one massage but tip both of us. We could take turns writing them down so we each get our commissions, and Mike won't catch on. You can have the first one," she said. My stomach twisted as I tried to envision what was being discussed. Jennifer said, "It's totally up to you. No pressure. I just know you need the money like the rest of us do!"

For the next few days, I continued thinking about it. I paid attention to how long Jennifer was in the room and how much money she was collecting afterwards. I noticed how quickly the men were "serviced." They came in to "get off" and then go on about their day.

The majority of the clientele during the daytime hours were businessmen. They visited the parlor during their lunch hour, or they would take a midday break to relax. Most of them were wealthy and very generous. They came in regularly, at least once per week, and sometimes more often. Almost all of them were nice, courteous married men with children and almost all of them visited in secret.

I finally got up enough nerve to agree to happy endings later that week. This was after getting only a $10 tip for a half-hour massage. Jennifer and Deb never got less than $50-$100 for the same time and less work! I plopped down in one of the outdated velvet chairs. "Okay, the next one I'll be ready," I said.

Wait, did I just say?

It's no big deal, I told myself. *Everyone else does it. It's what is expected!* I ran through this dialogue in my head trying to convince myself it really wasn't a big deal...but I knew it was. I was about to cross a line I could have never in a million years believe or predict I would ever even consider crossing.

Chapter 29

POOR NO MORE

*Don't trade away your happiness now in hope that if you make
enough money you'll be able to buy it back later. You
can't~Unknown*

I doodled nervously on the ticket book while we waited for the guy
to get showered and into the room. Jennifer was completely
relaxed, jabbering about what happened on the last episode of
Melrose Place. I was a nervous wreck, so I wasn't even listening to
her. I was consumed with my own thoughts. *Could I really do this? I
was about to participate in a sex act for money! Who is this girl?* I
heard that cynical voice in my head telling me this is the same ruined
girl I had always been. All anybody cared about was my body, and
the only worth I had was my sexuality. I had tried finding other jobs,
but I was never called. I was a college dropout with little work
experience. *What if I have to go back to night shift if I don't keep
getting requests? What if I was on some sort of unstated probation
period? What if I lose this job?* No, I could not let that happen! *It's
really no big deal...right?*

Because I was working now, Max and I were finally able to go to
a movie or grab food from Taco Bell once in a while. Would I be
letting him down if I got fired? Or would I be letting him down even

more by crossing this imaginary boundary line? What is it with me and boundary lines anyway? No matter what, they always get stepped over, either by me or by someone else.

I knew I would be stepping into a situation that was against everything I believed. I knew once I crossed this line, my life would never be the same, for my conscience could never let it. I knew what I was about to do was wrong, but at that moment, I didn't care enough to do what was right. I wanted that man's money.

That day and many others after it, I chose money. The love of money shamelessly led me straight into the arms of sexual immorality. Soon, I would find myself in bondage to a type of slavery that would entrap me for the next two years.

The lyrics to a famous song are:

Hey baby won't you look my way

I can be your new addiction

Hey baby what you gotta say?

All you're giving me is fiction

I'm a sorry sucker and this happens all the time

I found out that everybody talks

Everybody talks, everybody talk

Hey, honey you could be my drug

You could be my new prescription

Too much could be an overdose

It started with a whisper

And that was when I kissed her ("Everybody Talks Back."
Neon Tree, 2012)

I would be "his" addiction, and his money would be my new

prescription...because money talks.

You may have heard a similar whisper. An inaudible sinister voice reminding you of your weaknesses, failures, and mistakes. Mine sounded like this...*you've always been a bad girl. Now you can get paid for it. You know you deserve it--you crave the attention. And what harm can it do? You know it's just a hand job, right? No big deal. You want to fly home and see your family, don't you? Wouldn't you rather be shopping instead of scrimping? How do you like being broke?*

Suddenly, I was jolted back to reality when Jennifer asked, "You ready?" I thought I was going to throw up. "Yeah almost, hang on just a second," I replied. I grabbed my purse under the desk and made a beeline to the bathroom. I was so jittery, and I felt sick. I rummaged through my purse for something to calm me down. I had a bottle of Xanax; I always carried it with me. I popped one into my mouth and washed it down with the rest of my Sprite.

The whisper spoke up once more: *Get in there! Why are you acting like such a prude? It's not like you haven't seen one before...in fact, you've even seen this guy's! He's old. It will only take a second or two.* Jennifer lightly knocked on the door. I opened it. "If you changed your mind..." she started to say. I interrupted her before she could finish the sentence. "Nope, I'm good. I'm ready now," I replied.

I thought the Xanax would have time to kick in before we got to the happy ending part. I wasn't that lucky. I followed Jennifer through the "beads of shame." Once inside my eyes quickly adjusted, and I saw our customer sitting up on the massage table with his feet dangling. The plump man was in his 50s and mostly bald. He was wearing white tube socks and nothing else. The socks seemed to be alive as he excitedly swung his feet back and forth.

I had massaged this customer once before, but he never requested me again. When he saw me, he chuckled and said, "I was hoping you would change your mind. I'm not so bad." His belly jiggled as he said this. My stomach turned.

"Are we doing topless!?! he asked, like he was a kid asking if he can get a candy bar and a coke! Jennifer batted her eyelashes, and with a flirty response, she said, "Depends on how much you want to spend today." He nodded for her to look on the table. She walked over and held up two 100-dollar bills. "Okay, sugar! Topless it is!"

My heart skipped a few beats, and suddenly, I felt like I couldn't catch my breath. I wanted to leave. I really did, but I stayed. I watched Jennifer and followed her lead. She easily lifted her shirt up over her head and let it flutter to the floor. I did the same. Then she was very flirty, teasing him a bit before taking off her lacy bra, which was glowing against her flat, tanned stomach. With my heart pounding out of my chest, I followed, letting my bra slid off my arms. Our customer laid back facing upwards. Jennifer turned on some music and motioned for me to grab the oil.

Thankfully, it was over almost before it started. We both rubbed on his oiled chest and stomach, leaning into him as our hands glided across his body. He moaned and jerked a little, and it was done. Wait, did I miss something? Jennifer handed him a hand towel. He wiped himself off while she wet a washcloth in the large bowl of hot water and then rang it out. *So 's what the bowl is for*, I thought.

Jennifer continued acting sexy while she put the pink shampoo all over his chest and stomach. With the warm cloth, she cleaned him up by removing as much of the oil as possible. Then she sprinkled the powder on him. Again, I followed her lead and began to very lightly touch him, rubbing the powder into his skin. He smiled up at us satisfactorily when we finished. He happily slid off the table, wrapped the towel around his thick waist, and scurried off in his white socks. I watched him disappear behind the colorful, floor-length beads.

Jennifer and I slipped our clothes back on. She handed me a $100 bill, which I tucked into the back pocket of my frayed jean shorts. That crisp $100 bill felt good next to the measly $10 I had received from my last customer. Now, the Xanax was in full effect. At that moment, I felt no guilt.

As we ate lunch, Jennifer and I laughed and talked. "Did I miss something?" I asked between bites. She sipped her lemonade and then responded, "No, you didn't. Sometimes they get so excited you don't even have to touch it, especially when there are two girls!" Just then one of her regulars pulled up in a shiny black Jaguar. "Wanna do it again?" she asked. "This guy will love it!" I didn't really want to do it again, but I wanted more 100-dollar bills--it was just too easy.

Chapter 30

THE ROOT OF ALL EVIL

For the love of money is a root of all kinds of evils. It is through this craving that some have wandered away from the faith and pierced themselves with many pangs. ~1 Timothy 6:10

He who loves money will not be satisfied with money, nor he who loves wealth with his income; this also is vanity. ~ Ecclesiastes 5:10

I wish I could tell you I didn't do it again. But I can't. Not only did I do it again and again, but each time I did it, I felt less conviction as time went on. I became completely desensitized. My moral compass was beginning to spin out of control. What I once considered morally corrupt behavior; I was now engaging in with very little thought. The money was well worth it or so I thought at the time. My judgment became increasingly clouded. I justified every unethical, unfaithful touch as a necessary evil just part of the job. I assured myself what I was doing was not harming anyone or jeopardizing my emotional or spiritual wellbeing.

As for my marriage, I convinced myself if Max ever asked me about my job or how I was making that much money, I would tell him but *only* if he asked. I never hid any of the money from him. I would lay it all on the kitchen table when I emptied my pockets each evening. He got off work before I did, so he was almost always home when Jennifer dropped me off. He never asked.

Not too long after we started doing two-girl massages, Jennifer and I stopped at the mall to do a little shopping on the way home. We both had plenty of cash; we knew how easy it was to get more, so we spent it as fast as we could make it.

As Jenn looked through the racks of clothes, she casually mentioned some of the clients like to see her outside of the massage parlor. "They can spend more time and relax, not worrying about time or someone walking in," she stated. "By the way, I actually have a 'date' scheduled with a client tomorrow evening." She continued, "He likes two girls, but the girl who usually goes with me had to cancel. He pays really well, so I was wondering if you would wanna fill in for her."

My curiosity was piqued, so I asked, "Like how much...what are the deets?" She began, "Well, this particular client is a short ugly dude. He's kinda troll-like." She giggled and went on, explaining, "He's married and has a ten-year-old daughter. His wife doesn't like to have sex, so he pays for it." I stopped for a second to consider what she just told me, then I spoke again. "Wait, he pays you for sex?"

Jennifer looked at me like I was the dumbest girl on the planet. "Yeah, that's why they like to see girls outside of the parlor," she said. "It's totally cool if you don't want to. I just thought you might want the money. He's got plenty of it." I did want the money, but I didn't want to have sex for it. After all, I still had morals and boundaries.

I questioned her more about it. "So, would I have to have sex with him then?" I asked.

She replied, "No, he can barely last long enough for just one girl, but his fantasy is to have two there."

"So, what would I have to do?" I wondered aloud.

She said, "He's so easy. I could just tell him your rules, and he will respect them. He may pay you less, though."

"Okay, how much less?" I asked.

Jenn replied, "I bet you could keep your panties on and still get $250. Plus, he likes a whole date experience, so we always get free drinks and a fancy steak dinner." She continued, "This date was supposed to be a 'lingerie' date, so if you let him watch you try it on, he'll buy you anything in the store you want! That's how I get all my cute lingerie, bras, and panties!"

"You have got to be kidding me! Why would I say no to a steak dinner, free drinks, free lingerie, and $250 cash! And if I get to keep my panties on, it's a win-win!" I exclaimed. "What time are you picking me up?"

This conversation led to our first of what we later called "2-5-0 dates." As soon as we coined the term, we began pitching the idea to the men we knew could afford it and to the ones who hadn't already thought of it themselves. Our calendar filled up fast, and what we called our "cash stash" filled even faster. These meetups were known as "out-call" massages, meaning the women met the man outside of the massage parlor at a location of the man's choosing.

Occasionally, Randi the girl who Jennifer worked with before I agreed to go on dates with her--would join us. I didn't mind this at all because it was less pressure for me on the dates. They were both willing to have sex, and I wasn't, so it all worked out. Everyone was respectful of the comforts and boundaries of everyone else. Sometimes, Jenn and Randi would go, and I would babysit Jennifer's daughter while they were out.

Frequently, a client would request overnight, or they would want a date for an out of town business trip. I never did those for two reasons: those dates always required sex, which I didn't do, and I did not want to spend a night in bed with anyone besides Max. I know it sounds strange, but I had very clearly laid-out boundaries in my head for these dates. The boundaries closely paralleled the boundaries I set in junior high school. I was willing to participate in sexual activity as long as my panties stayed on.

So, Jennifer handled the overnight trips, and I gladly stayed home with Max and babysat her four-year-old daughter. She always paid me very well, usually $500. She would get paid several thousand dollars for the trip, so she was very generous with me for watching her daughter to make that possible.

Soon, Jenn and I decided we no longer needed to work at the parlor. We really had more than enough clients without spending eight hours waiting for them to come to us. We told our customers how they could get ahold of us should they want to see one or both of us elsewhere. Hotel rooms or rented apartments the clients kept for these occasions, or sometimes their own homes were our new meeting places.

Now that Jennifer and I weren't working all day but had plenty of money, we spent our days working out with our trainer, laying out getting our tans on, getting our hair and nails done at the salon, or shopping at the mall. We took pride in our appearances. It was our job to look beautiful, sexy, and in top physical condition. We were "high-class call girls," among the highest-paid girls between San Diego and Los Angeles.

I only had a few clients who I agreed to see alone. These were high-profile individuals who had more to lose than I did if our meetings were ever discovered. They had to be okay with the "panties stay on" policy. These few clients mostly just wanted company for the afternoon or evening and a topless massage with a happy ending. One particular client always had fruit and champagne ready when I got there. We would sit by his pool for an hour or so getting tipsy. There was never a rush since a customer had to pay for a two-hour minimum, which was at least 500 dollars. Depending on what else they wanted, the price went up from there.

For these men, money was never a concern, and they were more than generous on every occasion I saw them. I think they liked to pretend they had a girlfriend coming over because some would have gifts, chocolates, or flowers. I treated them with kindness and respect, and they treated me the same.

I almost felt sorry for some of the men. Not the ones who were married because I had little respect for them. The ones I felt sad for were the ones whose wives had died. They were generally older, past traditional dating age, very wealthy, and very lonely. I never rushed them. I tried to make them feel loved and special. I believe that's why they called me even though I didn't take it all off for them. These men had airplanes, yachts, beautiful homes, expensive cars, and large bank accounts, but they were emotionally bankrupt...and I was slowly becoming that way, too.

Chapter 31

ROCK BOTTOM

Real isn't who's with you at your celebration, real is who is standing next to you at rock bottom~Unknown

I had more than enough money to stop seeing clients. I drove a sporty white BMW. I purchased my husband a fire-red SUV he'd had his eye on, and we now could afford whatever else we wanted. We could travel and eat at nice restaurants. I wanted the money more than I wanted to stop making it. So, I didn't stop. I knew when I did stop, the money would eventually run out. Then where would we be?

As I had hoped, the next Christmas was indeed different. Max and I could afford to fly back home for holidays, and we showered our parents with big-screen televisions and other expensive gifts. I could even pay for my dad and my nephew to go on a hunting trip.

I spent the money as fast as I got it. Having it felt dirty and wrong. At first, I worshipped it, but one year later, I couldn't get rid of it fast enough. The immorality was taking its toll. I wanted to stop, but I didn't know how. I was caught up in money's unrelenting clutches. Sin, guilt, shame, and remorse were each taking their toll. I had plenty of cash, but these consequences could not be righted with any currency available to man.

There was only one way the price could be paid to redeem me from the slimy pit of sexual sin, greed, lust, unfaithfulness, fornication, guilt, and shame. Only the precious blood of Jesus could save me, and I knew it deep in my heart. I just didn't know if I could surrender and give up the fight. I didn't want to be poor again. Now I wasn't financially poor anymore, but I was poor in spirit. Looking back, I can see Jesus was waiting patiently for me with open arms, but I was running in the opposite direction into the arms of men with money.

Soon I would slide further into the slimy pit of immorality. At the time, though, I foolishly didn't see it coming.

This wasn't fun anymore. I was losing it emotionally. I found myself taking several showers during the day because one just didn't seem to cut it. I turned the water up as hot as I could physically stand it. My skin burned as I let the hot water pound down on me while scrubbing with a loofah soaked in scented bath gel. When the water would run cold, I dried off, then covered myself in perfumed body lotion. Even on days when I didn't see clients, I would do this.

The price was too high. I started to notice that besides the normal anxiety and depression I had always battled, I began having obsessive-compulsive behaviors. I did not ever feel clean. I almost always drank before and during dates, but now I was drinking after them also. I started to feel reckless and out of control. Irrational, obsessive thoughts haunted me. I worked out frantically, I drank more, and I turned up the music louder, but nothing seemed to help.

Soon, I added prescription pills to the mix through new friends. Jennifer and I had one client who paid us to go with him to strip clubs, and we made friends with some of the girls in the clubs. We were hanging out in the dressing room with the dancers so we could get away from our client because he was not one of our favorites. While we were back there, one of the girls offered me Valium. She said it was the only way she could get through her shift. I gladly accepted it. Others were saying Cocaine, Ecstasy, or Heroin were their drug of choice, but I liked the Valium and started taking it as often as I could get it.

Valium made me feel so completely relaxed that I honestly didn't give a $h*t about anything. As soon as it wore off, I wanted more. I started going out to bars just to party, and I would get so hammered I could hardly get up the stairs to my apartment.

The whispers were growing louder now. *You're such a disgrace...you really are a whore, but at least now you're smart enough to get paid for it. Just wait until Max finds out what you really do. He will hate you forever. Your family will disown you. You're such a failure. You will never get a real job, so you might as well start stripping too while you're at it. You should call that man back who wants you to be in the Playboy video. You know you would love the attention.*

These kinds of thoughts constantly rang in my mind. I couldn't sort them out. I turned up the music as loud as I could to drown out the whispers.

I began to let my guard down. I was careless about who I would spend time with. One day, Jennifer said a guy named Greg called her. He was referred by a friend and asked for a date, but she told him she didn't date men she didn't know alone. He agreed to pay for two girls, so she asked me to go along. Normally, I would have asked more questions and probably would not have gone, but I really was at a low point. Since we didn't know him, Jennifer and I agreed to meet him at a bar in San Diego.

Jennifer and I started drinking before we got there. When we met up with him, we were surprised. Greg was around Jenn's age, and he was handsome and seemed genuinely nice. We could tell he had money because his clothes, watch and ring, leather jacket, and boots were all expensive. The three of us sat in a booth drinking kamikazes, shot after shot. We danced a few songs, and I was three sheets to the wind. We stumbled out of there and got into his Range Rover. He drove us to the next club called Emerald City. It was not my kind of place.

As drunk as I was, I couldn't ignore a weird feeling telling me something wasn't right at Emerald City. The entire club gave me the creeps; a green neon light flashed all around, making it feel demonic. People were wall to wall. I pulled on Jenn's top and said, "Let's go. I hate this place." She leaned over to our date and told him I wanted to leave. He leaned over and yelled in my ear, "Just one drink, then we'll go. We gotta at least have one of their famous drinks!" Fine, just one drink and then we leave. I didn't say it out loud because it wouldn't have done any good.

Jennifer and I sat at a small cocktail table while Greg went to get our drinks. He walked over to our table carrying two slender glasses with green liquid sloshing out and running down the sides of the glasses. I noticed he wasn't drinking one, but I honestly didn't care. I wanted to down that glass and get out of there. Jenn and I made some cheesy toast no one could hear and then threw the glasses back, letting the green Nyquil-like liquid run down our throats. I spilled some of mine, but I drank enough to satisfy Greg so we could leave.

Almost immediately, I felt sick, and the entire place started spinning. It felt like I was on a cheap carnival ride. I was dizzy and disoriented. *What the hell was happening?* My legs felt like jello. I couldn't think, and I just wanted to sleep. I don't remember walking to Greg's Range Rover, and I have no recollection of anything that happened after I finished that drink. Everything went black.

I vaguely remember thinking Greg was on top of me...was he? *Where were we? Where was Jenn?*

I'm not sure how much time passed, but I tried to force myself to wake up. I was so out of it that I couldn't even lift my head. Sleepy and discombobulated, I let myself drift off again. Sometime later, I woke up to a bright light shining in the front windshield. I was sitting in the front passenger seat, which was reclined all the way back. My arm felt so heavy when I attempted to lift it to shield my eyes from the glaring light. I was still groggy. I tried to focus my eyes, but my contacts were dried out, which made opening my eyes more difficult.

Jennifer looked like hell, as she sleepily peered over from the backseat looking down at me. My clothes were only half-way on. With a raging headache, I attempted to speak, but my throat was dry. Jennifer seemed to feel the same way. Then the car door opened, so I slightly turned my head to the left. Greg was holding a sack, and he climbed back into the vehicle. Then he said, "Oh hey! You girls are awake. I'll help you get your seat upright." He leaned over me and adjusted my seat. He handed me the sack saying, "I thought you girls might be hungry, but nothing around here is open except this convenience store."

I didn't want food. I just wanted something non-alcoholic to drink and about forty-seven aspirin. Before I could ask for water, Greg said there were some snacks, a couple of Lunchables, soft drinks, and bottled water in the bag. I fumbled around clumsily for a bottle of water. "Where's my car?" Jennifer asked. He reminded us that her car was still at the first club we went to. "I feel like total $h*t. I want to go home," I said, the first words I could muster after a few sips of the ice- cold water.

I needed to pee, but I was afraid to stand. My legs still felt wobbly, and I was nauseous and dizzy. I opened the car door, nearly falling out onto the pavement. Jennifer got out, and we steadied each other walking to the bathroom.

I noticed my shorts were undone. Was this some kind of twisted sick déjà vu? It felt just like the night I ended up in a convenience store bathroom after I had been raped, but now I was in a different bathroom 1,500 miles away from my hometown, barely able to stand and slowly realizing it had happened again. I had been drugged and raped.

Greg drove us back to Jennifer's car. I didn't say a word. What could I say? I felt sick, completely, and utterly disgusted with myself. The whispers taunted me even louder. *It's all your fault. You deserved to be raped. Do you think you can be such a tease and get away with it?*

The voices continued. *The only thing you're good for is sex. You think you're a notch above other prostitutes just because you have a stupid rule about panties? You fool! You're a slut turned hooker...but this time you didn't get paid!*

I wanted to jump out of the car as Jenn drove us back to Oceanside. The evil voice whispered inside my head once again. *Do it! You should jump. You're no good. Are you going to go climb in bed next to your husband now? You don't deserve a husband. You're a dirty little tramp!*

I thought about taking all the Valium I had when I got home. An overdose would do nicely to end it all.

I thought about not even going home. I let my mind ponder the possibilities. What would Max do if I just didn't come home? Would he even care? I didn't deserve him.

Why could I not stay out of trouble?

The sun was coming up as I climbed the stairs to our apartment. I felt too weak and sick and just wanted a hot shower and a cold compress for my head. I had lost my purse somewhere during the night. I couldn't even remember when I had it last. Did I take it in the first bar with me? Maybe I left it in Jennifer's car. I hoped that's where it was. I couldn't recall having it at any time during the night.

The entire night was a sickening blur.

Chapter 32

PAID FOR

*Money is numbers and numbers never end- no matter how long you string them along~*Lee

*Flee from sexual immorality. All other sins a person commits are outside the body, but whoever sins sexually, sins against their own body.~*1 Corinthians 6:18

When I stumbled in looking like hell, Max was sitting on the couch reading a book. As his beautiful blue eyes pierced me, they showed only relief, love, and kindness; no anger in them at all. "Thank God you're alright. I was so worried about you," he said. I had no words. Looking past him, I walked into our bedroom. I wanted to go to sleep and never wake up.

After my ritualistic scalding shower and some Tylenol, I climbed into bed and prayed to disappear. Around noon, I woke up. Max was sitting at the kitchen table. His eyes searched me, but I was too broken to say anything. I couldn't face him.

Max should have been screaming and yelling at me, demanding to know where I was all night. He should have been mean and angry. He should have thrown me out and slammed the door in my face. He should have called me names and pushed me to the ground. He could have done any or all of those, and I would have had no defense. I deserved wrath, not kindness.

"Can I fix you something to eat?" he said while pouring a glass of orange juice. He set the glass on the table in front of me. A thick cloak of shame and guilt tightened around my throat, threatening to choke the life right out of me. I finally said, "No thank you." His loving kindness was too much for me to handle.

I wanted to run to him, fall on my knees, and confess everything. I wanted to give him every reason to leave me then beg for him to stay. Instead, I stayed silent. I didn't tell him...I couldn't. I couldn't that day and probably never could. Secrets, on top of secrets...on top of more secrets.

I tried desperately to put that night in the rear view and move forward. Jennifer and I talked about it several times over the next few weeks. She cried with me, but when I couldn't stop crying over it, she suggested I see her therapist. "It really might be helpful for you to talk to her. She is really nice and non-judgmental," Jennifer said. She handed me her business card.

I thanked her then stuffed it in my pocket and blew my nose on a wadded-up tissue. The night with Greg was difficult for both of us to cope with, but it was especially traumatic for me. I had never allowed any other males to touch me down there since I had married Max. I was serious about my boundaries, which up to that point, had not been compromised in my marriage.

Yes, I was a "call girl" in every sense of the word. I exchanged sex acts for money, but I still had my limits--I called the shots! I would have never consented to sex with Greg, but Jennifer would have. Why did he feel the need to drug and render us completely helpless and then rape both of us? I just couldn't understand it!

The more I thought about it, the more enraged I became. I didn't take it out on anyone but myself. I became even more obsessive, compulsive, anxious, depressed, and self-loathing. I was on a path of destruction. I stepped right up to the edge, put my toes over the line, and dove in headfirst, all the while sinking deeper and deeper in the sea of regret.

Max's duty reassignment was less than three months away. I was still seeing clients but was determined to wind it down. I had already made the decision to stop working as an escort once we moved. I didn't know how we could make ends meet once I quit, but I knew I was at the end of my rope. There was just enough rope left to tie a noose at the end of it and hang myself. I was drinking heavily and using drugs like candy.

In addition to Valium, Ecstasy and Xanax became my favorites. Of course, I smoked pot occasionally too. I hated what I had become. That night, I could hardly sleep. I was uneasy and restless. I lay in bed listening to Max's slow rhythmic breathing as he peacefully slept next to me.

I was living two lives. Max only knew about one of them. He knew I did out-call massages and that I made lots of money. But there were so many dirty little secrets he didn't know. He didn't know what was going on during those out-call appointments. He didn't know he was sleeping with a prostitute. He didn't know his wife was a highly paid call girl.

Because I was determined to get out of the business, I narrowed my work down to a handful of clients. Two of them I saw alone, and the other three men I saw with Jennifer. The rules had not changed--I was still off limits for intercourse, but Jennifer was available. Usually the date would end with intercourse between the client and Jennifer if he lasted that long.

One man, Bill, who we saw weekly, was not attractive physically, but he was very gentle and kind. He took good care of himself, and he was always courteous and polite. He was extremely generous, always paying more than we asked. I told him soon Jennifer would be working these dates with Randi because I was getting out of the business. He genuinely looked saddened by this news. He told me if there was ever anything, I needed big or small, he would be there for me. He was sincere, and I believed him.

On the second to last date with Bill, a conversation was sparked during dinner and drinks. He sat between us in a cozy booth inside a nice seafood restaurant. We had finished eating but still had plenty of fine wine left to drink. With Jennifer on one side and me on the other, we nuzzled up close to him with our legs draped over his. He loosened his tie as the wine started to kick in. I leaned into him, drawing small circles on his balding head with my painted red fingernails. If anyone noticed the three of us sitting together in that booth, they would not have to think too long to realize this man was paying for our hospitality.

Jenn and I were pros at this now, and we had it down to a science. Our goal--as is with any good hooker--was to get them off as quickly as possible. Then it's over, just like passing Go in Monopoly. You collect your $200 and move on. But in our game, it was to collect $500 each and move on. If we could accomplish most of the goal before we got to the hotel, we preferred that. The dialogue became coy to match our flirtatious actions towards him.

That is when it came up.

Bill looked over at me and said, "I know your rules and all, but I'm simply curious...how much would it take? You know money-wise, for just one time." Taken back, I said, "You couldn't afford me, plus why would you want to? You can have many other girls for way less." He smiled and said in a pouty sort of way, "But I want you."

I brushed it off from there, but he brought it up several more times that evening and during our time at the hotel. I reminded him of my rules and that I didn't even have a price because I never considered it to be an option. Finally, he said, "Just say a number, and I'll let it go." Being tipsy from the wine and not really thinking, I quickly responded. "Okay, you normally pay me $500, and I keep my panties on. Put a 2 in front, and I'll take them off." He just nodded his head in acknowledgment and said nothing further about it. We scheduled time and place for next week, and then Jenn and I hurried out the door.

On the way home, Jennifer and I giggled about my $2,500 price tag. We didn't give it much more thought. We both agreed once I gave in and said a number, he would drop it, and he did.

I only had about five more weeks in Oceanside. Max and I were starting to make moving arrangements. I wanted to create as much distance between my clients and my life as an escort as possible before it was time to move. I was still desperate with shame and regret, but I could see a light at the end of the tunnel. I would work just one more week, and then I would put that lifestyle, and everything associated with it behind me and never look back. I would have a fresh start back in Oklahoma and no one would ever find out about the California version of me, hopefully not even Max...especially not Max.

In the weeks leading up to our move, Jennifer and I spent a lot of time together—without clients. For me, there was never any romantic attraction to Jennifer or any other females, but I had grown to love her as a dear friend. She was really the only one who knew me--the me I had become--and all my secrets.

Everyone else, including Max, only got half-truths or all out lies. I couldn't tell the truth about anything to anyone. I was living a life of sexual sin and slavery to money. A life of spiritual and emotional isolation of my own making. *Just hang on for one more week...don't fall off the edge,* I told myself. *Just a few more dates...no big deal, right?*

The final week I was a "working girl," I saw all five of the remaining clients. I had become a remarkable actress. I was not one bit sad it was the last meeting with them, but they would not know that. The only thing I would miss about them would be their money. I never wanted to touch another man's body ever again except for my husband's. I never wanted another handsy, horny man to touch me ever again. There were certainly discussions about them flying me out to Cali for dates once I left, but I never even considered it. I just didn't tell them that. I needed to lead them on for just a bit longer.

Jenn and I added a few additional $500 dates since it was my last week. I started getting anxious about running out of money and being poor again. I despised the constant roller coaster of desperately hating what I did but loving the monetary rewards of it. It was a never-ending tug-of-war in my mind. *Maybe I should just go ahead and work that last month,* I thought. *What's another month? I'll do as many escorts as I can just to save up,* I told myself.

Why did the love of money have such a tight grip on my heart?

As Jenn and I took my white BMW to meet up with Bill for our final date, the soft California breeze whipped through our hair. We met at a Greek restaurant, and while I'm not a fan of Greek food in the least, I enjoyed the entertainment. Belly dancers twirled around the dance floor and danced right up to our table. They swung their hips rhythmically to the beat of the drums played by a live band. I drank more than usual that night because I didn't like the food.

As I sat there mesmerized by the Valium, the alcohol, and the beat of the music, my mind drifted back to my childhood. I fondly remembered going to these types of shows and entertainment-themed restaurants as a child with my parents. We took the grandest, most expensive vacations money could buy. We traveled to The Bahamas frequently, as well as visiting Martinique, Barbados, The Virgin Islands, The Hawaiian Islands, and many other places. Fine dining on exquisite gourmet foods, exclusive tourist excursions, captivating dinner shows, and fancy five-star hotels best describe our typical family vacations.

Suddenly, reality slapped me across the face. I was no little girl anymore. I was not sitting next to my loving father while innocently enjoying a dinner show. I was twenty-two years old, sitting next to a sexually hungry man whose intent that night was to have me for dessert. The thought sent chills down my spine. Right then and there, I got an agonizing notion Bill had not forgotten the conversation about adding the 2. I swallowed hard, trying to calm my pounding heart. My shaky hands held up the empty glass motioning the waitress to bring another Long Island Tea. I said, "Extra tequila, please!"

Normally, Jenn and I tried to move the evening along just to get it over with, but I was stalling. I certainly was not going to bring it up in case he had forgotten about adding the 2, but I had a strong suspicion that not only had he *not* forgotten, but he was looking forward to it.

When I could stall no longer and it was time to leave, I insisted this time we meet him at the hotel instead of him driving us like usual. I never again wanted to be in a situation where a way of escape wasn't possible. During the drive, I asked Jennifer if she thought he remembered about adding the 2. She said she doubted he remembered. I asked her to help me think of a plan just in case he did remember. I was trying not to overthink it, but the all-too-familiar warning signal was going crazy. We drove the rest of the way with Depeche Mode blaring in the car, and I had the same sickening feeling again.

Once inside the hotel room, my fears were realized when Bill smiled eerily and opened his wallet. He methodically counted twenty-five $100 bills, and then let them freely fall onto the bed. I was stunned! *Oh $h*t! Oh $h*t! This cannot be happening right now.*

I never thought he would pay it; I thought I had said a high enough amount that no sane person would ever pay! I had been around this industry long enough to know sex could be bought for as low as $10-$15 from street prostitutes. The girls I worked with charged $250 an hour, sex or not. We were technically referred to as "high class," but this is insane. I needed more Valium and fast!

At that moment, I actually felt bad for wanting to back out on Bill. Even though I didn't agree to it in the first place, I felt trapped with no way out. I can't explain why I felt bad about that but could be so casually deceptive to my husband. Why I was okay with breaking my word to people I actually cared about. Why I could break the law every single day with little remorse.

I immediately checked out mentally, retreating deep within myself. Then without any further thought, I mechanically lowered my body onto the bed. At the same moment, my capacity to feel anything at all disappeared into nothingness.

In the span of those few moments, something shifted. I realized how this must have felt every single time for Jennifer, Randi, Trisha, Jessica, and so many other girls I knew who sold their bodies. I assumed it was easy for them. I believed since they had done it so many times, they had become jaded, and it didn't bother them anymore. I thought since they were getting paid, somehow that made it an even trade.

I hadn't realized until then that sex for money was costing everyone involved their very soul. Each man took a valuable piece of a woman away when he used her body for his sexual satisfaction. At that very second, I saw the unimaginably high price paid during every encounter. The cost is more than anyone (the man or the sex worker) can afford to pay...no matter how much money is in their wallet.

I already knew that every girl, every single time she was used sexually, hated it with everything inside her. I knew this because I hated it, too.

There was no pleasure in it, only pain.

The cold reality of it all of it hit me in the face and left its mark.

For the first time, I realized how indescribably painful the act of allowing someone you are not married to and do not love to invade your body in any way is painful, even if it is consensual paid sex. Even if it's a seasoned prostitute and especially when the prostitute is your best friend. Jennifer had been shielding me from the truth she knew all too well. By sparing me the act of intercourse, she was protecting me in the only way she knew how.

Jennifer had paid more times than I could count. I did not realize until now what it really cost her to do so, and she had done it for me. She lived this every single day. This time, it was my turn to carry the burden. The tables had turned. This time, I was the one who was going to pay.

I would do it knowing one thing for certain...this would be the first and the last time anyone would pay me for sex.

It lasted less than two minutes from start to finish. I know because I watched the red numbers on the clock. Jennifer held my hand as if I were a child. I didn't cry, because in my mind, I wasn't really there. After it was over, I wasn't angry. I was numb. I knew I had put myself in the situation. It had all come full circle, and now it was finally over.

I knew without a doubt, I would never see him or any other "john" ever again.

The act of sex itself and all of the other stuff--the hand jobs, the blow jobs, the unmentionable and off-the-wall acts men will ask you to do for their sexual pleasure, the stripping, and the pretending it ALL lessens the soul.

During my time servicing men for money, I ceased being surprised at who called for a date: married and single, middle-class, and wealthy, young and old. Men in the political arena, high and low-ranking military personnel, white-collar and blue-collar workers, businessmen, high-profile and no profile, and even Hollywood celebs. A few names you would recognize, but most you wouldn't. All these men had a common thread tightly woven into the core of their being. They all had an insatiable appetite for intimacy, but they were looking for it in all the wrong places.

I, too, was on a quest for intimacy, but not sexual in nature like they were seeking; no, mine was of a different nature. I had a deep-seated need. No amount of attention, no drink or drug, no man or woman, no relationship, no friendship, no money, no beauty, no fame, and no fortune could fill the void crying out deep within my soul. I realize now the men doing the seeking and the women they were chasing were all empty. No matter how long, how deep, or how wide we search, we will all come up empty or partially filled at best.

The longing, the craving, and the seeking will overtake us all, forcing us down deeper and deeper still until the destruction has its way. Only remnants remain. What once was a whole soul, fearfully and wonderfully made, is now tattered and torn. We are left holding mere fragments.

We've all heard the saying, "all good things come to an end." I would add, "all bad things eventually come to an end, too." The remorse, guilt, and shame I carried around daily was so heavy I couldn't carry it much longer.

Our eyes implore someone to see us in our brokenness, to help us gather the fragments and carry them to "The One." There is One and only One who can fill every empty place in our soul. The One can put us back together again and make all things new.

I know Him now, THE ONE I speak of-- and He has other names, as well.

PART 2

Beauty For Ashes

To appoint unto them that mourn in Zion, to give unto them beauty for ashes, the oil of joy for mourning, the garment of praise for the spirit of heaviness; that they might be called trees of righteousness, the planting of the LORD, that he might be glorified." Isaiah 61:3 KJV

The story of my life could easily be divided into "before and after." There are significant events that define moments, and during those defining moments, something happens deep within your soul that changes you forever. Something is either added, or something is taken away.

I wonder if the best way to describe it might be to think of life in general; my life or yours as a never-ending, complicated series of math problems. In Algebra, which is just highly confusing math with many unknowns, the goal is to solve the equation called an "expression" by solving for "x," which is the missing part or the unknown.

This solving is done very methodically. Some rules simply must be followed. The calculations must be accurate. Steps cannot be skipped or misaligned. This set of rules is called "the order of operations." The order must never be altered or confused. If it is, the answer will most assuredly be wrong. It is imperative that adding, subtracting, multiplying, and dividing be done in the right order. If there are parentheses, brackets, or braces inserted anywhere within the problem, those must be dealt with first--using the same order of operations needed outside of them.

A "problem" with a complex set of integer consonants, variables, and sometimes exponential numbers thrown into the mix is that you are left on your own to figure it out. Hopefully, you never forget these rules, or you could end up with a mess of irrational numbers instead of the rational ones that are most desired. Then there are negative numbers, which occur when more is taken away than they have to give.

Sometimes, I feel like a negative number.

In the Algebra class of life, a substitute teacher sits idly by, watching you struggle to find the answers, but you get it wrong time and time again. With glasses situated low on his nose, the substitute peers over his lenses, squinting to get a better look at your failures. You're afraid to raise your hand and ask for help because the last time you did, he reminded you of how many times he's been over this and over this with you--but you just don't seem to get it. You must pass the test. If you don't, you will fail again...but you are running out of chances to get it right. So, you resort to doing things you never thought you would do to come up with a passing grade. You lie, you cheat, you steal, you compromise your values, and you reduce yourself to a lower standard while striving for a higher mark.

You try and try over and over to sort out the variables. Then you must start all over... but wait, what is an integer again? No matter how hard you try or how long you sit there agonizing over this set of problems you were assigned, you just can't do it alone.

Discouraged and defeated, you crumple up the paper and throw it in the trash. You're tired, so you give up. You've failed again, and you will never measure up...you'll never amount to anything.

But then, suddenly, and unexpectedly, the REAL teacher walks confidently into the room. He knows the answers, and He knows how to teach you in a way you can personally understand because He understands YOU. His demeanor is not critical or condescending, for He is patient and kind. He has all the time in the world to sit with you and help you to sort it out.

He walks over to the trash can and retrieves the crumpled-up papers that represent your failures. He sits down beside you and begins to smooth out the wrinkles. He shows you where you messed up in a non-judgmental, caring way; then He shows you how to fix it. He puts the pencil back into your hand, but He doesn't leave your side.

He sits with you, never getting frustrated or bored with your mistakes. He gently corrects, time and time again, showing you in the "book" how to get it right. This book has all the answers. He lays it down beside you and says He'll help you to understand every word of what it says. This is your guide through all the problems you will ever be faced with in life.

Suddenly, the light bulb flashes on. It's no longer dark and confusing. It's still a challenge, but not one you can't figure out with His reassuring guidance. Now you understand, maybe not all of it, for you will still need Him to sit with you... but it starts to get easier, little by little. He works with you patiently, through every step. HE IS THE ANSWER, and He is THE ONE. His name is Jesus. He is everything you will ever need.

I struggled through life continually messing up, getting it wrong repeatedly, and never measuring up. My failures were huge, and my mistakes seemed unredeemable. Until I met THE REDEEMER! I knew OF Him before; I had even invited Him into my heart as a child, but I kept Him at a distance. I didn't want to let Him come too close. I drifted further and further away from Him and into a life of sin which led to torment, which led to desperation and defeat. At the verge of giving up, I found Him at the end of my rope.

Jesus was there! He was with me the entire time. He didn't interrupt, He didn't intrude, and He didn't insist. He was just there quietly waiting for an invitation to rescue me from the pit of despair. He is the greatest lifeguard of all. He even walks on water!

Drowning in a sea of despondency, I reached for Him, and without a moment's delay, He pulled me up from the pit. He cleaned me up and gave me a new start, a second chance. Now life is different. He walks with me still, but now I acknowledge and welcome His presence. I talk with Him, and He lovingly directs and guides me unto all truth. The TRUTH about who I really am. The TRUTH about what HE says about me. I no longer listen to the cruel voice whisper lies about me. I now KNOW THE TRUTH. It is IN HIM! JESUS is THE WAY, THE TRUTH and THE LIFE. HE IS THE ONE!!

As I wrote at the beginning of this section, life can be divided into "before and after." The main difference--yes, the defining moment changed everything--was when I made JESUS my LORD, not just my SAVIOR. There is a distinct difference between the former and the latter.

Please allow me to explain. When Jesus is your savior, that means you are going to heaven when you die. But when Jesus is your Lord, not only are you going to heaven when you die, but while you are living, you are in close fellowship with Him. You care about what He cares about. You allow Him to have a say in your life because you know He knows best. You look to Him, not the world, for answers.

The first part and the second part of my life lived this far is distinctly divided between "before Jesus" and "after Jesus."

Continue to walk with me through my story, and you will see the difference. My life will not always be free from disappointment, grief, pain, and loss. Unfortunately, those threads are also woven into the second part of the story, but the difference will not be a lack of brokenness; in fact, it will not lack anything ever again.

Instead, it will be the addition of THE ONE who never fails. The

One whose love never runs out, whose goodness never ends, and whose love always abounds. The One who is willing to forgive because He is the only one who can. The One who will never leave or forsake us, who is an ever-present help in times of trouble.

Chapter 33

MAYBE BABY?

The decision to have a child is momentous. It is to decide forever to have your heart go walking around outside your body~Elizabeth Stone

When Max and I returned to Oklahoma, we soon learned the queasiness I felt in my stomach the day we left California was because I was carrying a precious gift from God I was carrying a son! And this little boy would be the new start we had been longing for. A sweet, innocent baby boy would change everything. From the moment I found out I was expecting, I never touched another cigarette or illegal drug. Alcohol no longer had a hold on me. God delivered me from my dependency by blessing us with a child.

I prayed many times after the abortion for God to give me another chance to be a mother. I made a promise to God and myself that if He gave me another opportunity, I would strive with my entire being to be the best one mom I could possibly be. God was sending us a son, and in doing so, He saved my life.

After we settled into our modest three-bedroom rent house in Moore, Oklahoma, my only focus was learning to be a Godly wife and preparing to be a mother. I spent time praying and reading the Bible as well as many other books written by Christian authors. In my sobriety, I was slowly learning to lean on the Lord.

I had decided after that final night in the hotel room when I compromised everything that I believed in for a stack of one-hundred-dollar bills that I would never again compromise my values for anything or anyone.

God used a little brown-eyed, curly headed baby boy to alter my course. I was on a path headed for destruction, but God knew how to save me. By giving me a baby, He gave me a purpose. That purpose is to be a Godly wife and to raise children in the honor and admonition of the Lord. And for that, I am exceedingly and eternally grateful.

Now...having said all that, one might think life would be easy from that point on. You know, living a Christian life means only sunny days in the forecast with no cloudy days or threatening storms on the horizon until we arrive safely in heaven. Yeah...that's what I thought, too.

When I first became Christian and by that, I mean someone who actually *follows* Christ this is how I thought life would go down, in five simple rules:

1. Once you give your life over to the Lord and surrender your will for His, then life would be peachy.
2. As long as you are "living right," meaning free from immorality and sin (well, for the most part; after all, no one is perfect, but you really are doing your best), then God should protect you, your family, and everything and everyone you care about from anything bad.
3. If you avoid all the *major* sins and commit only the *minor* ones occasionally, then God would have your back. And let's not even talk about sins of omission...what are those, exactly?
4. God will keep anything bad from happening in my life. He is not governed by free will. He can eliminate the consequences of sin or other's choices if He feels like it.
5. God will and should always answer my prayers when and how I want Him to because it's all about me isn't it?

SIDENOTE: I know these "rules" sound silly. I hope I'm not the only one who ever believed myths like this or had unrealistic expectations about God. Back then, as a new Christian, I had a lot to learn. I still do, but I've come a long way, baby!

Now after spending more than twenty-five years learning of the Lord, drawing close to Him, reading, praying, studying, and getting it wrong many more times than I've gotten it right, I've made progress. I believe I have a firm grasp on His character, on who He is, and on who I am in Him. The road has not been easy.

We can live for Him or against Him and I hate to tell you this, but it's really only one or the other. There is no in between. I have done it both ways, and it's far better to live for Him.

So, back to the story.

Chapter 34

ROCKING CHAIRS AND
BABY PRAYERS

For this child I prayed and the Lord has granted the desires of
my heart~1 Samuel 1:27

Max was enjoying his new duty station. His office was in the Alfred P. Murrah Federal Building on the 6th floor. The hours he worked were long. I missed the days when he would get home around 5:00 p.m. daily.

Our life in Oklahoma was vastly different than it had been in California. Instead of being out with strange men doing unthinkable things, I was at home reading my Bible. I no longer had a desire to be anywhere except with Max. Drugs, alcohol, cigarettes, clubs, or parties no longer had any appeal. I did not seek approval from anyone except the Lord Jesus and my husband.

Before long, Max and I found a local church and began attending three times per week. We didn't know anyone there at first, but it didn't matter. I was not there to make friends. I wanted to get more acquainted with my Maker. However, the people there welcomed us, making us feel like we belonged.

I had to continually fight against feelings of unworthiness, though.

The accusing whispers were not gone, and they cruelly continued to remind me of my past. They told me lies like, *if these people in the church knew the kind of girl you really are, they would reject you. You are a fake and a fraud! You're really just a slut dressing up for church instead of a bar, and just because you clean up nice in a church dress doesn't change anything. You're still a dirty little whore.*

Battling these unrelenting and accusing thoughts day after day made me feel worthless, anxious, and depressed. But I was learning to look in my Bible and read what God's word says about who I am. I read over and over 2 Corinthians 5:17. I constantly reminded myself, "I AM a NEW creation in Christ Jesus." This and many other scriptures became my battle weapons. The struggle was real, but eventually, I would get the victory over the cynical voice. It took months of practice, but very slowly, The WORD took root in my heart. I was becoming new from the inside out.

Financially, we were in a different situation, too. Max and I sold my BMW and other "luxury" items we had accumulated while I was living a double life. We lived paycheck to paycheck again, but this time, it did not bother me like it had before.

And after we moved, I did not give our new phone number to anyone I knew in California. Not even Jennifer. I knew I needed distance and time to heal emotionally.

I was content to be a stay-at-home wife, and soon, my days would be filled taking care of a newborn. During the day and on weekends and evenings when Max was at work, I read. Any extra money we had, I spent it on either something for the baby or on books about pregnancy, nutrition, and parenting. I read about how to be a better wife, how to be a mother, and how to be a Christian. I was hungry for sound teaching and Biblical advice.

One day in a little gift shop, I ran across a book called *Supernatural Childbirth*. I bought the book and began reading it at night before I went to sleep. The book was about pregnancy and childbirth God's way, and at the end, it has prayers to pray over your unborn baby. I started praying these over my baby months before he was even born.

That book helped me learn how to pray and how to stand in faith on scriptures in the Bible, believing God would answer. I took the book with me everywhere I went, and I highlighted the scriptures I was praying in my Bible so I could find them easily.

Day after day, I sat in a brown wooden hand-me-down rocking chair with a torn blue cushion, rocking my unborn baby and praying for him. I tried not to think of the baby I had lost, but most days, I couldn't help it. I imagined that child and the one I was carrying now, playing together when the baby got older.

One afternoon, I had been grieving that loss throughout the day, and it was still on my mind when Max returned home from work that evening. Knowing it was a difficult question, I carefully asked, "Babe, would you have still married me if I would have been able to have that baby?" Max thought for a few seconds before he responded. He gently said, "Yes, I still would have. It may have been hard at first, but I would have loved you and that baby."

I was relieved but wept bitterly for what might have been yet never would be.

As we prepared to become parents, the bond between Max and I grew even stronger. He was attentive and caring throughout my pregnancy. Max wanted children as much as I did, and I had no doubts he would be a great dad. We talked about who we thought the baby might look like and who he might become.

To get us started, the ladies at church kindly hosted a baby shower for us. Then, the military wives hosted one, and our families also got together and hosted a baby shower for us! God was showing me He was not just meeting our needs but *abundantly* meeting our needs. My faith was increasing as God's faithfulness was abounding.

Every night without fail, I continued to pray over our baby, our marriage, and our future. I asked God to give us a healthy and strong baby boy and to give him a desire to serve God. I prayed he would be a blessing to everyone he met. I also asked God to provide him with long beautiful eyelashes.

Max and I excitedly transformed an empty spare bedroom into a nursery for our soon-to-arrive baby boy. As we were coasting through the last weeks before the baby's arrival, putting the final touches on the nursery and deciding on a name, something evil beyond description happened.

Chapter 35

A DAY WE CAN'T FORGET

She had the choice to sulk in the disaster or find beauty even from the ashes~S.S. Jubilee

Wednesday, April 19, 1995, began as normally as any other. My body was indicating our blessing would be arriving soon. I was cramping and uncomfortable with a constantly aching back. When Max's alarm went off early that morning, I begged him to stay in bed longer. I had an unrelenting feeling something was wrong. "Please call in today. My back hurts…what if I'm in labor? I need you here with me," I whined.

Max replied, "I'm sorry, babe. I can't miss work today. But I'll have lots of time off when the baby gets here." I pleaded, "But what if the baby gets here today? Please don't go in, or at the very least, skip PT and go in later." Max ignored my request and proceeded to get his uniform ready and pack his gym bag.

I laid in bed a little longer, trying to think up something else to keep him home. Nothing came to mind, so I got up and readied myself for the day. Max kissed me goodbye before he hurried out the door. I wondered what was the matter with me. Why was I so clingy and insecure all of a sudden?

During the week, I usually babysat a little boy to make extra money, and this was the last week I was scheduled to watch him before we had our baby. His mom dropped him off about ten minutes before nine. As I went into the kitchen to fix his bottle, I flipped the TV on. When I returned to the living room, the show I normally watched was in the opening lines. It was 9:00 am on April 19th, 1995. I bent down and picked the baby up to feed him, and I was still holding him when the program was interrupted by an urgent news bulletin. I wasn't looking at the television, but when I turned to get his bottle, I saw a glimpse of the chaos and absolute mayhem on the screen. The reporter was saying something about a bombing in downtown Oklahoma City. The reporters were frantic.

My knees buckled. I thought I was going to pass out. I quickly laid the baby down so I wouldn't drop him. I stared in disbelief at the television screen and watched as the horror was shown. At first, they were reporting the bombing had occurred in the Federal Court House, which is directly across the street from the Murrah Federal Building. The blood drained from my limbs as I collapsed onto the couch. I was dizzy and felt disoriented, and I couldn't think. *Was Max okay?*

I waddled to the phone, holding my stomach as if my baby was going to fall out of me. I was willing myself to stay calm. I thought, *if it's the courthouse, Max would be fine because he didn't work in that building*. I picked up the phone and called his office; it was 9:05. The call rang and rang, but no one picked up. *Someone should be there*, I kept thinking! *Someone should pick up. Please God, let Max be okay,* I prayed as I hung up the receiver.

Just then, my phone rang, and I quickly answered. It was my mom who was with one of my sisters. "Lee? Honey are you okay?" my mom said, speaking faster than normal. I replied, "Yeah, I was just trying to get a hold of Max, but no one is answering."

I was shaking so much I could barely hold the phone to my ear. I quickly checked on the baby, who was just playing with a rattle as if nothing in the world was wrong. My mom's voice brought me back to reality when she said, "Lee! We are on our way over to wait with you. I've called your dad. He's leaving work and headed there also. Lee? Are you there? Honey?"

I slowly processed what she just said. I asked, "What? Wait with me, why? It wasn't even Max's building." I was confused and scared; then my mom spoke again.

"Lee. Yes, it was, it was the Federal Building. Max's building, not the Courthouse, was bombed. Lee? Lee? We are on our way!"

I couldn't say anything, and I couldn't move. I just stood there frozen, holding my stomach while crying and praying.

Back in 1995, there were very few cellular phones. It wasn't common for everyone to have a phone like it is today. I did not have a way to reach Max. At that moment, time seemed to stand still. I sat for several gut-wrenching hours, watching the minutes on the clock slowly tick by. I kept my eyes glued to the television, flipping from one channel to the next, seeing nothing but panic and devastation. The initial blast at 9:02 a.m. killed 168 people, including children, and injuring more than 500 others.

On every local network station, the scenes were the same. It looked like a war zone; zombie-like victims were walking around on scattered debris and broken glass. Rocking back and forth, sobbing helplessly on the couch, I sat and waited. I waited to find out if my husband was a victim of this hellacious crime against humanity. *God, please let him call me or walk in the front door! PLEASE GOD!*

After waiting over two hours, my prayers were answered. I finally heard my husband's voice. Max called, but I could hardly hear him because the sound of devastation and chaos in the background was louder than he could speak. Max was highly emotional and shaken to the core but thankfully unharmed.

For Max and me, the outcome of that day was positive. My husband came home, but two other military families from Max's office grieved the loss of their Marine who did not. Countless families had a vacancy at their table for dinner that night and many nights after. Mommies and daddies were missing who were not home to say bedtime prayers with their little ones, and there were little ones who were not there to be tucked safely into their beds.

May we never forget. April 19, 1995 was a day of "before and after" for hundreds of families, including mine. A typical day for some was a catastrophic day for others. Days like these draw a line in the sand of time defining "before and after."

Chapter 36

MY SONSHINE

For you created my inmost being, you knit me together in my mother's womb~Psalm 139:13

After forty long weeks and three days of anticipating, waiting, longing, and praying, the joyous day finally arrived! On May 1st, 1995, Max and I became parents! Our hearts could hardly contain the vastly enormous love we felt when we welcomed our healthy 7-pound, 12-ounce baby boy. We chose to name him Zachariah Tyler…Zachariah, a strong biblical Hebrew name meaning "The Lord has remembered," and Tyler for Max's middle name.

I knew the second I saw my son's big eyes brimmed with long, beautiful lashes that God heard our prayers and answered every one. Our beloved firstborn son, right there in my arms, captured our hearts from the moment we saw him. We were parents! The first fruits of our marriage lay peacefully suckling at my breast. Our Zachariah was fearfully, perfectly, and wonderfully made right from the start.

This adorable, tiny person made me a mother. I would look at Zach, almost in disbelief that someone as perfect as him could come from me. Max and I were fascinated with everything about our son. Those big brown eyes and soft brown curls melted our hearts.

I never wanted to put Zachariah down. I rocked him for hours on end, singing gently in his ear as we rocked. "You are my sunshine, my only sunshine, you make me happy when skies are gray. You'll never know dear, how much I love you. Please don't take my sunshine away." Zachariah felt like heaven in my arms.

I never wanted those days of his infancy to end. I didn't know it was possible to love another person so much...every day, I loved my son more than the day before.

Max and I felt stronger than ever in our marriage, and the sinful desires and lust for money no longer plagued me. Joyfully, I had the privilege and freedom to be a full-time mommy. I could care for my husband, son, and our home, and we even had an amazing dog! Since I couldn't bring myself to leave Zach in the church nursery, we even joined the kid's ministry team at church.

This was a chapter full of happiness! We loved each other and our son, we were active in church, I was reading my Bible every day, and I even had my pre-baby figure back yet something felt off.

The continual battle with anxiety and depression had taken its toll on me. Over the years, I had used drugs, alcohol, sex, money, reckless behavior, and men to cope. I didn't understand it then, but I was constantly on the run, playing hide-and-go-seek with disaster. Looking back over my life, the apparent common thread was anxiety and depression. The only thing that changed over the years was how I coped with it or didn't depending on the circumstances.

Thankfully, I no longer used the crutch of drugs, alcohol, or other harmful behavior to cope with "the common cold of mental illness," also known as anxiety and depression. But because I hadn't truly dealt with my wounds, I was in for a long road of recovery.

Chapter 37

TURN OFF THE DARK

Monsters don't sleep under your bed, they sleep inside your head.

I am a 23-years-old with a six-week old baby. I was quickly coming apart at the seams and no one, including me, knew what was happening. I was stricken with severe panic attacks that were terrifying and vengeful; they came seemingly out of nowhere. The severity of these attacks literally rendered me helpless. When they hit, feelings of sheer terror would bring me to my knees. No place felt safe, not even home.

Anxiety hunted me down like a hungry beast stalking its prey. Nothing I tried helped. I prayed and asked God to take it away. I asked for prayer at church. My parents and Max prayed for me. I kept reading my Bible. But no matter what I did or what I avoided doing, the panic found me everywhere I went.

I became agoraphobic, only leaving the house if I absolutely had to and only if my husband or one of my parents were with me. Sometime over the next couple of months, I stopped driving. I went from a social butterfly to a complete shut-in.

I did go to the doctor about this a few times, but they would tell me nothing was wrong. They were partially correct; nothing was wrong with me physically, but mentally, something was very wrong. The whispers, the ones I thought would leave when I became a "good Christian," taunted me even louder, telling me lie after lie. Despite my loving husband and precious son, I thought I was going crazy.

The voices got louder. *You're so stupid. You think living for God is better? Even when you were high, you weren't this crazy! God doesn't love you. He is punishing you for all the stuff you used to do. You'll never be good enough for him to love you. You're trying to be someone you're not by "playing house." You're still a slut dressed up to look like a church girl.*

On and on the internal dialogue bantered back and forth, and I desperately tried not to believe the accusing whispers. But it was evident to me and everyone else I was coming unglued.

No one knew what these attacks were, and medically, there didn't seem to be any answers. There was no internet then, so googling it was not an option. Everyone had an opinion, though. My mom, my sisters, my friends, and people at church everyone was willing to dish out plenty of well-meaning advice, but none of it helped. I felt like a complete failure.

The only ray of sunshine was Zachariah. Taking care of his needs brought joy and purpose to my days. Holding him, rocking him, feeding him, changing his diapers, and wiping his little nose were the responsibilities that kept me going when I wanted to give up. I knew no one in the whole entire world loved him more than I did, and I wanted to be the one taking care of him. I was terrified if I kept having these "attacks," someone might try and take him away.

After having these episodes for about six months, one of my friends suggested a night out with Max might help. "I would be crazy too if I was cooped up in the house all day with leaky boobs and dirty diapers," she said. But I loved my leaky boobs; they were full of life-sustaining milk for my infant son. And for the first time in my life, I felt good about my body. I had given life to another person, and that was my only real accomplishment…if I was unable to be his mommy, then I didn't want to live.

But I thought if a night out with Max could cure me, I was more than willing to give it a try. I arranged for my parents to babysit and made plans for the upcoming weekend. Max bought tickets to a ballet, which we couldn't afford, and then we planned a romantic dinner afterwards, which we also couldn't afford. But I was looking forward to spending time alone with Max. I was just so apprehensive about leaving Zach for the evening. He was six months old, and I had never left him with anyone. I knew my parents would take good care of him, but the thought of leaving him in anyone's care but mine made me nervous.

It would all come to a head that night.

Chapter 38

PSYCH WARD

*Hey darlin', your crazy is showing. You might want
to tuck that back in.*

Our date night arrived but not without me dreading it. I tried to
talk Max out of it a hundred times, but he wouldn't let me back
out. He encouraged me by saying, "Babe, you cannot live your life in
fear. This is not like you at all. I'm worried about you! A night out
will be good for you."

Logically, I knew he was right but none of this felt logical! *Why
was this happening to me,* I wondered for the millionth time. Finally,
after stalling until the last minute, I went to get ready. I was washing
my hair when an anxiety attack invaded my shower; the physical
symptoms of panic completely overwhelmed me. I quickly rinsed the
shampoo out of my hair. Trembling, I turned off the water, stepped
out of the tub, and then crumbled onto the bathroom floor in tears.

*You're never going to get over this. You might as well just give
up. This is God punishing you,* said the cruel whispers. *You suck at
being a wife and mother, but you were a great hooker. Max and Zach
would both be better off without you.* Without relenting, the whispers
taunted me on that bathroom floor.

Somehow, I pulled myself together to create the illusion I was not completely off my rocker. On the way to the ballet, Max did his best to make small talk and put me at ease. His demeanor was almost always calm anyway, but no matter how much gentle reassurance he offered, it didn't help. The closer we got to downtown Oklahoma City, the more anxious I got.

As the images of the recent Federal Building bombing flooded my mind, I didn't feel safe. *Keep it together...just calm down. Nothing bad is going to happen. You're going to be okay. Just breathe,* I told myself repeatedly while Max found a place to park.

We parked, and when Max came around to my door, I didn't want to get out of the car. "Come on babe, you can do this. Hold my hand, and once you get in there, you'll be fine. You will love the ballet," he lovingly encouraged. I knew he was right. I knew my fears were irrational, but it didn't make them less significant or scary in my mind. I finally agreed to go in and try to enjoy the evening.

As we were walking up to the building, it happened a severe panic attack immobilized me right there in front of God and everyone. *Why was He letting this happen to me?!* The fear inside me was suffocating. I felt like I couldn't get any air in my lungs. *What the hell is happening to me? WHY?*

I buried my face in Max's jacket and cried.

Then I screamed in Max's face, "Take me to a psychiatric hospital now! I need to be committed!" I sobbed until I was empty. I told Max I wanted to go pick Zachariah up so I could see him before they locked me up. Max drove me home, and with no explanation to my parents, I swooped in and grabbed Zach. Holding him close, I kissed his face as fresh tears ran down mine. We got back in the car with Zach and drove to the nearest mental hospital.

I had never been in a psych ward or in any building with sliding doors that could lock you in. I clung to Zach as we walked up to the emergency entrance. Bouncing my smiling, happy boy on my hip, I announced to the lady sitting in an area secured behind a plexi-glass shield, "I need to see a psychiatrist. I think I'm going crazy."

I imagined any minute, the doors would slide open and two orderlies dressed in white would walk out, put me in a straightjacket, and cart me off kicking and screaming, never to be heard from again.

Thank God, that did not happen. Instead, I held it together and calmly walked to the back area where I would willfully submit to a psychiatric evaluation. A nice lady put me inside a small room with shiny eggshell-colored paint on the walls. There was no artwork or anything to distract me from the reality of where I was and why I was there. A black plastic and metal chair sat next to a small writing desk attached to the wall. There was another identical chair which I occupied.

Gosh, I hope I'm not REALLY crazy, I thought while I waited. Looking down at my high heels, I mused to myself, *Man, I am sure overdressed for this place.*

Soon, the nice lady brought me a bunch of paperwork to fill out. She smiled as she handed the papers to me and said, "Take your time, but please answer every question as honestly as you can." Then she left. I wondered what Max and Zach were doing while I was behind locked doors. I wanted to run out there saying, "I'm free, I'm free! They let me go," but I didn't. I scooted up to the desk to begin my task.

I laughed a little under my breath when I noticed a ballpoint pen secured to a chain attached to the wall. I guess they didn't want the pen to escape. I sat there for an hour or so answering every question as truthfully as I could. It felt like I was back in high school taking a standardized test. For whatever reason, I wasn't nearly as anxious "on the inside" as I had been just a few hours before while driving to a ballet with my husband.

It wasn't too long before the nice lady returned to get my completed paperwork. *Was she going to grade them now?* I imagined her looking over the forms and saying, *Let's see, on a scale of 1-10, how crazy is this girl?*

It seemed like forever before I heard a soft knock on the door. A very nice middle-aged man walked in. He looked like he could've been one of the clients I used to service. The man extended his hand and said, "Hello, I'm Dr. Blaine. I'm wondering what brought you in tonight."

Since I had never sat down with a psychiatrist, I didn't know what to expect, but Dr. Blaine put me at ease. He asked me many questions, scribbling notes as I talked. He looked at the forms I had filled out, and I noticed he had marked some with an asterisk. He inquired further about specific questions he had.

Soon my official psychiatric evaluation was concluded. Dr. Blaine put all the papers down on the desk before crossing one leg over the other, sitting up a little straighter in his chair. Finally, he spoke and said, "Well, you put down here that your biggest concern was going crazy, and somehow lost your mind. Is that what you think has happened to you?"

I didn't know how to answer. I was afraid I was going to say the wrong thing, which would confirm my suspicions and give him reason to lock me up. But I really did think I was crazy and that something was clearly wrong. I didn't want to live like this anymore. I needed someone to help me, so I said the only thing I could: "Yes, I think I may be crazy."

Dr. Blaine' smile reassured me as he gently chuckled and said, "Well, I have some good news for you. You are NOT crazy, not even in the least." I could have jumped up and hugged him. I was so relieved, but I remained composed and asked, "If I'm not crazy, then what is wrong with me?"

Dr. Blaine then explained I had repeated and frequent panic attacks, and he confirmed many people feel "crazy" when they have them. He told me he suspected I had developed a full-blown panic disorder from the frequency and severity of the panic attacks. He added that most likely I also had obsessive-compulsive disorder (OCD), and I was borderline agoraphobic.

I felt somewhat relieved, but those words sounded foreign and scary. "So how long do I have to stay here?" was my next question. He responded, "Oh, you don't have to stay here. You are of no danger to society, and you are of no danger to yourself, so you're free to go. I'll send you home with some medication to help you through these attacks over the rest of the weekend, then you will follow up with me in my office on Monday."

So, I took the medication Dr. Blaine gave me and followed up with him on Monday. I continued to be a psychiatric patient of his for many months. I was officially diagnosed with Generalized Anxiety Disorder, Anxiety/Panic Disorder, Post Traumatic Stress Disorder, Obsessive-Compulsive Disorder, and Agoraphobia. Contributing factors included all of the following: hormonal changes from pregnancy and childbirth, a chemical imbalance, heavy drug, and alcohol use, compiled and unaddressed shame, guilt, depression, and fear along with a genetic predisposition.

At first, I met with Dr. Blaine several times per week, and these sessions helped immensely. He was so patient and kind. He helped me sort out my fears that had led me to his office in the first place. Over time, I learned coping strategies I could use when anxiety attempted to render me helpless. We eventually found the correct balance of medication to keep me regulated.

When I discontinued weekly therapy, Zachariah was almost two years old. At that time, I still needed medicinal support. I continued taking prescribed antidepressants and antianxiety medications. Even though the struggle with obsessive/compulsive tendencies and panic attacks was ongoing, many of the self-imposed limitations had been eliminated. I was far from "over it," but I was able to function more regularly, and I was beyond thankful for that.

Chapter 39

MORE SONSHINE

Children are a gift from the Lord, the fruit of the womb is a reward~Psalms 127:3

Despite all my internal chaos, Zachariah was thriving. As he grew, our love for him grew even more. There was wisdom in his big brown eyes. We knew God had plans for him and that one day his influence on this world would make it a better place. Zach and I spent the days together while my husband worked two jobs to ensure I could be home with our son.

I couldn't imagine being anywhere else. I cherished every moment, and I'm grateful for each one. I observed Zach in amazement as we played I could see his little mind working to figure things out. We did puzzles, read books, built towns out of blocks, baked cookies, and made "art" out of objects around the house. We were active and happy.

Soon, we knew Max would be getting transfer orders, so our time in Oklahoma was ending. I was still taking medicine to combat the anxiety that was always lurking nearby, threatening to knock me down when I least expected it. But little by little as the weeks turned into months, I was getting stronger. I felt ready to wean off of the medications...baby fever will do that to you.

Max and I both wanted to give Zachariah the gift of a sibling, so we educated ourselves about the risks versus benefits of taking these medications during pregnancy. We did not want to take even the slightest risk of causing harm to an unborn baby, so with my doctor's guidance and blessing, I stopped all medication.

Once I got adjusted, I felt good most days. We waited a few months for all the meds to get out of my system. Then just after we celebrated Zachariah's second birthday, the timing felt right. We knew we were ready, so after much prayer and consideration, we started trying for baby number two. I replaced medication with prenatal vitamins and folic acid.

Every day, I spent time reading my Bible and praying, building up my faith little by little and learning to trust God more and more. I continued to read books by Christian authors to help my understanding of what I was learning during my Bible time. My love of books grew right along with my faith. I wanted Zachariah to love books as much as I did, so I read to him every day.

At barely two, Zach was already mastering the early fundamentals of reading. We worked on letters, letter sounds, blends, and numbers. I made flashcards out of a package of index cards so he could "read" his favorite words. Dinosaur, moon, stars, Woody, Buzz, Toy Story, pizza, ice cream, bug, and pool those were some of his sight words, and our smart boy knew them all. I saw this emergent reading quickly develop into a love of books.

Life was peaceful, but the closer it got to our move, the more tired and ran down I felt. I was having unusual cravings for pizza and waking up queasy and nauseated. That could only mean one thing. *Maybe I was pregnant?*

About a week later, after a long day of packing for the move, Max walked in from work smiling ear to ear, and I could tell something was up. Zach ran to him, dropping his flashcards along the way and yelling, "Daddy!" Max leaned down to hug him and ruffled his hair. Max sat down, unbuttoned his jacket, and then lifted Zach into his lap.

I smiled and said, "Hey babe, do you mind if we have pizza again for dinner tonight? I think Zach is hungry for it." Max and I both knew I was the one who wanted pizza again. "Pizza!" Zach exclaimed as he quickly sorted through his flashcards, finding the one that said "pizza."

Max grinned, "Yeah! Pizza sounds good, and by the way, I have something to tell you." I wasn't surprised because I could tell he had something on his mind when he walked in. I said as casually as possible, "Okay, and I have something to tell you too. You go first!" I couldn't wait to hear what he had to say.

Max was still holding Zach in his lap, bouncing him on his knees. Max said, to Zach, "Hey buddy, do you like pineapple?" Zach looked up at him brushing his curls back away from his eyes. "Yeah, Daddy! I wike 'em." Then Max continued, "Well that's good then, because you will have the chance to eat them a lot! Guess where we're moving?!"

Zach couldn't guess but I could! Hawaii!

"Ok, now what did you have to tell me?" Max inquired.

I couldn't think of a creative way to tell him, so I just blurted out excitedly, "I'm PREGNANT!"

Chapter 40

HAWAIIAN RAINBOWS

"When it rains look for rainbows, when it's dark look for stars."~Oscar Wilde

Saying goodbye to family and friends was harder than when we first got married and moved to California. Emotions ran high as we pried Zach away from his grandparents.

I was thirteen weeks along when the wheels of the airplane touched down in Honolulu. Except for the morning sickness, the pregnancy was going wonderfully. With Zach, I had a sometimes-queasy feeling, but with this baby, it was a throw-your-guts-up feeling every single day.

Hawaii was absolutely gorgeous, and in the beginning, I was free of panic attacks. It truly felt like we had landed in paradise. Max's paycheck still didn't amount to much, so living on the base was our only option. We were given a three-bedroom unit in a quadplex. Our neighborhood consisted of identical quadplex buildings situated in rows; the building colors alternated between tan and pea green.

Our quadplex was pea-green, and might I add that was not just on the outside, but a paler shade of pea-green adorned the interior walls as well. The day we went to see our housing for the first time, I started to cry. The place was run-down and ugly. The floors were an industrial linoleum with no carpeting. It had no air conditioning, no ceiling fans, and no window coverings. This was not where I wanted to live for the next three years!

As we walked through the unit, I began to calculate the cost of fixing the place up. Tears escaped my eyes. Zach noticed, and in his dutchy little voice, he said the sweetest words I will never ever forget. "Mommy, why are you cwying? This house is purfect for us...I willy wike it!" I wiped the tears from my eyes, then knelt down to hug my little angel on earth and thank him for the encouragement.

But the thought of Zach and the new baby having to play on those cold floors made me anxious. I had not worked since we left California three years before except for odd jobs or babysitting, so money was extremely tight. Having to purchase blinds, rugs, fans, and wallpaper to cover parts of the hideous paint color on the walls would be expensive but necessary. The cost of living in paradise was apparently beyond our means.

But we buckled down. To reserve fuel and save money, Max walked to work. I did not go anywhere during the day unless it was a necessity. In the evenings and weekends, we stayed home or walked to the beach. We resorted to racking up credit cards, quickly becoming financially strapped once again. The difference this time was we had a two-year old little boy and another on the way. I began to get anxious all over again. I handled it the best I could because I was determined to be thankful for what we did have and not focus on what we didn't.

Several months passed, and slowly but surely, we got settled into the empty house and made it our home. Once we got unpacked and bought what we absolutely needed, like blinds on the windows for privacy and ceiling fans for air circulation, it felt better. But even with the house fixed up, we spent most of our time outdoors.

My very favorite place to be was our own backyard. I can still hear the children's laughter when I think back to those days. In the far corner of our yard was a mature plumeria tree. The large, fragrant tree provided just the right amount of shade to cool us off from the hot afternoon sunshine. Each day, the tree released a new batch of white, sweet-smelling plumeria flowers with pink edges and yellow centers. The fragrant flowers floated to the ground, settling on the soft green grass below.

Zach and I collected the scented flowers in a repurposed Easter basket, then we spread out a large lemon-yellow satin blanket that had been my grandmother's. We spent many afternoons stringing the flowers on a piece of yarn with a large blue plastic needle, making leis to give to the neighbors. During the months of afternoons spent under the plumeria tree, it turns out Zach was right--this house was "perfect" for us.

Zach and I also spent many fun-filled days sitting on the golden Hawaiian sand near the vast, salty ocean, watching the huge waves roll in and out. One day, Zach was horrified when one of those big waves took away his shovel and pail and knocked his sandcastle down. It may have been the first time in his whole life he realized just how unfair life could be.

Another of our favorite pastimes was to go outside at night and study the sky. Looking into his big, beautiful eyes with long lashes fluttering like the wings of a butterfly, I could see eternity. He would point his chubby finger towards the navy velvet sky, attempting to count a million stars. Zach's eyes looked as large as the full moon he stared at while gazing far up into the galaxy. "To infinity and beyond," he would exclaim while holding Buzz Lightyear up as high as he could reach.

In his little voice, Zach would ask a thousand questions about God and His world. "Where did the dinosaurs live, Mommy? How many stars are there? How did God get here? Why did he make some snakes venomous and some not? How much does a spider weigh?" The questions were endless, but I never tired of him asking. We talked about the universe and all it held. We talked about dinosaurs, and he could name them all. His gentle heart was as big as his imagination, and Zach was wise beyond his years.

Each night, before we went inside, we would sing a little song to the moon and thank it for shining down on us. After Zach fell asleep, I would lay there beside him and run my fingers through his soft curls, just listening to him breathe, wondering what he was dreaming and thanking God I was his mommy.

Chapter 41

KEEP YOUR EYES ON JESUS

Cast all your anxiety on him for he cares for you~1 Peter 5:7

When I was seven months pregnant, Max was required to go out to sea for extended training. When he told me, I completely fell apart. The anxiety I thought was under control returned with a vengeance. The thought of being left alone on the island with a two-year old and no family anywhere around for thousands of miles while also pregnant was too much. I lost it.

Multiple panic attacks plagued me daily, and there was nothing medicinally I could do to reduce the severity because I was pregnant. I had been spending time praying and reading my Bible regularly for more than two years, and my faith was stronger than it had been when I started, but nonetheless, I was a nervous wreck. I had made friends with my neighbors, which was some security for me, but knowing Max would be away sent me over the edge.

I called my parents and begged my mom to fly out to stay with me while Max was gone. I was terrified to be left alone. Constant worry and fear burdened me, and I wasn't sleeping or eating much at all. My mom called me back a few days later and said she would not be coming to my rescue. She explained she didn't want to come now because she wanted to come when the baby was born. I still had a few months to go before our baby was due. My biggest concern was not being able to make it to the due date with the severe stress I was undergoing.

But once it was settled in my mind that there was no way to avoid being alone for the next few months, the only thing I could do was to push through and get through it.

At that time, my mother gave me this advice, which I have never forgotten. It has been valuable, not only during that time but also several times since. She said, "Lee, just keep your eyes on Jesus." She reminded me of the story in the Bible when Jesus and His disciples were out to sea, and there arose a terrible storm. The disciples were terrified and cried out in fear. Jesus came to them in a very unusual and unexpected way; He walked out to them on the water. Seeing Him walking on water, they were frightened. Jesus told them it was Him and to not be afraid. Peter doubted and said, "If it's you, bid me to come." It was indeed Jesus, so He said to Peter, "Come." Peter was brave enough to step out of the boat.

You see, a miracle had happened. As long as Peter kept his eyes on Jesus, he was able to walk on water, but if Peter allowed fear to shift his focus from Jesus and onto the circumstances, he began to sink. Of course, Jesus didn't allow Peter to be overcome by the storms. He saved Peter. The point of the story is this: as long as Peter kept his eyes on the Lord Jesus, he was fine, but when he took his eyes off of Jesus and focused on his circumstances, he began to sink.

I decided the only way I could survive my "storm" was doing what Peter did. I was still learning, and I was making progress. Now I had the ultimate opportunity to put it to the test. I would literally fix my eyes on Jesus and put my faith in Him, trusting Him to get me though.

A few days later, Max left around 5:00 a.m. When Zach and I awoke, I fixed his favorite breakfast: dinosaur oatmeal and orange "boost." He adorably called orange juice "orange boost." I sat down at the kitchen table with him. That's when the cramping started. I tried to ignore it and to resist the fear it triggered. *Please God,* I prayed, *don't let me have this baby with Max out to sea!*

The cramping didn't ease up, and neither did the anxiety which accompanied it. I was terrified to drive across the Ko'olau Mountain Range to Tripler Army Hospital where my doctor was. The narrow and winding mountain roads, which went through several tunnels, always made me feel on edge. I had never done that drive without Max, and the thought of it sent me into a full-blown panic attack. I was afraid to go, but equally as afraid not to go.

Finally, I decided to walk down to my neighbor Audrie's house and ask her to ride with me. In a heightened emotional state, I found myself failing miserably at "keeping my eyes on Jesus." That's when my sweet little angel boy helped me overcome my fear. Even at his young age, it was clear to Zachariah I was struggling. He stopped playing with his toys and confidently walked to where I was; he put his chubby toddler-sized hand on my large round tummy and spoke the sweetest words I will never ever forget.

Zach sweetly said, "It will be alright Mommy, remember…'casting all of your cares on Him, for He cares for you'. 1 Peter 5:7."

I looked into Zach's big brown eyes; in them, I found the courage to do what I needed to do. I knew Jesus was speaking to me through my precious son. I wiped my tears and said "Zach, let's go for a drive." It was an unexpected and proud mommy moment.

I had been helping Zach memorize that verse because I knew it was important to us to teach Zach to "hide God's word in his heart." That day, God used a two-year-old child to "teach" a verse back to me when I needed it the most. The old saying is certainly true: "for out of the mouth of babes."

Once we arrived at the hospital and I was waiting for the doctor to come in, I tried to pray. I wanted so badly to be brave and not give in to the fear tormenting me. Those cruel whispers reminded me of all the mistakes I'd made. They hissed; *you don't deserve to have this baby because you didn't stop the abortion. God is mad at you, and you are not forgiven. He is punishing you for your past.* I couldn't stop the torrents of tears. I had so much regret, guilt, and fear. I cried until I was dry heaving when the doctor arrived.

Thankfully, everything checked out fine with the baby. However, I was put back on antidepressants. I felt like a complete failure because I so desperately wanted to get through the pregnancy--and the rest of my life, for that matter--without medication. But it wasn't to be. The doctor felt the risk to the baby was higher without me taking medication than it was if I took a low dose just to get me through the next couple of months.

The last month of the pregnancy was the hardest. I begged my doctor to let me stop taking the medication so I could nurse the baby. He reluctantly agreed, but he told me at the first sign of trouble, I would need to resume taking it.

We chose to name our second-born son Joshua Tyler. We wanted a strong biblical Hebrew name for him also. Joshua means *Yahweh saves* or "is salvation," and Tyler was after my husband and Zach. Our precious new baby was as unique and special as our first.

Max was only able to stay home with us for one week before duty called him back to work but being a mommy of two was a pretty easy adjustment for me. As long as I was at home taking care of the boys, I felt okay, but if I had to leave the house for any reason, it was panic chaos.

By the time Joshua was about two weeks old, I could no longer cope with the mounting anxiety. I was strongly advised to resume antianxiety/antidepressant meds; but in doing so, I felt like a complete failure once again. The negative self-talk played loudly like an old familiar record. I prayed and fought hard against postpartum depression and anxiety, but I was losing the battle.

Before we celebrated Zachariah's third birthday and Joshua turned one month old, I was right back in full-blown panic disorder...only the second time was worse than the first. Thankfully,

Joshua was sweet-natured, calm, and happy.

Everything terrified me, and I do mean EVERYTHING! I lived in constant fear and could not fend off irrational thinking. Anxiety was an enemy that had returned with a vengeance, and I was too weak for the fight. I was imprisoned by agoraphobia once again. Nowhere felt safe, and I was suffocating as my world closed in more and more. The sadness and desperation was stifling.

Even though we lived in one of the most beautiful places on earth, I was too afraid to go outside. Despair found me on an island in the Pacific, right beneath a vibrant double rainbow. The rainbows were frequent and always breathtakingly gorgeous...but where was my pot of gold? There was nowhere to run; I was surrounded on every side by a raging sea. The vibrant beauty of this gorgeous island faded into gray...my world had lost its color.

Even though my body had recently birthed new life, I was dying emotionally. *God! Where are you? Why are you letting me sink back into a pit of despair? PLEASE HELP ME!* The cheap living room rug was worn thin from my pacing and crying out to the Lord.

Soon, my OBGYN doctor referred me to a psychiatrist. The psychiatrist then recommended I also see a cognitive-behavior specialist weekly to further assist me in learning to cope with the severity of my disorder. Obsessive-compulsive thoughts convinced me if I did not obey their every whim, I would be met with some sort of impending disaster.

Over time and with medication, therapy, and prayer, I slowly improved. The only joys in life were my husband and little boys. God used them to keep me moving forward when I felt too weak to fight. Each day, I drew my strength directly from my Lord. No matter how bad I felt, I opened my Bible and continued my quest. I had a firm grasp on the hem of His garment, refusing to let go.

After a month or so of therapy, I was able to enjoy going outdoors again. We started taking the boys to the beach and spending most of our time outside, just like before. God was slowly teaching me how to believe what His Word says about me instead of what I believed about myself.

In Him, I could do all things through His strength. Praise and worship music lifted my spirits, helping me through the toughest days. Fixing my eyes on Jesus was the only way I was going to get through this. I was beginning to understand all peace, joy, strength, happiness, and fulfillment comes through Christ and Christ alone.

Chapter 42

GOIN' BACK TO CALI

*"I will love the light for it shows me the way, yet I will endure the darkness for it shows me the stars." * ~ Og Mandino

We left the little pea-green home that we ended up growing to love when Joshua was almost two years old, and Zachariah was nearing five. San Angelo, Texas became our next home; San Diego, California after that. We followed Max everywhere; the military allowed us to go. The places we could not accompany him, we stayed back trying to make the best of the unwanted separation.

The boys grew closer and closer in their relationship; no matter where we lived and whether or not their daddy was with us, Zach and Josh always had each other. Our two boys were two peas in a pod, one with soft brown curls and one with blonde.

I continued the long emotional journey of healing from the pain and shame of the past. After about four years of therapy and learning of the Lord, I was getting stronger. The OCD and panic attacks were well-controlled, but I continued to take medication as prescribed and stayed under a physician's care for maintenance.

One September morning, we awoke to alarming news. We had

just moved into a nice home on base in Mira Mar, California. Upon hearing the news, my neighbor was hysterical. She burst in my front door and shouted, "Turn on the television! The Pentagon is on fire, and the twin towers in New York have been hit! America is under attack!!" Soon our lives, like millions of other Americans, would be altered. Max and many others, both military and civilian, would be called into action to protect and defend American soil.

A few weeks prior, we had received an upsetting phone call from Max's mother, Beverly. She had just been diagnosed with colon cancer. She was scheduled to undergo surgery to remove the cancer and then chemotherapy would follow. We were so far away and just getting the kids settled in our new home. Zachariah had started Kindergarten, and Max was getting acquainted with his new unit. Max's siblings and stepfather would be with his mother during the surgery and recovery, so we decided to stay in California.

During my mother-in-law's surgery, it was discovered the cancer had metastasized. Fifty percent of her liver was cancerous; they called it stage 4 and told the family she most likely would not survive. Beverly began a fight for her life, and we took an "emergency" leave to go back to Oklahoma to be with her. Max's unit had just been given deployment orders to the Middle East, but because his mother was dying, he was given permission to temporarily join another unit in Oklahoma until she passed away.

Our family of four packed up our household and once again made the long trek across the desert to join Max's family. When we arrived in Oklahoma, Beverly was not doing well. The boys were three and six years old, and sadly, they could scarcely recognize their Mimi. The once strong and vibrant lady was now lying helplessly in a hospital bed, losing the fight.

We spent Thanksgiving with Beverly in the hospital. The doctors kept her heavily sedated to keep her pain under control. The doctors advised that everyone say their goodbyes to her before they left that evening. Max's mother lived only a few more days before the angels lovingly carried her spirit back to God. As heaven celebrated her arrival, we mourned her departure. The beautiful lady, who had given my husband life, was now gone from ours.

I loved Beverly deeply. She had been a second mother to me. I fondly remembered the birthday cake she baked for my seventeenth birthday. Beverly was a wonderful mother and Mimi, and to this day, we all miss her terribly.

During that holiday season, Max and I were able to spend Christmas and New Year with our families before Max had to rejoin his previous unit, which was already overseas. The thought of Max going into a volatile situation was frightening. The boys and I stayed in Oklahoma with my parents while Max bravely flew into the unknown. With my ongoing mental issues, it was best for me and the boys to stay close to family.

When Joshua was about eighteen months old, he was diagnosed with asthma. He had already been hospitalized twice in his young life. Soon after Max left, I found myself sitting inside a pediatric oxygen tent alone with our little boy. Watching Joshua struggle to breathe caused my anxiety to escalate. I knew I was not cut out to be a single geographical parent

I missed my husband, I was still grieving the loss of my mother in law, and now our little boy was in the hospital. I did not sign up for this! Life as a military wife is highly unpredictable and stressful in the best of circumstances.

Thankfully, Joshua recovered and was released from the hospital. We celebrated Zachariah's seventh birthday and Joshua's fourth birthday that spring while Max was still deployed overseas. I continued my quest to stay strong through it all.

For the most part, the panic attacks were controlled. I was able to go about my daily life taking care of the boys. But soon, I would make a very unexpected discovery that would cause me to question everything...including my identity. Once again, life as I knew it was about to unravel.

Chapter 43

IT'S COMPLICATED

"When did you stop caring?" He asked

"When did you start noticing?" She replied

Lang Leav

It's a commonly held belief that babies in utero become aware of their world through the sounds and voices they hear even before they take their first breath. No wonder I have issues. I was wanted and I was planned, but not in the traditional way. My life began as a result of an illicit affair another story within a story within a story in my life.

My parents knew each other as young children, but they came from quite different families. My mother was second to youngest in a family of six children. Her family had very little money, requiring all six children to help with household chores and to work small odd jobs to help with the family's needs. My father was the oldest of two children. His father owned a family business in its third generation when I was born, providing financial stability to his family that my mother's family did not have. My dad worked in the family business as well as starting several additional business ventures on his own.

Their love story began at least for my dad when he was a young boy. My mother knew she was beautiful and used her beauty to her advantage, turning male heads everywhere she went. At ten years old, my dad knew he wanted to marry my mother. And as time would tell, my dad would eventually marry her, but he would not be her first husband.

When my parents were in high school, my mother became pregnant with my oldest sister by another young man. She married him, but their marriage wasn't stable. When their baby was three months old, my mother discovered she was pregnant again. The pressure was just too much, and the couple divorced.

My mother, while still a child herself, had given birth to two baby girls and went through a divorce all before she finished high school. But in spite of it all, my father loved her and came to her rescue. After a short courtship, they flew to Las Vegas and tied the knot. My dad's feelings for my mom and her two little girls were unconditional. Unfortunately, it was only a marriage of survival for my mother. She did not love my dad the way he loved her. She saw him as a generous man who loved her and would be a wonderful provider for her and her daughters. He did, and he was my dad officially adopted my sisters and raised them as his own with a sacrificial and unselfish love.

A few years into their tumultuous marriage, my mother became pregnant with another baby girl. My dad was over-the-moon excited for a biological daughter, although he loved all his girls the same. But their marriage was already in trouble even before the honeymoon was over; it was hanging by a fragile thread of secrets, lies, and infidelity when I was conceived. Let me fill you in on a bit of the back story the day after I was born:

My daddy loved his girls. There were three in the nest and the fourth had been born the night before. He couldn't wait to bring the three older girls to meet their new baby sister. As he bundled them up, his mind began to wander to the recent past. Anger seethed within him as he buttoned and zipped their coats on that frigid December morning. While he continued his task of getting the girls ready, he tried not to focus on the unthinkable betrayal. He refused to think about any of it now. This was going to be a happy day; he was determined to make it so.

When his car was pulling into the parking lot at the small-town hospital, another car was pulling out. It was not the car of a nurse coming off of night shift or the car of someone who had spent a sleepless night tending to an ailing loved one. No, this car was driven by a man who was once my dad's best friend. Robby, a man who knew my dad's deepest darkest secrets. These childhood playmates grew up together, spending the summers tightening a bond of friendship and true brotherly love.

Although the two men were not brothers, they did share a common bloodline. They were cousins. The two families were close even though they lived miles apart. The cousins took turns spending the summers at each other's house. Those were carefree, fun-filled days of childhood and adolescence. They looked forward to the holidays every year when their families would reunite. No one could have predicted that one day, the bond between cousins would be completely severed. The families would be separated--not by distance in miles, but by a painful division. A line was drawn because a line was crossed.

These men, the two cousins, stayed in touch but hadn't seen each other in several years. While my dad was busy raising a family and running the family business, Robby had been serving in the military. One day, my dad got an unexpected call from Rob. He told my dad he had recently been discharged because of a medical issue. He was without a plan and had very little money, so my dad invited Robby to stay with our family until he could get back on his feet.

Robby moved in, and it wasn't long before he fell in love with my mother. The feelings were mutual, and they began an affair, creating a heartbreaking situation for all involved. When my dad discovered their relationship, he gave my mother an ultimatum: either she would discontinue the affair, or he would divorce her.

Although my mom loved Robby deeply, she had three little girls to consider. My dad was an excellent provider and father. Yes, he had his issues, but she knew staying with my dad was best for her daughters. My mother made the decision she would end it with Robby...but not before a child was conceived. She wanted him, but if she couldn't have him, then she wanted his child.

My mother carefully calculated this conception to ensure the man she wanted--but could not have--would be the biological father of her next child. Once she was pregnant, she told my dad she had ended it with Robby. Loving her and the girls as much as he did, my dad tried his hardest to put the whole thing behind them. As my mother's belly grew, so did the doubts, fears, and suspicions. My father was crushed and betrayed on multiple levels. Out of concern and kindness, he had invited Robby, his cousin and lifelong friend, into his home. Now the deep wound from the knife in his back almost paralyzed him.

One week before Christmas, just after dusk, air filled my lungs for the first time. My dad was waiting right outside the delivery room doors and when he heard my cries, he decided right then and there that DNA had no say in the matter. The tiny blonde baby girl was his, and nothing could change that. He loved me unconditionally from the very start.

Hours after I was born, my dad left that evening to care for my three sisters at home. My mother then called Robby to tell him their daughter had been born. Robby immediately drove more than two hours to the hospital to meet me. He spent the night at the hospital with my mother and me. The next morning, he left just moments before my dad arrived with my sisters.

Robby told me many years later that as he drove to the hospital that night, the stars were exceptionally bright and more numerous than any other night he could remember. He said he thanked God for his baby girl and decided no matter what my mother named me; he would call me Star.

My dad loved me dearly, but he was not sure who my biological father was. To keep him hanging on, my mother lied and told him she thought I might be his. A DNA test thirty years later would scientifically prove what my mother had known all along, confirming what I had always felt: I was not his, and I did not belong.

Despite promising to end the affair, my mother continued going back and forth between Robby and my dad until I was four months old. After finally having enough, my dad told my mother as much as it pains him, he wanted a divorce...oh and by the way, he would be fighting for custody of all four of his daughters! With that, my mother permanently ended the affair. Robby moved to Nevada, and the three of them all agreed they would never breathe a word of any of this to anyone.

My dad never wanted me to find out; in fact, he had spent his entire life protecting the secret. He selflessly sacrificed his relationships with all of his extended family because it was far too painful for him to be around his cousins, aunts, and uncles after what Robby and my mother had done. He also felt he couldn't ask Robby not to show up at family functions, so my dad avoided the get-togethers.

When I was a child, my dad was never able to explain why we were so estranged from his side of the family and why we never went to any family holidays or functions with his relatives. Now I understand why we never saw them.

Growing up, somehow, I always felt different, like I didn't quite belong. Sometimes, I even felt out of place in my own family. I questioned my mom from time to time over the years. She just casually brushed it off, saying something like, "Of course you're ours!" I believed her...mostly.

In what felt like hundreds of times, I looked through the family photo albums searching for some sort of clue, even though I didn't know what I was searching for. I didn't find any evidence to support my suspicions that maybe I was adopted, but I heard rumors all my life that I was not my dad's biological child. People would jokingly say, "You belong to the milkman!" or "We don't know where the heck you came from!" It didn't make sense to my young mind. I knew the milkman--he was a Hispanic man named Oscar, and I didn't think I was the fruit of his loins.

During heated arguments between my parents when I was little, I was the topic of many of their arguments, but I was too young to make sense of any of that. This made me   extremely insecure, and I felt like there was something wrong with me. I felt it was my job to fix whatever was wrong between my parents, and it was also my job to keep them from killing each other.

I felt I was to blame. Neither of them ever purposely did anything to make me feel bad; in fact, they both tried to protect me in every way they could. They were just two broken people trying to hold an unhappy marriage together for the sake of their daughters.

From the outside looking in, our family appeared to have it all together. We had a gorgeous home, an airplane, and several sports cars. We went on amazing vacations and had every conceivable material possession anyone could want.

But behind closed doors, we were far from being one big happy family. For almost forty years, my father tried making my mother love him, but he never succeeded. No amount of diamonds, pearls, rubies, emeralds, or sapphires could make her love him. Instead, she loved someone else.

As a result, my mother battled severe depression. She spent her younger days drowning the pain with prescription medications. The majority of her time at home was spent sunbathing or sleeping. The older she got, the less she wanted to live and the more reclusive she became. Sadly, she was never able to find what she was looking for.

Happiness eluded her...while she spent her life chasing it, my dad spent his life chasing her.

Chapter 44

EXPOSED

*For all that is secret will eventually be brought into the open,
and everything that is concealed will be brought to light and
made known to all.*~Luke 8:17

Since Max deployed, six months had slowly passed, and the boys and I missed him terribly. We still lived with my parents, and the school year had just ended. One ordinary day in early summer, the truth of the distant past came crashing in and blindsided me with a life-changing family secret. I learned everything I had believed was a lie.

At thirty years old, I had long since forgotten to question my identity. The last time it had even crossed my mind was when I was first diagnosed with anxiety disorder at age twenty-three. The psychiatrist asked for a complete family history, and I gave him the information about my parents and siblings as I knew it. He questioned me further, telling me the severity of my disorder indicated a genetic link. I told him neither of my parents or my grandparents suffered from anxiety disorder, so after several times of asking me and my answer not changing, he dropped it. But in the back of my mind, it made me wonder.

Then after I gave birth to Joshua and started with a new

psychiatrist, the same thing happened. The doctor also told me all signs strongly pointed to a genetic connection. My mind wandered back to my childhood when I had heard the snide remarks about my paternity. I went home and wrote about my doubts in my journal, trying to process everything in my head. I told both doctors that my mother had depression but neither of my parents had issues with panic or generalized anxiety. The topic was discussed briefly and then dismissed.

Throughout my life, when doubts would occasionally arise, I thought it was just my own insecurities. I never wanted to believe the rumors could be true. As usual, though, instead of confronting and dealing with any issues, I pushed everything under the rug, refusing to consider the possibilities.

Since the boys and I moved in with my parents, I had noticed my mother's behavior was out of character. While my dad was at work, she was spending hours talking on the phone with her bedroom door shut or typing away on the computer in the den. She was also upbeat and peppy.

I asked her several times who she was talking to for so long and she nonchalantly answered, "Just a friend." Hmmm...a friend? I chose to not question her further because, after all, I was living in her home. I wondered; s*he couldn't be talking romantically to a man...could she?* This went on for a while, and occasionally I asked her, "What friend?" She brushed me off and acted offended at my inquiries, so I didn't push.

Then one day, I accidentally discovered her secret.

I had asked her to watch the boys while I ran some errands. I returned much sooner than expected. The boys were being very rowdy and loud when I walked into the house. It was obvious she wasn't really watching them. I walked into the den to let her know I was back, but the boys were making so much noise that she didn't notice when I walked up behind her.

She was on the computer reading an email. I could tell by her quick reaction to clear the screen that it was something she did not want me to see. But her response was not quicker than my ability to scan the contents of the email. I saw enough to deduce she was conversing with a man. I also saw enough to know me, and my boys were the topic of discussion.

I don't know how I dared to blurt out what I had suspected throughout my life, but in a matter-of-fact tone, I asked, "Are you talking to my biological father?" My bold question surprised me, but her quick answer surprised me even more. My mother quickly responded, "Yes! How did you know?"

My world as I knew it had just collapsed, and she thought absolutely nothing about it. I stammered my response through muffled tears, trying hard not to cry. I said, "I didn't KNOW. I guessed." I don't remember what else was said. Completely caught off guard and not knowing what to do, I walked out of the room. I felt strange and lost, and I didn't want her to see me cry. Retreating in a large walk-in closet was my pathetic attempt at hiding from the world, where I fell to the floor in a heap of tears.

Feeling sick, anxious, curious, and sad all at the same time, shame and fear enveloped me. I couldn't get a deep breath. I felt worthless. I didn't know who I was...my whole entire life was a lie! These secrets exposed made me feel small and vulnerable again just like when I was a child. *How was I going to tell the rest of my family? Would they reject me? What about my dad? Did he know? What if this destroys him and it's all my fault?* My husband was a world away, and I had no one to turn to. I felt completely alone.

I quietly rocked myself, just like I used to rock my dolls. I had so many questions, yet I felt ashamed and guilty for having them. I wanted to know everything, but at the same time, I wanted to go a few hours back in time and not discover the secret. Was it better to know or not to know? But I could not go back and unknow the truth. It was too late for that.

It was time to find out who else knew. *Did my dad know I wasn't his biological child, or would finding out this terrible, awful secret send him over the edge?* I had to find out if he had known all these years. *How will he react to me knowing the truth? How would he react when he finds out about my mother getting re-involved with Robby?*

On that beautiful, otherwise calm summer day, my dad would soon arrive home from work to find his entire life in pieces. I felt it was all my fault because I was the "love child" of an illicit affair. It was my fault I accidently discovered the secret, and it was my fault my dad was about to come completely undone right in front of my eyes. It was my fault his heart would be shattered into a million pieces as everything he had spent his entire life building and protecting was destroyed. My very existence was about to wreck my whole family.

To protect the privacy of other family members, I will avoid disclosing all of the details, but my dad did find out my mother was communicating with Robby once again. It was the proverbial straw that broke the camel's back. My dad immediately filed for a divorce. At sixty years old, my daddy was heartbroken; I stood helplessly by as he packed up his personal belongings and drove away from everything and everyone he loved.

I had failed. Their break-up ended up being because of me. The whispers taunted me: Y*ou are a failure. You are worthless!*

My dad moved into an apartment where sadness was his constant companion. He sat alone in his apartment grieving all that was lost and all that would never be again. Life as he knew it was over. His family was completely severed, and there was not one damn thing he could do to fix it. I can still hear the sounds of his sobbing as he grieved for his family. My sweet daddy loved my mother with his whole heart. His sacrifices for her and for all of us were many. He lived his entire life striving to make her happy, to please her, and to make her love him back, but unfortunately, it was all for nothing. She never did.

My mother and Robby began seeing each other again, attempting to rekindle an old flame. Robby moved to Oklahoma to be closer to my mom and to get to know me and my sons. I wanted to meet him to help me learn more about myself. I found out after Robby moved to Nevada when I was a baby, he got married and fathered three other children. I had two brothers and one sister. I wanted to meet my siblings and learn about their lives.

I was completely torn. I wanted to get to know Robby and learn everything I could about his life, my siblings, and my other family. I knew his life would give me genetic clues to my own. I felt an instant connection to Robby and a strong love for him, but at the same time, I felt sick for the way it made my dad feel.

When I made the decision to meet Robby and introduce my boys to him, my dad felt the sting of betrayal deep in his already wounded, fragile heart. My dad told me he was livid with me for allowing Robby to meet Zachariah and Joshua. My dad felt they were his grandchildren and I was his daughter. He didn't want Robby anywhere near us.

First, my mother had betrayed my dad, and now I had. The pain was almost more than my dad could handle. We met at an ice cream shop to sit down and talk about it. At that meeting, my dad told me although he always knew the probability was high, I wasn't his child biologically, it never mattered to him. He accepted and loved me as his own, and he shared his worst nightmare was I would one day find out. His nightmare had become a reality, and now Robby was back, once again taking away what was precious.

My dad did not force me to choose between him and Robby, but the entire situation caused a tremendous strain on my relationship with him. The hurt, anger, sadness, and grief turned my dad into someone I didn't know. He became very depressed and withdrawn. His desire to live greatly diminished...almost to nothing.

My mother and Robby, however, had no trouble picking up where they had left off thirty years ago. I couldn't be happy for them because

I was so burdened for my dad.

My parent's marriage of almost forty years officially ended in a bitter divorce that August. Their separation and divorce also separated and divided our family. Some family members felt they must take sides, so lines were drawn, and relationships were weakened. Our family was far from perfect--very far--but at least we were intact; now the threads that held us together were no longer strong enough, and we fell apart.

During the time Max was deployed overseas, my dad and I had become very close. Our relationship was thriving. We hung out together watching movies and taking the boys on fun outings. We were filling a void in the other's life because I missed Max, and my dad needed someone to talk to and pass the time since my mom was so withdrawn from him.

But now that my parents were divorcing, my dad was depressed and emotionally closed off. A huge "DO NOT ENTER!" sign was written across his heart in invisible ink. I desperately tried to remain as close as possible to my dad while he was going through the worst crisis of his life.

My parents were in the midst of an ugly. This left my boys and me stuck smack dab in the middle. Not knowing what to do, I rented a house for us, and my mother moved in.

During this time, Robby visited my house often to see my mother. The boys and I were just sort of a part of the package. He cared for us, but his desire was for my mother, and hers was for him.

Meanwhile, my dad, who the boys called PaPa, could no longer fill the role of father and grandfather emotionally. And my mother, who the boys called Pooh, was focused entirely on Robby. She and Robby behaved like two love-stricken teenagers, and I was the adult trying to protect my kids from the confusion they were feeling.

The boys wondered where PaPa was? And why was this strange man kissing and holding hands with their Pooh? It was such an awkward situation for all of us. Anxiety attacks plagued me, but I had to put my needs aside and focus on providing stability for my boys. Their world was turned completely upside down with their daddy overseas and now their grandparents divorcing.

No matter what happened in the past, I had an enormous love and respect for my dad. Besides Max, there was no other man on this planet I loved more, and no one biological or not could ever take his place in my heart. God had provided the perfect man for the job, and he would forever and always be my daddy.

When it comes to Robby, though, I want to be fair. Robby never wanted or tried to fill the role of my father. He wanted to get to know us, and I think he did love the boys and me, but he never wanted to be a parent to me or even a grandparent to my sons. Robby knew my dad had raised me and that he was my only daddy Robby respected that, never trying to separate us emotionally from my dad.

Constantly, I worried about my dad and spent as much time as possible with him. More than anything in this world, I wanted him to be okay. I longed for him to find happiness and someone who would love him with her whole heart...to love him for who he was, not what he could give them. Sadly, my dad never found that love on this side of heaven.

Chapter 45

MOURNING GLORIES

Morning glories...whether purple, violet or blue...they all remind me of you.~Lee

Autumn's frigid temperatures chased the emerald chlorophyll from the leaves, making way for the vivid colors of yellow, orange, and red hues to display their fall splendor. As the winds of change blew and the colors of fall announced the trees were preparing for their long winter's rest. I could not have known the visible signs of the coming winter would usher in a life-altering change for all my seasons to follow. Now each year when the leaves change their color, I am brought back to a season of deep loss that occurred on a stark day in October.

The students at Zachariah's elementary school had been working hard for the upcoming Open House. The boys were missing their PaPa, so I asked my dad if he would like to go eat dinner with us and then go to Zach's Open House. When we picked him up after work, he was unusually quiet in the car. I could tell his arthritis had flared up as he warmed his stiff fingers against the car vents.

Sitting across from him in a booth at his favorite Mexican restaurant, I studied his demeanor. He had never looked so small and childlike as he did in that red vinyl booth. The wrinkles around his eyes were more pronounced, making him look sad and tired.

"I'm worried about you Dad. Are you feeling okay?" I said, reaching across to place my warm hands on his, which were cold and trembling. He replied unconvincingly, "I'm fine, hun. I've just caught a cold or something." But I knew better.

I knew he was suffering from a broken heart, not the common cold.

After our food was served, Dad attempted a few bites before putting his fork down and pushing his plate away. He had no appetite for his favorite Mexican cuisine. He finally spoke the words that conveyed the condition of his aching heart. He said, "I just don't have anything to live for anymore. You girls and your mother are my whole world. You girls are all married to wonderful men who will take care of you from now on, and your mother has chosen a life without me. So, I guess it means my job is done. My life is over."

Desperately, I fought the tears, which spilled from my eyes. "Dad, that's not true. You can't just give up! We still need you! We all do-- your daughters and your grandchildren. Your life is not over; you just have to begin again. You have plans this weekend with your sister. Please go and enjoy your time with her. Now you are free to build relationships with your family that you have sacrificed all these years!" I pleaded.

The boys finished their sopapillas, and then we went to the Open House. Dad did a good job acting interested in the artwork proudly on display, but I knew his mind was somewhere far away from that classroom. We visited with Zach's teacher and had refreshments before we made our way back to the car. The boys talked amongst themselves in the backseat while I drove back to my dad's apartment. Dad was deep in thought as we drove, but he did not offer to share any more of what was on his mind. Sadness as thick as fog rode in the car with us that night.

Back at his apartment, I leaned over and gave him a hug and a kiss on his forehead and said, "I love you, Dad." He replied that he loves me too and would call me tomorrow. As he got out of the car, I said again, cheerfully, "Bye Dad, I love you! Have fun this weekend! I can't wait to hear about it when you get back. And don't forget, next Saturday, Boomer Sooners!"

This is the last time I would see my sweet daddy alive.

The next day was ordinary...until it wasn't. Friday evenings were pizza and family game night. I had just taken the first bite of pizza when the phone rang. My oldest sister was on the other end of the line. When I heard her voice, I knew something was terribly wrong. "Lee, Dad was in a car wreck. He was hurt badly, and he didn't make it," she said through her sobs. "Oh my God, NO!!" I screamed into the phone. "Are you sure??" *How? I just saw him last night! He was fine. How could he not be alright now!? I just kissed his forehead!*

Suddenly, my legs would not hold me. I slumped onto the floor, screaming NO, over and over again. When I stood up, I was unable to make my legs work. Doubled over, confused and still unable to process what was happening, I continued to cry. My mom and Robby were there, and they tried to comfort me. "Get away from me!! This is your fault!" I screamed at them.

My mother's reaction or really lack of reaction showed just how truly disconnected she was to the man who had cared for her, loved her unconditionally, and sacrificed any potential happiness he may have had in life to stay in a loveless marriage for almost forty years. My mother was sad, I suppose, but not devastated like the rest of us.

My little boys were scared, sad, and confused; they sat softly crying, quietly huddled together on the loveseat. The emergency number to reach Max overseas was posted by the phone, but of course, I had hoped we would never need to use it. My mother called the number, and soon, I was screaming "I'M DYING!!" into the receiver.

Up until that day, the most significant loss I had endured was the traumatic loss of my unborn baby ten years earlier. We were still grieving the loss of Max's mother less than a year before. But this felt different. I truly felt like the pain was going to kill me. I did not want to live without my daddy, and honestly, I didn't know if I could.

The details of the crash that took my father's life too soon were investigated and later revealed to us. We learned that an irresponsible person who was living in the US illegally (and did not have a valid driver's license, legal tags, or insurance) had carelessly ran a stop sign, causing his speeding pick-up truck to smash into the driver's side of my dad's vehicle. The impact from the collision caused massive head and internal injuries, which my dad did not survive. My beloved father was pronounced dead, while the driver of the other vehicle only had a dislocated shoulder.

With the support of our husbands and children, my sisters and I lovingly laid our dad to rest next to his parents in the family burial plot. It was one of the most difficult days of my life.

My dad was a dedicated and loving husband and father. He selflessly raised, nurtured, and protected four daughters. Daddy was as close to perfect as any man I know; he loved his wife and daughters fiercely. I miss him terribly. I wish his life could have been different...it was one long heartbreak that ended in tragedy. Our family has never been the same since he was suddenly taken from us.

After the funeral, my mother moved out of my house and moved in with Robby. This caused even more strife, anger, and confusion in our family. My sisters resented them both terribly, and there was no way in hell any of them or their children would ever give Robby a chance.

The boys, Max, and I were caught in the middle. Robby was my biological father, and he was dating my mother, which put us in a very awkward position. One big happy family we were not. Robby and his wife were still married at the time he and my mom started communicating again. Robby filed for divorce from his wife when my dad filed for divorce from my mom. As a result, Robby's three other biological children resented me and my mother. They wanted nothing to do with me, my children, or of course, my mother.

My sisters wanted nothing to do with Robby or his family, so it was even.

The relationship between my mother and Robby was doomed from the very start. In less than two years, they split up. Robby moved back to Nevada to be closer to his children and ended up remarrying his ex-wife. His ex-wife hated me and did not want Robby to have anything to do with me or my children. It was a hellacious battle between them. Robby said they constantly fought, and I was at the center of it.

Robby's attempt at reconciliation with his wife failed, and they divorced for a second time. I was told it was all my fault.

Now I had wrecked two families.

Chapter 46

HOLLOW

I wanted to write down exactly what I felt but somehow the paper stayed empty...and I could not have described it any better.~WTM

When the dust settled, back to counseling, I went. Anxiety, depression, and a sense of loss and brokenness defined me once again. I knew I could not sort this out on my own. Tears ran in torrents for months. My self-worth tanked again, and I felt more worthless than ever.

The unraveling of my story was unraveling me. My parents had made some difficult choices years ago, but wrong choices, shrouded in secrets--even though they had the best intentions--almost destroyed me. All the deep emotional wounds began to resurface with a vengeance. The hidden truths and all the deception that had been so closely guarded for over thirty years had now surfaced. I was at the center of everyone's pain. It all came crashing down on me. I couldn't stand up under the weight.

The tormenting whispers returned, reminding me I was trash from the beginning. *You were conceived as a result of an illicit love affair. No wonder you are such a screwed-up mess. Your dad just felt sorry for you. That's the only reason he raised you. You were a constant source of heartache for him. Every time he looked at you, he was reminded where you came from.*

Guilt and shame took up residence in my head once again, and I didn't have the strength to resist. I hated thinking about the pain my dad suffered because of me.

I missed my dad. I wanted to tell him how sorry I was. We were just getting our relationship back on track and then he was just suddenly gone because some careless person who had no business driving took him away.

Now that my dad was gone, I felt remorseful for letting Robby into my life at all. This choice of mine hurt my dad immensely, but at the time, I didn't know what to do. I did want to give him a chance. I needed to know where I came from. I struggled with whether to continue a relationship with Robby or lose him, too. I could see so much of myself in him. I looked like him, we shared similar personality characteristics and I had the exact same emotional issues as he did. Now I finally seemed to fit. But the fitting felt wrong.

When I first met Robby and began getting to know him, he shared some interesting family history I had not known, but more importantly, he shared his medical history, which had contributed greatly to my own. Robby had suffered most of his life from severe and debilitating anxiety and depression. It was to such an extent that he had to be on disability and could not hold a steady job. His condition led him down a path of confusion, fear, unresolved frustration, and anger. Now, I finally understood what the doctors had been trying to piece together to help answer questions about my ongoing psychological condition.

During all this emotional upheaval, I became pregnant with our third child. It was unplanned but a much-welcomed pregnancy. Being pregnant gave me something positive to look forward to. Zachariah and Joshua were both school age. Max and I wanted more children, so this new addition was going to be a light in our darkness. Max and I had both lost a parent within a year, and we were ready for something good to take away some of the heartache.

More change was coming. Though Max loved his career as a Marine and had proudly served his country for fourteen years, his position, called MOS, required him to be deployed for months at a time. I really needed him at home with the boys and me.. He was missing so much of their daily lives and activities. Plus, I was still grieving the loss of my dad, and now I was pregnant.

Reluctantly, Max made the difficult decision to put his family and our needs over his military career. He separated honorably from the Marine Corps, but he will always be a Marine at heart. He settled into a regular job to provide for us and enrolled in college to finish his bachelor's degree.

We purchased our first home in a lovely neighborhood close to the boys' elementary school. The neighborhood had a huge community pool, walking trails, and a private lake for fishing. It was perfect for our growing family. We loved having Max all to ourselves and not having to worry about duty calling him off into the great unknown. I was going to therapy and starting to feel better emotionally. There were still some hard days, but overall, things were looking up.

Then one weekend, when I was about twelve weeks along, I started spotting. I tried to stay calm and lay down and rest like my doctor advised. Resting didn't help, and within a few hours, the spotting became heavier. I called a good friend who was a labor and delivery nurse, hoping she could give me helpful advice and reassure me. She advised me to continue resting, but if the spotting got any worse, I should go to the emergency room to be checked out.

The spotting soon became heavy bleeding. Trying to remain hopeful and calm, we loaded up the boys and drove to the emergency room. Max and the boys stood nearby, and we all focused intently on the screen of the ultrasound machine. The young man performing the ultrasound was quiet as he moved the wand around in the gel on my stomach. He pushed buttons on his keyboard and became solemn as he finished his work. He said the doctor would be right in before he slipped quietly from the room.

Max tried to keep the boys occupied while we waited for what seemed like forever. When the doctor finally came in, I knew from his demeanor what he was about to tell us wasn't good. I felt so sad for Zach and Josh, realizing they were about to hear more bad news. The baby we were expecting was not going to be born after all...the heart was no longer beating. I was experiencing a miscarriage, and my husband and little boys were, too. Two grandparents and now a baby were gone.

I didn't want our boys to think life was always cruel.

I wanted to scream up into the heavens and accuse God of not being good.

We drove away from the hospital with hearts full of sadness. The accusing whispers reared their ugly voice in my head. *You deserve this! It's all your fault. You are such a screwed-up mess. You killed one baby, and now this one died because God doesn't love you. Just admit it--you are unlovable! Don't ever think you deserve anything good. Remember you are still a slut. God doesn't love you, and He hasn't forgiven you either!*

In the middle of the night, the cramping became severe. I crawled out of bed and into the bathroom. I lay in the fetal position on the bathroom floor, crying as much from the emotional pain as from the physical. I wept for two babies. I would never hold either of them this side of heaven. The loss of one reminded me of the loss of the other. I wanted them both. These precious innocent babies, once carried in my womb, would now both be carried safely in my heart.

I recovered physically long before I recovered emotionally. I felt guilty, as if I had let Max and the boys down. I had failed them. Max tried to reassure me he didn't feel that way. He told me I did nothing wrong. He said he was happy with our family just the way it was. But no matter what he said, I was convinced I had to prove to him I could have more children.

Feeling sad and defeated, my thinking was askew, but at the time, the only thing I wanted was a baby. Being pregnant felt like I was contributing something good to the world. I thought a baby would take away the emptiness in my soul. My faith was wavering. I was trying to be a "good Christian, but my striving was moving me in the opposite direction. I was mad at God and I wanted Him to make it all up to me. I was struggling.

Within a few months, I became pregnant again. I told Max, but we agreed not to tell the boys until I was past the twelve-week mark. If I could carry past the first trimester, we would tell them and the rest of our family.

But it was not meant to be. For unknown reasons, I miscarried again.

This time we hadn't told anybody, so I suffered the loss in silence. I felt ashamed, broken, and alone. No one sent a card, or flowers, or brought over a pie like the last time. I laid in bed weeping, now for three little lives. Because of the "secrecy" of that pregnancy, grieving the loss felt similar to the first baby.

LORD, where are you? Why are you letting all this happen? I feel like You don't even care. I want to believe you are good, but You're just sitting far off in heaven, letting my life fall apart. Why aren't you answering my prayers?

I thought You loved me.

Chapter 47

SURRENDER

Surrender your heart to God, turn to him in prayer.
~Job 11:13

Despite my grief, I began to seek God with all my heart...really seek His face, not just His hands. I was saved, I was filled with the Holy Spirit, and we went to church, but something was missing. I was found, but I still felt lost.

My aching soul was searching...but for what? I had been doing life my way, and I wanted HIM to do it MY way instead of ME doing things HIS way. I wanted to run my own program...and God was lovingly showing me I had not fully surrendered my will and accepted His. We had been playing tug-of-war for over thirty years. I was finally ready to give up and finally let go.

After the second miscarriage, I realized that it was HIM I was desperate for. Not another child, not an identity, not money, not my husband, or my dad. I needed to make room in my heart for Jesus and give Him control and free reign. I needed to truly SURRENDER everything I was--and everything I was not--to Him.

By this time, I had knowledge of the Bible. I could quote some scripture, and I even listened to praise and worship music in the car and at home. Let me tell you, I was spiritual!

I wanted so badly to please God, to make Him see I was good (knowing I could never be good enough) without really believing He was good. I had given a part of my heart to the Lord, but I had a tight grip on to the other half. Sometimes I believed the whispers that told me I couldn't trust him; that maybe He wasn't really good.

But I knew God was calling me deeper. He wanted me to go ALL IN with Him. Not in my words or actions but in my heart.

I FINALLY learned I could NEVER be GOOD enough. No matter what I did or didn't do, God could never love me anymore or any less than He did right then! I realized when I was deep in a sinful life, He LOVED me, and now that I was a "good Christian," He LOVES me. His love is unconditional. It doesn't waver depending on our actions.

That day, I felt the peace of God wash over me, and I decided to fully surrender ALL OF ME...to lay it all down at His nail-scarred feet. I crawled into His lap and have been resting in His unmerited love, grace, and acceptance every day since then. That wonderful day, Jesus did ANOTHER work in my heart and reintroduced me to HOPE.

Over the next four years, I worked on surrender, trust, and obedience--in that order. I was determined to let go of any and all of MY expectations and wait for God. I had never been good at waiting on God or on anyone else for that matter. I studied patience, perseverance, self-control, joy, hopeFULness, faithfulness, righteousness, grace, love, surrender, and forgiveness.

I immersed myself in books and Bible studies. I listened to my favorite Christian speakers, preachers, and teachers daily. I spent time in prayer and read the Bible with an urgency and an open mind. I really wanted God to teach me, heal me, and guide me. For the second time in my life, I was DESPERATE for HIM. I wanted God more than I wanted anything else. I wanted more of HIM. I learned of His faithfulness, I learned of His goodness, and I learned of His peace that passes my understanding.

I surrendered the need for another baby, an education, a career, a social life--everything. While those are not bad accomplishments to desire, I knew I needed to let go and give myself fully to God.

At this time, my focus was on God and my family. I wanted my boys to have a strong Biblical foundation to build their lives on, so I taught them at home. I cherished each day with my boys. They were truly enough. I didn't need any more children--I was beyond blessed with the two I had!

Soon, Max finished his degree and was offered a position with an oil company in the Texas Panhandle. The job paid a lot more money than the job he currently held and had opportunities for personal growth. It would give Max a sense of accomplishment and provide great benefits for the family. We prayed about it and decided to move our family to a much smaller community in nearby Texas.

We relocated that summer and were settled in time for the first day of school. The move to Texas ended our homeschooling days, but the memories remain special to all of us. Our boys developed a love for literature, language, and science, and I developed a love for teaching.

That fall, Zachariah started sixth grade, and Joshua started third grade. They both made friends easily in our new community and quickly acclimated to small-town life. Everyone embraced and welcomed our family with open arms, and we felt confident God led us here.

Even though the boys were enrolled in public school, our habit of spending family time studying and reading God's word daily continued to be a precious time of bonding and connecting with the Lord and each other. The boys continued to surprise us with their comprehension and growth in their faith. Every evening during the week, the four of us gathered in the living room. I read aloud while

Max and the boys listened. We didn't just readout of the Bible; we continued to build on our homeschooling days and nurture our family's love of inspirational stories as well as uplifting, educational literature. I wouldn't trade those days for anything.

The first two years flew by. Zach was involved with the school's athletic programs and showed great potential physically, which excited the coaches, but he was more academically inclined and began to show an interest in art and music. Because such emphasis is placed on small-town Texas football, many young men feel pressured to play. Zach was not one to be pressured into anything, but he didn't want to let others down, so he continued to play football until his Junior year of high school, but his heart just wasn't in it.

Josh gladly attended and supported his older brother until he was old enough to play in junior high. Josh soon found his heart wasn't in it, either. He still battled asthma, which made participating in sports more challenging. Since he preferred other activities over athletics, he only played through junior high. Max and I didn't care as long as both boys were happy and kept their grades up.

After the miscarriages, I really let myself go. I didn't lose the pregnancy weight and gained an additional twenty pounds. I had never been overweight in my life and carrying around unwanted pounds felt like bondage. As soon as we moved to Texas and got settled, I decided to get in shape.

I started working at the YMCA during the day while the boys were in school. After school, they walked the short distance with a large group of friends to hang out. I enjoyed watching them interact with their peers and really got to know their friends on a personal level.

One of the benefits of working there was a free membership. I began to focus on my health and got certified as a nutritional counselor. Within about six months of concentrated effort on exercise and nutrition, I lost twenty-five pounds. With the excess weight gone, I felt great physically, and my mental state was vastly improved. Life was finally back on track.

Since I was making these lifestyle changes, I attributed missing my period once to my recent transformation. I never considered pregnancy as an option. But when I missed my next period, I began to entertain the possibility. I just didn't want to get my hopes up. I had surrendered my plans and desires to the Lord, deciding whatever God had for us was exactly what we needed.

I finally took a test at home, and it was positive! I nervously scheduled an appointment. The pregnancy was confirmed, and I got referred to an OBGYN doctor in a town about forty-five miles away. The experience of having two back-to-back miscarriages was still fresh in my mind, and I was afraid of getting too attached to this little one. I was still taking antidepressant medication, and the doctor determined with my history, the pros of taking the medication outweigh the cons; she advised me to stay on the medicine.

I found my worn and well-loved book of prayers called *Supernatural Childbirth*; the exact book I clung to during my pregnancies with Zach and Josh. I faithfully said the prayerful confessions over my baby every single day. I took excellent care of myself, making sure to drink lots of water, take prenatal supplements, eat healthy, and get plenty of rest. I wanted to do everything I possibly could to ensure our baby would arrive safely.

At thirty-seven years old, I was considered high risk because of my advanced maternal age. My doctor recommended genetic testing. I consented to the tests she recommended. The results of one of the tests, called Maternal Serum Alpha-Fetoprotein Test (AFP), came back elevated. The doctor explained it may be indicative of a birth defect or possibly a genetic defect, and then she recommended further testing.

I agreed to all the advanced screening tests except for amniocentesis. I refused that procedure; because of its invasive nature, there is a slight risk of miscarriage. I was not willing to risk pregnancy for any reason. The doctor had us go to genetic counseling to be informed about the possibilities of what could be wrong with our baby. Max and I did not care, and we were not shaken by the news.

The pregnancy was easy and seemed to fly by. Zach and Josh were looking forward to the new baby as much as Max and I were. We knew this child was a gift, and no matter what, he was ours, and we loved him already!

On May 21st, 2009, with Max's loving support and coaching, I gave birth to a perfectly healthy, genetically typical baby boy. Waiting just beyond the delivery room doors were Zachariah, Joshua, one of my sisters with her daughter, my mom, and my aunt. They could not wait to meet him!

We had narrowed the name choices down to three names we all liked. Zach and Josh came into the room to meet their new baby brother, and as I held him close to my breast, Max sat next to us on the bed. Zach walked over to the bed, proudly admiring the baby.

Zach said, "Mom, he looks like a 'Micah!' Can we name him Micah?" I looked up at my tall, handsome, fourteen-year-old brown-eyed, first-born son and lovingly responded, "Absolutely!"

In His perfect timing, God blessed our family with another son. We were all so proud and honored God had chosen us to raise him. Micah Tyler—he shares a middle name with his dad and brothers-- continues to amaze us.

Micah is smart, kind, and full of compassion for others. As of this writing, he is ten years old. I cannot wait to see how God uses Micah for His glory, as he lives for Him.

Chapter 48

DREAM GIRL

"You. I've spent my life waiting for you."~Melissa Marr

Having a new baby in our lives was a dream come true. Micah renewed our sense of wonder by bringing out the "inner child" in all of us. Joy filled our hearts as we watched the older boys play with the same toys, they had long forgotten but now shared with their baby brother. Zach and Josh set up Hot Wheel tracks, made Playmobil cities and villages, and played with Legos, Star Wars toys, and of course, their most favorite, well-loved Toy Story characters. All were lovingly introduced to Micah.

Our family continued our habit of reading aloud in the evenings. Max, Zach, and Josh played quietly on the floor with Micah while I read to them. Then we discussed what we just read and talked about the practical application while playing patty-cake and peek-a-boo with Micah.

When Micah Ty was fifteen months old, I started feeling run down and tired. Could I be pregnant?

It's no surprise I had longed for a daughter since I was a child playing with dolls, tucking my beloved Bananas into her pink and white cradle. I prayed for the daughter I had seen in my imagination hundreds of times. When Max and I fell in love as young teenagers, I believed one day we would have a daughter. And when I was sixteen years old, I privately named this special little girl.

For thirty-five years, from time to time, I would think of our daughter and long to hold her in my arms. I often wondered if one of the babies I had lost might have been her. Every time I had been pregnant, I had hoped for her. When I was first pregnant with Zach, Josh, and Micah, I thought they might be her until I found out they were boys.

Could I be carrying her now? I was too afraid to hope.

A little pink + sign told me I was pregnant. But everything about this pregnancy felt different. And soon, an ultrasound revealed our baby was, in fact, a girl!! As the months went by and my tummy grew to accommodate her, she was by far the most active of any of our babies. She kicked and somersaulted and flipped and flopped almost non-stop.

By now, the cherished *Supernatural Childbirth* book of prayers was worn out. The pages were earmarked, tearstained, and highlighted; the front cover was torn, and the back cover had fallen off during my pregnancy with Micah. I knew this baby would be the last one I would need the book for.

During the second trimester, I was considered a "geriatric maternal patient" since I was thirty-nine years old. My doctor wanted to run the same tests they did when I was pregnant with Micah. Just like with that pregnancy, the AFP test came back abnormally high. It was of no real concern because we had just been through this, and Micah was born with no genetic abnormalities. We had all the recommended follow-up tests except for an amniocentesis procedure. I refused it for the same reason I did with Micah. I did not want to risk a miscarriage.

During the genetic counseling, they told us our baby showed no signs (which they call markers) of having any abnormalities. I faithfully prayed over our daughter just like I had prayed over her brothers. As her due date approached, I could hardly contain my excitement! We were finally having a little girl, making our family circle complete.

Everything was ready for our baby girl's arrival--pretty pastel-colored dresses with matching bows and headbands hung neatly in the closet. Pink seemed to dominate the house. How could one tiny girl already own so much stuff, and she wasn't even here yet?

Joyfully, we celebrated a birthday with each of the three boys shortly before our girl was due. Zach was sixteen, Joshua thirteen, and Micah two years old.

I had many dreams of being a girl mom. I was so excited about everything a girl typically does with her mother. I thought of taking her shopping for cheer shoes, school clothes, prom dresses, and eventually a wedding dress. I imagined proudly sitting in the audience at her dance recitals or watching her cheer at local football games. I wondered what she would be when she grew up, maybe a nurse or a teacher. I knew she would be a wonderful mommy someday. The possibilities were endless, and my mind considered them all.

On a hot windy day in June, three weeks before she was due, a deep ache in my back told me our little junebug was coming early. The older boys wanted to be there when she was born. Max drove all of us to the hospital which was forty-five minutes away. I was in active labor when we arrived at the hospital, already dilated to seven. The labor went quickly, and the delivery was the easiest one yet.

That evening, our long-awaited baby girl made her long-awaited appearance. Her arrival was proudly announced to the boys waiting just outside the door. A pink glow filled the room! After quickly looking her over from head to toe, Max exuberantly said to me, "Lee, it really is a girl! She's beautiful!"

Chapter 49

TEN TINY TOES

Her tiny feet have yet to take a single step, yet she has already left an imprint an indelible imprint on our hearts~Lee

A nurse lovingly placed her at my breast. Max took photos of the first moments between mother and daughter. What the camera captured and documented, though, included a solemn look of concern on my face. The second I saw her, I knew something was different...not wrong necessarily, but different. My mind refused to tell me what my heart already knew.

As I held her, studying her through the window of her eyes, the shades of pink quickly faded from her face and limbs. Pink turned to milky white, with a tent of azure, then to deep tones of blue and purple right before my eyes. As the pink hues of a healthy newborn drained from her cheeks, alarm and fear seized my heart. Looking up, with tears in my eyes, I forced the words from my mouth, "What is wrong with my little girl?"

A nurse swooped in and began an assessment. Max and I watched helplessly as our daughter lay there looking like a rag doll while being poked and prodded. Minutes turned to hours as we prayed, watched, and waited for her to "come around."

It soon became evident this small-town hospital and its medical staff, including my doctor, were ill-equipped to handle our daughter's quickly declining condition. My doctor left, leaving the inadequate nursing staff fumbling around, not knowing what to do.

No one there could start a pediatric IV, the rural hospital did not have pediatric oxygen-support equipment, and the "makeshift" dome contraption they were attempting to use was failing miserably. Our tiny daughter could not suckle effectively, so the sugar water solution they attempted to give her wasn't helping.

Max and I watched our daughter's oxygen saturation levels repeatedly dip dangerously low into the 70s. Max and I both expressed our growing discomfort and dissatisfaction with the situation, and we demanded the doctor be called back. When she arrived, she assessed our daughter and then told us to give it a few more hours to see if her condition improves.

The doctor told us then that our daughter may have Down syndrome.

Max and I sat in stunned silence for a few moments. I heard the doctor's words, but I couldn't comprehend their meaning. Suddenly, fear tightened its grip on my heart, and it was hard to breathe.

Confused, I asked the doctor, "What do you mean? Down syndrome? I don't understand." Gently, she explained our daughter has some "markers" which point to Down syndrome, and our baby would need further testing and blood work to confirm a diagnosis. I steadied myself, trying not to fall completely apart before I nervously asked, "What markers?"

The doctor then gave us a rundown. She said that for our baby, there were several indicators: the gap between her toes, a crease across her palm, her floppiness (called hypotonia), her lower-set ears, and her overall appearance. All were strong signs of Down syndrome.

The doctor then told us our beautiful daughter was most likely mentally retarded.

I don't remember what other questions we asked or her exact words when she answered them, but the longer we talked and the more information we were given, the worse it felt.

Down syndrome, mental retardation, medically fragile...*how was this happening to us?* Suddenly, with two devastating words, our hopes and dreams for our daughter were dashed, and our hearts broke a million times over.

Over the next hour, our daughter's condition did not improve. My husband's patience had run out. The futile attempts by the medical staff to help our baby were not working. With authority I had never seen him use; Max demanded our daughter be transported somewhere equipped to treat her. Her condition was worsening, and she was growing weaker by the minute. Max did not let up, and finally, the doctor made the call to have our daughter transported to OU Children's Hospital.

Before she was five hours old and even officially named, our helpless little girl was loaded into a helicopter and flown off into the night. Our arms were empty, and our hearts were broken, but finally she was in the care of a capable medical team.

Now all we could do is pray.

My mother took the three boys' home to wait for an update. Neither Max nor I knew what to tell them or anyone else who wondered what was wrong with our baby.

My doctor would not allow me to leave the hospital since I had given birth just five hours before. Max and I spent the following seven hours in a hospital room staring at an empty bassinet where our newborn girl should be. We prayed and cried most of the night, counting the minutes until we could be with our daughter. Everything felt wrong--we were grieving, but our child was alive.

Our sadness felt shameful and wrong. How do you grieve a loss when no one has died?

Fear of the unknown tore at our hearts as we wrestled with all the what ifs. What if she really does have a mental and/or physical disability? What if the oxygen deprivation AFTER she was born had done its damage; maybe she didn't have anything wrong at first, but now she does? Maybe lack of oxygen made her disability even worse? What if she doesn't survive? Why us?? What did we do to deserve a mentally handicapped baby? Is God punishing me for having an abortion? What will our lives look like trying to parent someone with a disability?

We tried unsuccessfully to sleep, hoping when we woke up, it would be nothing more than a bad dream. Sometime during the sleepless night, we decided on her full name. We knew the name she would be called--it had been established for more than twenty years--but we needed to officially decide what her full name would be. In all the uncertainties surrounding her birth, no one had even asked us her name.

All our boys had Biblical Hebrew names. It was important to us for our daughter to have a strong Hebrew name, too, but all the Biblical names we liked were already taken by other family members. And I wanted to see her and hold her, like I had done with her brothers, before I committed to a name.

We decided since she may have an extra 21st chromosome, we would give her an extra middle name.

Around 6:00 a.m., I rang for the nurse and asked her to bring the birth certificate paperwork to us. I told her we were ready to fill it out. We wanted to do something to feel like we were taking care of our baby even though she was hundreds of miles away.

We named our baby girl Tylee Annissa Brielle. "Tylee" is my first name and Max's middle name combined. The "Ann" in Annissa is my middle name, which means "grace and favor," and Brielle, a name we both love, means "God is my might."

During the early morning hours, I also called a trusted friend who happened to be a NICU nurse at the hospital where Tylee was transported. I tearfully explained the situation, and she said she would go be with her until we could get there.

And I was ready to leave. After Tylee was named, I signed the discharge papers. The papers I signed underscored the risk I was taking by leaving before the recommended time, but I didn't care.

I was released twelve hours after birth. I could not wait to hold Micah and hug my older boys. The two older boys were leaving for church camp in a few days. Max and I didn't want their lives disrupted more than they had to be, so we felt like they should both still go to church camp. We had no idea what we were facing or how long Tylee would be hospitalized.

Since Zach had a driver's license and a summer job, the boys were fairly independent. Zach and Josh were both trustworthy, responsible teenagers, so we agreed to let them stay home under my mom's supervision. We hastily packed a suitcase for Micah and one for Max and me.

The thought of our family having to be separated was heartbreaking. Who would read to the boys at night? I still read to them and tucked them all in! I bawled at the thought of leaving, but I couldn't bear the thought of not going either. I cried as Max loaded our belongings into the car. He placed Tylee's diaper bag, which contained her going-home outfit, into her empty car seat. Our baby girl needed us, so we hugged Zach and Josh tightly, and then reluctantly said our goodbyes.

I still hurt physically from giving birth, but nothing could have prepared me for the emotional pain I felt. But I was not bearing the emotional pain alone--it was a burden Max and I would carry together. We were mostly quiet on the drive to the hospital, but occasionally, I saw Max wipe away a tear that had escaped while he was driving. In my mind, I kept repeating the same words over in disbelief: *There has to be some other explanation. She just can't have*

Down syndrome.

Denial was already setting in.

When we finally arrived at the enormous hospital, we were led to our baby girl. I was so afraid of how I would handle this. Doubts, fears, and worry flooded my mind. I had never been around anyone with a disability in my whole life. I always felt sorry for "them" and the people who loved them, but I never thought I would have a child who had "problems."

Being brutally honest here, I worried whether I would love her as much as my "typical" children. I wondered, *Would I be able to love Tylee no matter what she had or did not have? Could I love her unconditionally? Would I think less of her and focus more on what she couldn't do rather than what she could? What would my family and friends think of her? Of me? Of us? Could I bond with her as deeply as I had my other babies? Has God made a mistake and given us the wrong baby?*

Those were the thoughts I had been secretly wrestling with since they took Tylee away and left us sitting with our fears. I did not share my thoughts with anyone, not even my husband. I felt ashamed of myself for even allowing those questions.

Our baby was alive. Why wasn't that enough?

When we walked into the NICU room that held our daughter, my fears were momentarily put to rest as unconditional, unimaginable, unfathomable, and pure LOVE burst forth from the core of my being when I first saw her lying peacefully, perfectly swaddled in soft pink blankets.

Tylee was the most perfect baby girl I had ever seen. At that moment, I could not have loved her more, and I couldn't have cared less about any scary diagnosis...all that mattered was that she was safe, she was beautiful, and she was ours.

Chapter 50

LOVE DOESN'T COUNT CHROMOSOMES

"And I'd choose you in a hundred lifetimes, in a hundred worlds, in any version of reality, I'd find you and I'd choose you." ~Kiersten White-The Chaos of Stars

From the time they whisked her away twelve hours ago, she looked one hundred percent better. When we last saw her, she was fifty shades of blue and struggling to breathe. Then, her hair still had remnants of afterbirth, and she looked swollen and blotchy.

Now, she was bathed, clothed, and sucking sweetly on a vanilla-scented pacifier. Her coloring was pink, and the swelling was immensely improved. She looked completely healthy and normal. I could not see any signs of Down syndrome as she peacefully slept. Her head was perfectly shaped with a little tuft of blonde hair standing proudly, as if waiting for the placement of a small pink bow--which I just happened to have.

Tylee's tiny fingers curled around her daddy's as she opened her almond-shaped eyes to greet us. We were mesmerized and overwhelmed with gratitude. I checked her over from top to bottom, carefully lifting and then replacing the small blankets. All I saw was God's loving grace and absolute perfection.

I had been praying for a miracle and I really believed we had been given one...that or the small-town doctor had been mistaken. We did not share her suspicions with anyone, not even our older boys. I did not believe Tylee had any chromosomal abnormalities and refused to "confess" it out loud for anyone to hear. We just told everyone Tylee had a difficult time getting acclimated to life outside my womb.

Technically, Tylee was a preemie, so I used that as a reason, too. The pediatricians told us it would take about a week or so to get the results of the genetic testing, and all during that time, I rebuked Down syndrome, praying for our daughter to prove them wrong.

At OU Children's Hospital, there were a plethora of doctors, nurses, therapists, social workers, students, and various others who were in and out of Tylee's room. I was so confused at the differences between the types of doctors who were taking care of our daughter. Helping Tylee to get her best possible start included an impressive cast: medical students, interns, residents, fellow (post resident), and attending physicians, not to mention the genetic specialists, the pediatric cardiac and pulmonary doctors, and the pediatric hematologists.

I distinctly remember correcting several of these doctors/interns for just "assuming" our baby had Down syndrome without the results of the tests confirming the diagnosis. I listened to their words as they discussed a treatment protocol for our daughter. I felt a surge of defensive anger rise up when one of them would say something about her having an extra chromosome. "You don't know for sure. We don't have the results back yet," I would say. "We are hoping and believing she does not have any chromosomal defects. Thank you very much for waiting before you label her."

Looking back now, I see how I was in denial. I was unable to process the fact my child may have a lifelong disability. I was praying against all the odds God would take it away and correct any mistakes He may have made when creating Tylee in my womb. All the while, I knew full well God is incapable of making a mistake. He is perfect in all His ways.

Although Tylee was healthy overall, she did have several medical challenges to overcome. She struggled to keep her body temperature regulated, so she was placed under a warmer. Eating was exhausting for her, so she needed nasogastric intubation. It was difficult for her to maintain adequate oxygen saturation, so she needed oxygen support via a nasal cannula. Her bilirubin was high, so she needed to spend time "tanning" under the lights. She was floppy, called hypotonia, and her blood was thicker and stickier than normal, so treatment was needed for that.

It was also discovered Tylee had a small hole in her heart, called a ventricular septal defect (VSD). We were praying over that condition and hoping it would correct itself and close on its own.

Even with all these medical challenges, Tylee was considered extremely healthy compared to the other babies in the Neonatal Intensive Care Unit. She looked like a mini-Sumo wrestler, weighing in at a whopping eight pounds and five ounces at birth, while lying next to these teeny-tiny, one-pound preemies who were barely clinging to life.

Tylee's first little roommate sadly lost his fight and passed away. We saw other families grieving for their infants who were too sick, frail, and weak for this world. The constant beeping and blaring of monitors and alarms kept us always on edge. We didn't want to leave her side for even a minute.

The nurses calmed my nerves and reassured us our baby was healthy. I remember one cheerful nurse saying, "You guys hit the jackpot! If your baby does have Down syndrome, it's the least critical and scary of all the genetic abnormalities!"

She said it as if Down syndrome was something to celebrate instead of grieve.

When Tylee was about a week old, I sat in a rocking chair holding her carefully as not to disrupt all the various tubes and wires. I sang to her while she gave her best effort to drink my breast milk from a small, skinny two-ounce bottle. At that moment, it felt like this big world only contained the two of us; we were lost in each other's eyes. With her tiny fingers curled around mine, I searched her dark blue eyes, pondering what God may have planned for this little girl of ours.

I could hold her for hours, never tiring of the weight of her in my arms.

Soon, though, my thoughts were abruptly interrupted by a brief knock on the door, "Mrs. Monty? We have some test results. May we come in?" Intimidated by all the official-looking people filing into the room, I stuttered over my words and said, "Yes of course, but before you say anything, I want to have my husband here."

Max and Micah were just down the hall in a playroom for siblings. I texted and asked him to come immediately. Soon, Max entered the room carrying Micah, and he looked frightened. I was already crying before a single word was spoken.

The entourage of medical people wearing white lab coats and various colored scrubs parted so Max and Micah could make their way to where I was sitting with Tylee. Once everyone was situated, one of the lab coat wearing personnel began to speak. I did not look up; I just couldn't. I continued looking into Tylee's eyes where I felt safe. This room suddenly felt foreign, like a place we didn't belong. I wanted to gather my husband and babies and find a secret place to hide.

On a piece of paper with pairs of curved, yarn–like, squiggly lines side by side with a number from 1-22 underneath each pair, we were shown how Tylee's DNA looked different from ours. My eyes were blurred with tears, but I quickly scanned each row of these paired squiggly lines. When I came to the fourth row, there it was, circled in red: right above the number 21, there were three curved lines instead of two. Every single cell in her body has a third copy of the twenty-first chromosome. It was confirmed that our baby has trisomy 21, more commonly referred to as Down syndrome. We were crushed.

I don't know who said what since I couldn't look at any of them. I watched my tears fall like raindrops onto Tylee's soft head and blanket. I don't know who I was crying for the most. I cried for Tylee who would have to live with this disability, but I realized Max, me, and the three boys would have to help Tylee carry the weight of her disability.

I cried for all of us.

Someone breaks the silence and asks, "Mr. or Mrs. Monty, do either of you have any questions?" I don't know who asked because I still can't look up. I don't know what my husband is doing or thinking because I can't look at him either. I fear if I look at any of them, I will completely lose it, and they will think I'm unfit to be her mother and take her away.

I want to keep Tylee no matter how many chromosomes she has. No, this isn't the baby I expected, and I am grieving for her and for the lost hopes and dreams I had for our daughter.

I don't know how to cope with this, and I don't know how to grieve for a baby who didn't die. I'm forced to abandon my expectations like one would leave a broken-down car on the side of the road.

I must leave behind what might have been. I am crying for all that isn't and for all that is.

So *yes*, I wanted to shout--*I have questions! A million of them, to be sure.*

I also have doubts, fears, and uncertainties. I'm afraid of the unknown.

I want to escape, but where would I go?

Then they tell us there are social workers who can help us in case we decide not to keep her. The thought of NOT keeping her sends me right back to crying. Of course, we are keeping her. She is ours. She is a gift we didn't know we should ask for.

I love her. I love everything about her.

I continue to look at Tylee as we rock, for holding her is soothing. She breaks my heart, and she heals my heart all at the same time. I don't ever want to put her down. I don't care that there is a room full of strangers watching us.

This is a defining moment.

This is the moment we embrace her for all she is and all she may never be. This is the child we were given, and this is the child we will cherish, encourage, and love unconditionally. We will learn everything we can about her extra chromosomes, and we will learn everything about what makes her different and what makes her the same.

Somewhere intermingled with the tears and sadness, there is hope and gladness. The bond I feel with my daughter is indescribable. Conflicting emotions each give way to others in rapid succession. Holding Tylee, I suddenly remember sitting in my bedroom as a little girl, rocking one of my favorite dolls. I pretended she was special, and I was the only one in the world who could be her mommy.

Now I realize, I am holding that little girl in my arms. Now she is real. God had been preparing me for this child since I was a child. God had given me a healthy, beautiful, amazing, capable little girl. I am the only one in the world who could be her mommy. I slept in the hospital room with her every night. Even though nurses were close by, I wanted to be the one to care for her.

Tylee worked extremely hard to prove to the doctors and nurses she was strong enough to go home. Overall, she was healthy; she did not have the heart defects or any other issues common to babies with Down syndrome. The small hole (VSD) closed on its own, without the need for surgical intervention; and her blood consistency leveled out on its own without the need for a blood transfusion. She began to breathe room air, eat, and maintain her body temperature without support--these were all answered prayers!

Physical stamina was her biggest challenge; at three weeks old, she was barely able to finish a two-ounce bottle. But she was getting stronger every day, proving to the world she is a fighter and she is here to stay.

Our Tylee was released from the NICU when she was three weeks old.

On July 3rd, 2011 we brought her home and introduced her to the world. That year, July 3rd represented happiness, love, and joy unspeakable. We took photos, ate homemade ice cream, and cuddled on the couch together as a family. That night, it felt as though the colorful firework display was a celebration just for Tylee!

All four of our children were at home. We were together at last, one big happy family! The older boys were so happy to have us home; they had never been away from Micah, and they missed him terribly. They got to hold Tylee for the first time that day. Tears of gratitude trickled down my cheeks as I watched this bonding between brothers and their baby sister. It was beautiful, it was perfect, and it was everything I could want. God blessed our marriage exceedingly, abundantly above all we could ever ask for, hope for, or imagine...just like He promised.

Our family circle was complete, our nest was full, and our hearts overflowed...July 3rd that year was one of the happiest days of our lives.

Chapter 51

PERFECT LOVE

There is no fear in love, but perfect love casts out fear.
~1 John 4:18

We were no longer a typical family. We were now a "special needs" family. The denial stage passed during her long hospital stay, but there were still feelings of disappointment, sadness, and bewilderment. I had accepted the fact our daughter was different, but what does that really mean? I had many more questions than answers. We were beginning to navigate an unknown territory where we would live the rest of our lives.

Several of my friends were pregnant at the same time, and our babies were all due within a few weeks of each other. Tylee was early, so that meant all four of us delivered the same week. All their babies were typical and healthy, but my baby was different.

I was very guarded about telling people. Once we got the results of genetic testing, we told our close family members the outcome, but I wasn't ready to tell everyone. I had failed to produce a genetically perfect baby, and I didn't want others to find out our child was "imperfect." I felt overwhelmed with complicated guilt. I wanted to hide our daughter from the world, not because I was ashamed of her, but because I wanted to protect her from the cruel people in this world who might not see her value.

There was no doubt I loved her fiercely; Max and the boys did, too. But I was scared and unsure what others would think of her.

I knew that disabled people are often marginalized, underestimated, and misunderstood. I was terrified of what Tylee's future may look like. Stereotypical images of various handicapped people flooded my mind and kept me awake with worry at night. Crossed eyes staring blankly into nothingness, large tongues, drooling, adult diapers, and mismatched clothes came to mind. Bad haircuts and hygiene, short and overweight with thick necks, crooked teeth, low set ears, and mental retardation...what if my baby ends up like this?

These disturbing thoughts horrified and terrified me. My thoughts vacillate back and forth like the fan in the corner of the room. I love her, I want her, and I need her, but she scares me. I'm afraid of her. The tears don't stop.

Every parent dreams of the life they expect their child to have. I, too, had great expectations for her and for all my children. I took for granted my children would grow up, go off to college, have a career, get married, and eventually have a family of their own. My expectations for Tylee have come to an abrupt half.

What if she can't do any of those things?

I want Tylee to dance ballet, jazz. and tap. I want her to take piano lessons and play the violin. I want her to be a lifeguard at the city pool like her brother. I want her to make straight As.

I want so much for her, and now I sit with crushed dreams in utter disillusionment. So, I must adjust. I have to change MY desires...now, I hope she can learn how to talk and one day learn to read. I want her to love books as much as I do.

What if she never learns to read?

I decide if she doesn't, I can read to her. I know I can at least do that.

I look up images of children with Down syndrome on the internet because I want to know everything I can. I want to prepare myself for what's coming. I order every book I can find about trisomy 21. We can't afford them, but books are my lifeline.

I decide to throw away all the tiny headbands I bought before she was born; they do not flatter her, so she will always wear a bow instead.

I don't know what to say about her...I don't know whether to tell everyone she has Down syndrome. Do I make a public announcement on Facebook or put that fact on her birth announcements? Or should I even send announcements at all? Maybe I should just wait and see if someone notices? If they do notice, do I say, "This is Tylee, and she has Down syndrome." I think if I don't tell them, then I'm hiding who she is, but I don't know myself yet who she is.

Does her extra chromosome define her? Is it dishonest not to tell people her genetic map looks different from theirs...or to just let them figure it out on their own?

With these questions, doubts, insecurities, and fears, I wrestle day and night and night and day. My thoughts are consumed with what ifs. My other children need me, especially Micah--he's only two. I cry for him, and I wonder if he will get into fights with other children on the playground when he overhears them making fun of his sister.

I know Tylee's brothers would defend her, but I hope they don't have to.

Will one of my sons end up having to assume the responsibility of her one day when Max and I get too old?

I feel isolated and alone. I don't know any other mothers who have a child with special needs. Mothers of typical children cannot relate to me, and I can't relate to them anymore.

I am no longer a typical mother. I have special needs now, too.

Our house becomes like Grand Central Station with the comings and goings of therapists and early intervention specialists over the next three years. I am always behind. I have to have my house picked up and ready for the weekly in-home appointments. Some days I wish everyone would just leave us alone, but I know they are here to help, and I do need their guidance.

One nurse visit early in our journey really helped. I was having a hard time with all the unknowns, and the tears did not stop during her visit. Over time, I began to feel close to these ladies whose job it was to help us navigate all the unknowns at the beginning. As trust built, I confided my inner struggles, and these ladies became a sort of therapist to me.

That day, I was overwhelmed with sadness about what Tylee might look like when she got older and what she may become as an adult. I know it was years and years away, but I still worried. The nurse kindly said, "Tylee will look like you and your husband, just like your other children do. She still has your DNA. She will look like she belongs in your family. She will resemble your other children. And, although she will have a lifelong disability, it doesn't mean she won't be smart and accomplish great things."

Her words encouraged me and lifted my heavy heart.

I had all these images of other people's children who had Down syndrome in my mind, and I had been focused on the stereotypes on the day she reminded me Tylee was a unique individual. I had neglected to consider and needed to be reminded of what I already knew--God has a special plan for Tylee.

Her disability was no surprise to Him. He had a purpose far greater than any of my plans for her could ever be. I just needed to give Him my fears, lay my expectations at His feet, surrender my will, and trust that His ways are always perfect. God would meet every need she would ever have, and it was up to Him to fulfill her destiny.

I remembered the Bible verse that says *He who began a good work would be faithful to complete it.* My job was to lean on Him, trusting Him with her future and ours.

SIDENOTE: I'm sure you will remember that I've been in this place before--the surrender-all part.

After that day, I slowly let go of my expectations and allowed the Lord to give me new ones. I still struggled, but I was adjusting little by little.

Chapter 52

MORE UPS THAN DOWNS

Thank you for making me so wonderfully complex! Your workmanship is marvelous how well I know it.~Psalm 139:14

One day, I was letting my emotions get the best of me; doubts and fears rose up while I was folding a load of laundry. I felt like I was ALWAYS doing laundry! With a husband, two teenagers, a toddler, and an infant, I could hardly keep up. I was feeling sorry for myself as I literally cried over dirty laundry. Micah was playing with a bucket of brightly colored blocks on the floor, and Tylee was taking a nap.

As I carried an armload of clothes I had just removed from the dryer, I tripped over some toys and accidentally knocked over Micah's architectural masterpiece. He cried, I cried, and the commotion woke Tylee, who then cried. I picked her up and laid her on the warm towels fresh out of the dryer. I sat on the floor to help Micah rebuild and then nursed Tylee back to sleep.

Once the disaster was averted, neither of them were still crying...but I was. *God, this isn't what I asked you for!!* I poured my heart out to the Lord. I expressed my anger and told him all of my fears. His response was quick and gentle.

He said to my heart, "You asked me for a healthy baby girl, with blonde hair and blue eyes. A child who would make the world a better place. Isn't that what you asked me for?" I thought for a moment then answered audibly but softly: "Yes, that is what I asked you for."

The Lord then spoke tenderly straight to my heart: "I gave you what you asked for. I gave you a healthy baby with blonde hair and blue eyes, and she WILL make the world a better place." Over the next few hours, God patiently helped me work through the disappointment and pain. He reminded me that Tylee's spirit, just like everyone else's, is eternal. Her physical body and mind will one day be made new. He told me she will teach me more than I could ever teach her.

I realized then that God doesn't compare his children, and I decided that I would never compare her to another child ever again (that's been a tough one!).

God "read" my every thought that day. He reassured me Tylee is a prize--not a punishment--and that I did nothing to cause her disability. He showed me her value far exceeds her abilities and that she is not worth LESS because she is "differently-abled." God loves ALL His children the same.

God told me I should not worry about society's expectations for her or our family. Tylee is fearfully and wonderfully made, and she is a unique individual capable of much more than I can imagine. She is a gift to be treasured, and she will indeed touch the world.

A few nights later, I decided it was time to send out a birth announcement. The Lord gave me a poem about her which I wrote down and included in her birth announcement that we mailed out to family and friends. I'll share it with you now:

Dear family and friends,

We would like to express our heartfelt appreciation for all the love,

support, and kindness shown from all of you during these first few months of Tylee's life. We have had tremendous support and our words could never explain how much it has meant to us.

As most of you know by now, our beautiful baby girl was diagnosed shortly after her birth, with trisomy 21 (Down syndrome). She struggled for several weeks in the Neonatal ICU, but Tylee has already proved she is a fighter! Her name means "God is my might." She has overcome so much and continues to impress us with her determination! Tylee is doing wonderfully, and we fall more in love with her every day.

We have been given a special gift from God in the form of this precious baby girl. Please join us in our continuous celebration of our little girl Tylee Annissa Brielle Monty!

We will raise her to love the Lord her God and to be a blessing to everyone! Please keep her in your prayers. We love you all very much!

Love,

Max, Lee Ann, Zach, Josh, Micah and Tylee

Tylee's Poem

Why all the sadness, why all the tears?

Please give me a chance, let God calm your fears.

For I have a special purpose, He has a wonderful plan.

Before too long you'll see, you'll be my biggest fan!

I'm just like every other baby; I'll need lots of love and care.

And as you get to know me, a special bond we'll share.

As time goes on, you'll know it, I'll laugh, I'll sing, I'll dance and play.

I'll look forward to walking up and embracing each and every day.

I'll learn all I need to know; I'll take it day by day.

I'll show you unconditional love in my own special way.

You'll see your life has changed now, it's better because of me.

My big blue eyes, my contact smiles, oh how happy I will be!

Love me as I am, and soon you will see what a precious gift I am!

Love,

Tylee

Born June 13, 2011, with something "EXTRA" special, trisomy 21

My fears and concerns about how people would react to the news of Tylee's extra chromosomes were quickly put to rest. Our family, friends and people in our community have accepted and embraced Tylee for who she is. We have received so much love and encouragement from everyone, and for that, we are profoundly grateful.

One of the big concerns was related to Tylee's financial future. Max and I were entering our 40's, and we needed to be thinking about retirement. We still had two teenage boys to send to college and a toddler who would grow up to need a college education, too. Tylee's educational, financial, medical, and all other future needs were big unknowns. I began to diligently pray for a way to prepare for Tylee's future.

One day I was browsing boutiques online looking for some cute affordable outfits for Tylee. I didn't end up ordering anything, but God planted an idea in my mind, and then a dream grew in my heart. A new online boutique called Brielle Boutique was born, shortly after Tylee was!

The boutique's sole purpose is to provide a way for Tylee--with the help of her family--to generate her own income when she is an adult. It can take years to build a viable and profitable business, so I wanted to begin building while she is young. As Tylee grows, so will her business. Over the years, we will teach her the ins and outs of running her business, and by the time she is an adult, she could run it with little assistance from us.

Max and I also knew from the beginning that this boutique would expand, and God will use it as a ministry to help others for His glory. We are still learning what that looks like. Just like the poem says, we will take it day by day, leaning on our faithful Lord for strength and guidance.

Eventually, all the questions we had in the beginning did get answered, but there are always more. Although the brunt of the sadness has passed, as I watch her grow, I still get sad from time to time when I think about the many activities, she is unable to do. I think about the girls who excel in academics, gymnastics, pageantry, cheer, or sports. I think about the birthday parties and sleepovers she is excluded from. I long to hear her secrets, her hopes, and her dreams, but she is unable to convey them to me verbally.

I see how much effort Tylee has to put into what comes so easily for most. I watch her struggle to do basic skills like talking, climbing, and writing. She works so hard for her teachers and therapists at school, and sometimes her accomplishments go unnoticed. She tries to express herself, making her wants and needs known, but at times, we just don't know what she is telling us. She has to practice basic skills over and over, but those same tasks, her peers can learn with ease. Her sheer determination amazes me. She is independent, and she finds creative ways of accomplishing her goals.

I pray a lot.

Tylee doesn't learn as fast as other children, so I pray for her teachers, that they will have unlimited patience with her.

Tylee is slow, so I pray for others to look past her slower steps and see the potential she holds.

I pray for the other kids at school, that they will treat Tylee with kindness and that she will not be teased or made fun of by her peers.

Tylee loves to freely share her talents with the world, so I pray for others, that they would embrace her ability instead of her disability.

Tylee has a big heart full of love, so I pray for all who know her, that they would see her through a filter of love and acceptance.

Tylee doesn't understand human cruelty, so I pray for her protection against all harm.

Tylee is beautiful and trusting, so I pray that others would not take advantage of her naivety.

Tylee is vulnerable, so we are fiercely protective of her.

Tylee's passion for life is reflected in her sparkling blue eyes that shine like diamonds.

Tylee is pure sunshine, and she gladly shares it with the world!

Each day, like the American theologian Reinhold Niebuhr, I ask God to "grant me the serenity to accept the things I cannot change, courage to change the things I can, and the wisdom to know the difference."

Chapter 53

ANCHOR OF HOPE

This hope [this confident assurance] we have as an anchor of the soul [it cannot slip and it cannot break down under whatever pressure bears upon it] a safe and steadfast hope that enters within the veil [of the heavenly temple, that most Holy Place in which the very presence of God dwells], where Jesus has entered [in advance] as a forerunner for us, having become a High Priest forever~ Hebrews 6:19-20 AMP

Life was busy for us, and the next three years seemed to fly by. Although we were not perfect, we had each other, and we were happy. A party of six and life could not be more wonderful.

Then came 2014, the year our family would be forever changed, the year one of us would be taken. The year we became five.

Time. It's a master of disguise, an illusion that makes a fool out of all. We live our days carefree and unaware; foolishly thinking there is plenty of it left. We don't know when the granules of sand in someone's hourglass is about to run out. We think there is always more time...until there isn't. The last few granules have slipped quietly by while we are completely unaware, planning for more tomorrows.

Suddenly and without warning, we are harshly slapped in the face with the sobering reality that time has run out. It's gone! It's all gone! No second chances and no going back, for we haven't the ability or the power to turn the hourglass over and start the flow once again.

Numbly we stare into the emptiness while dying inside and longing for more...please God...please...just...a... little...more...time.

This part of the story is by far the hardest to write. As an author and a creator of stories, I desperately want to change OUR story, OUR harsh reality. I want to rewrite the events of that night differently. *God, please...please let me hold the pen! It's all WRONG!* I want to change the ending and keep our family intact. I want to keep a firm grasp on the pen and forbid a devastating loss from rocking us to the core. I wanted a happy-ever-after script to be our family's story.

I hate this plot twist...I HATE IT! I don't want any of us lost-- gone from the face of the earth. How could I have known for one of us, the pen was almost out of ink... there were only a few blank pages left?

How does a day of basking in the sunshine on a lovely afternoon in June with those I love most in all the world turn into the chaos of a hellish nightmare, all in less than twelve hours?

Even though five years have passed, it's still difficult to wrap my mind around what happened. Oh, how I wish it were only a bad dream, I could wake up from. The nightmares of my childhood had stopped, but the nightmare of this June night would live on.

I didn't see it coming. I never really even considered it a real possibility. Hadn't I been through enough loss, pain, and grief already? Hadn't I paid my dues? I had lost three babies, my daddy, and my mother-in-law.

Sorrowfully, I also had to watch my beloved grandmother die right in front of me. I tried everything I could to help her cling to this life a little longer until adequate medical attention could be rendered, but she slipped away into eternity as I begged her to stay.

Yes, I had been through enough in my mind anyway but I was cruelly reminded that the ordinary rhythm of life can be abruptly interrupted by unsuspected tragedy. I had spent the past nineteen years of my life trying to protect my children from any lurking danger, keeping an ever watchful eye on them. But then, unexpectedly, death swooped in like a hungry vulture; and in an instant, one of my beloveds was gone.

My favorite times with all four of the kids was when the six of us were together at home: no agenda, not doing anything special, just spending time together as a family. Zach would get out his ukulele or his guitar and play songs for us. The little ones would dance and be silly while my husband and I captured those fleeting moments in our hearts and on our cameras. Our last day together as six was one of those sort of days. We had just returned home from celebrating my brother-in-law's 50th birthday. There was so much laughter and so much love.

The day before, Zachariah had returned from Ceta Canyon youth church camp, called One Way, which had been the highlight of Zach's summers all throughout his high school years. This was the last year he could go as a "camper" because he had just graduated high school and turned nineteen. All of the summers before, he returned from camp with a renewed relationship with the Lord and many new friends.

But this year when he returned on a Friday, he was set ablaze. He had encountered the Lord on a whole new level; his passion to live for God was rekindled. A spark was ignited deep within his heart, a new fire was fanned into flame, and Zach was ready to conquer the world for Jesus!

After a long day of sunshine and celebration, we were all exhausted and settled in for the night. Zach shared his excitement about being invited to return to camp the following week to be a counselor for the younger kids. He could hardly contain his joy over the opportunity to minister the love of Christ to others. Zach was an influencer, and people were naturally drawn to him. He was immensely popular, smart, and talented; this would be a chance to use his talents for the glory of God!

It was true Zach had many friends, but his favorite friend in the whole world was his younger brother, Joshua. Zach was remarkably close to Micah and Tylee also, and he paid special attention to them to make them think they were his favorite. But there was something undeniably unique and special between the two older boys. They were truly best friends.

Never have I ever known two siblings to be as close as those two boys. The normal quarreling and rivalry between siblings just did not exist with them. Their brotherly bond was strong, and the love they had for one another never faded as they grew. As young boys and eventually teenagers, they were inseparable...until the tragic day they would be separated by a thin veil even a love as pure as theirs could not penetrate.

About 11:00 p.m. Saturday night, Zach and I were sitting on the couch talking about his experiences over the past week at camp. I was getting sleepy after a full day of chasing the little ones underneath the hot summer sunshine. They were tucked safely into bed, and Joshua was already in bed, too. I wanted to stay awake to spend some quiet time with Zach while his clothes swirled around in the washer and dryer. We had one more load to wash and dry to get him re-packed and ready to go back to camp on Monday for another week. I loved those fleeting moments with him.

As I looked into his deep brown eyes while he shared from his heart, I could still see a glimpse of the precious little boy who had grown into a man right before our eyes. Joy and excitement flowed so freely when he spoke. He said, "Mom, one of the youth pastors at camp prophesied over me, and he said, 'God has called and appointed me as a leader.' Isn't that the coolest thing?!? I wrote it in my journal. Here! I'll show it to you!" When he stood up to go get his journal, I marveled at God's grace. I didn't deserve a son like him; in fact, I didn't deserve anything good in my life. But that's where God's grace comes in. Because of Jesus, God gives us good gifts we don't deserve, and He spares us from the punishment we do deserve.

Zach was an easy kid to raise, and honestly, he never gave us a moment's trouble. Yes, he went through the typical teenage orneriness, but he never pushed the limits too far. Overall, he was the model child.

I was not ready for him to be all grown up and headed to college in a few months. Zach was incredibly determined and decisive. He had chosen Texas State University, and that's the only school he applied to. Good thing he was accepted!

Max and I could not have been more proud of him as we stood posed for his high school graduation photos in the high school gym foyer. We all smiled big for the camera and celebrated his accomplishments as that day was frozen in time. If we had only known those would be the last photos we take together as a family of six. The date was May 30th, 2014. We had no idea his hourglass had almost run out.

A late-night text followed by several phone calls changed everything. While Zach and I chatted on the couch, he received a text message from a close friend. Zach excused himself from the room to make a phone call to Jake, who had just texted him. This friend was a friend in need.

Micah had woken up and sleepily walked into the room. He snuggled up next to me on the couch. Zach talked for a few minutes on the phone before coming in and sitting down next to me. He said, "Mom, I need to go. Jake is not in a good place right now. I'm going to go talk to him. I want to spend some time with him and share my experience at camp. He's a spiritual person, but he doesn't know Jesus."

He paused briefly before he continued, "He's really messed up, and I'm worried about him. I don't want to leave for camp again without telling him about Jesus." Who could argue with that? He wanted to go to share Jesus with a friend.

More people need a friend like Zach.

But Micah suddenly looked startled, as if he saw something scary. He lifted his head long enough to say, "Zach, I don't want you to go. Bubba, please don't go...."

As Zach pulled his shoes on, he ruffled Micah's hair and said, "I won't be out too late. I'm going to church in the morning." With that, he leaned down, kissed my cheek and Micah's cheek, and parted with these words: "Love you, buddy. Love you, Mom." Then he walked out into the warm night air, hopped into his car, and drove less than two miles to his friend's house.

That was the last time I heard my son's voice, the last time I saw my son's beautiful face and his radiant smile, and the last time I felt my son's touch. The last time I saw my son alive in his earthly body.

Zach's suitcase was open on his bed. His Bible and his journal lay beside it. Clean clothes were waiting in the dryer to be folded and re-packed. He was almost ready to head back to camp where he would worship his creator. But God had a different destination in mind; the place Zach would be going, he wouldn't need clean clothes, a journal, or his Bible.

No, where he was going, he would be WITH The Word. Zach would be worshiping his creator the giver of life face to face.

Chapter 54

PLEASE DON'T TAKE MY SONSHINE
AWAY

My God, my God, why have You forsaken me? Why are You so
far from saving me, so far from my words of groaning?
Psalm 22:1

At about three o'clock, Jesus called out with a loud voice,
"Eli, Eli, lema sabachthani?" which means "My God, my
God, why have you abandoned me?" Matt 27;46

I almost always waited up for the older boys to get in for the night before I went to sleep. Even though Zach was nineteen and had graduated high school, I still wanted to make sure he was safely at home before I went to bed. I got into bed and started to read, but soon drowsiness overcame me, and I fell asleep. Zach had not planned to be gone long, and I was exhausted, so I laid down to read knowing if I fell asleep, he would wake me up when he got home.

Instead of Zach waking me like I expected, I was awakened by Micah at three o'clock in the morning. He said in a hushed, sleepy voice, "Mommy, I want to sleep in your bed. I had a bad dream. Where's Zach?" It only took a couple of seconds for his question to register. I groggily looked at the clock and then sat up startled with a sick feeling. Where was Zach? Had he come in and woken me up? Did I just not remember because I was so tired?

I jumped up while fumbling for my glasses. I went to Zach's room and flipped on the light. He was not there. I knew he hadn't been there because his suitcase still lay exactly as he left it with his toiletry bag, Bible, and journal still untouched.

Trying to remain calm and telling myself there is nothing to worry about, but knowing in my heart something was terribly wrong, I picked up the landline and tried to call Zach's phone. No answer. I hung up and tried again...still no answer. Starting to feel panicky and dizzy, I went to get my cell phone off the charger so I could text him.

I texted and waited a minute or two for a response. Zach was very considerate and responsible, so he ALWAYS responded or called right back, especially in the middle of the night. I knew if he were able, he would be getting right back to me.

I tried calling his phone again. This time someone answered, but it wasn't the voice I desperately needed to hear.

There was a bunch of background noise so I could not hear the person who answered very well. Did he just say this is Deputy somebody?

"Hello? Hello Zach??"

"No, this is Deputy Clark."

"Deputy who? Guys, this is not funny. Put Zach on the phone now!" I thought his friends were joking around with me.

"Where's Zach? Give him the phone now!!" I pleaded.

"Who is this?"

"I'm Zach's mother. Put him on the damn phone!

"There has been an accident. There was a car wreck. They are working on Zach. He's been injured...."

My mind could not make sense of these words. I was angry and confused. I couldn't comprehend what he was saying even though he was doing his best to explain. The officer went on to say there had been a car wreck, but Zach was not in the car wreck.

Oh, THANK GOD!! I thought, then I said, "Put him on the phone then, please...I NEED to talk to him!"

"Ma'am, he cannot come to the phone. He has been injured because of the accident. He is being worked on."

"Worked on?? Why? If he wasn't in the wreck, how could he be injured!?"

"They are trying to get him stable enough for transport."

Oh my God. Oh my God. Oh my God. Please God. What is happening with my son?!

"Where are they taking him?" I asked.

After a confusing silence, he came back on to say Zach was being transported via ambulance to our small-town hospital. Knowing they were bringing him back to our community hospital--which is not equipped to handle trauma or complicated injuries--gave me a small sense of hope and comfort that Zach would be okay.

I told the officer we would meet them at the hospital and then hung up. Shaking so badly I could barely function, I tried to pray while I walked back to our bedroom to wake Max up.

"Babe, wake up, wake up...Zach is hurt! He's on his way to the ER. Let's go now!" I wanted to say it calmly, but I was frantic and terrified, and there was nothing calm about the entire situation. Max quickly jumped out of bed, pulling on a pair of shorts and a t-shirt. He said, "Tell me what happened."

Stumbling over my words trying to explain, I fumbled around in the semi-darkness looking for some clothes to put on. I don't know what I said. My memory is foggy at this point. I didn't want to wake the little ones or Josh. I wanted them to sleep through this nightmare and wake up to find their brother at home sleeping safely in his bed. But that's not what happened.

As I was trying to describe to Max what I had been told on the phone, he was nervous but calm until I said the part about Zach encountering live electrical wires. That's when Max came completely undone. He knew much more about electricity than I did, and he knew at that moment what I had been unwilling to consider.

He knew our son was likely never coming home.

A gut-wrenching cry from the depths of Max's being, accompanied by a physical reaction of him punching his fist hard against our dresser, sent me into a heap of tears. I didn't want to know what he knew.

All the banging of drawers, crying, and emotional chaos woke up everyone else. I told Josh that Zach had been hurt and was on the way to the ER. I asked him to stay at home with Micah and Tylee while we went to get Zach. He reluctantly agreed to stay home with the littles and pray.

When we tried to leave the house a few minutes later, neither Micah nor Tylee would stay. They both started to cry. Micah was rubbing his eyes and whined, "I want to go get my Bubba. I told him I didn't want him to go." Tylee, being too young to understand, just wanted her mommy. We loaded the little ones in the car, and I told Josh not to worry; Zach was going to be fine and we would all be back home soon.

I didn't mean to lie.

It took us less than two minutes to make the short drive to the hospital. I expected the ambulance to already be there when we arrived. It wasn't.

We arrived to find a bunch of Zach's friends pacing, weeping, and waiting. They were trying to convince themselves this was really happening while trying to convince me Zach was going to make it. Most of them had either been there at the time Zach got hurt or had arrived on scene shortly after. Even though I did not have any details of what had transpired besides knowing what I have already described, it was clear they had been drinking, and several of them were highly intoxicated.

We had not yet learned what had taken Zach to the scene of the car wreck in the first place; these were facts we would not know until later. At the time, none of that mattered anyway. All anyone cared about was whether Zach was going to be alive to tell the story himself.

"Why is it taking so long?? Why aren't they here yet? Why isn't a doctor here yet??" These are questions I demanded answers to while we paced and prayed.

An older nurse who had likely experienced hysterical parents before calmly said, "They have to get your son stable enough for transport. Once they do, they will be here."

Her statement created even more questions for me. "If it's that serious, then why are they bringing him here?? Why not take him to Amarillo or Oklahoma City!?! Why hasn't Lifestar been dispatched? Where is a doctor? I want to talk to a doctor!!!"

I crumbled to the floor in a heap of hot, burning tears.

All of a sudden, I realized I didn't know who had my little ones. "Where are my kids?!?" I cried. Several friends and parents had come, and someone had taken them for a walk. I wanted to hold them. I wanted ALL my babies!!!

I paced the stark, lonely hallways pleading to God in the heavens to let my baby live! I begged and wept until I had no more voice. I spoke to God and reminded him He PROMISED according to Psalm 91 and many other scriptures to watch over my children. I had prayed these prayers over every one of my children since before they were born.

How could this happen? There must be some mix up in the heavens! God, there has been a mistake!! Zach loves you! He went to tell his friend about you! Jesus...why did You let him get hurt??

I commanded Zach to live in Jesus' name, and I firmly rebuked the Spirit of Death. I spoke life and healing over him while they were working on him in the ambulance before he arrived at the hospital. I did everything I knew to do to cover him in prayer.

Chapter 55

DARK NIGHT OF THE SOUL

Maybe I'll wake up tomorrow, but today I'm still dreaming~Zachariah Monty

It seemed like an entire lifetime passed before the headlights of the ambulance carrying our son's lifeless body turned into the driveway with lights flashing and sirens blaring. Time seemed to stop while we watched the ambulance back into the receiving bay of the hospital. The doors swung open and gave us the first glimpse of our son who was no longer clinging to life. We helplessly watched and wailed while the first responders continued CPR. Nurses and our doctor quickly went into action trying to bring our baby back to us.

Completely torn to shreds, we stood by crying while they worked tirelessly to save a young man's life. A young man who was vibrantly healthy and alive only a few hours before. A young man who had his whole life in front of him. A young man who had a bright future. A young man who loved the Lord with all his heart, all his mind, all his strength, and loved others as himself. A young man whose family and friends would be crushed and completely devastated by his loss. A young man who was kind, compassionate, loving, giving, patient, obedient, handsome, talented, strong, smart, and amazing.

A young man who I was certain I could not exist without.

Merciful God, please don't take him!! Please, please let him stay, Lord Jesus, we need him here. Please don't take my sonshine away!!

The doctor stepped out into the hallway and led Max and I into a small room nearby.

Don't you dare say it. Please don't!

Yet he spoke the words I was silently begging him not to say. "There is nothing more we can do. I'm so sorry. Would you like to go spend some time with him?"

The doctor walked us back into the treatment room where they had been attempting what had become impossible. He told the first responders and nurses to discontinue the life-saving protocol; that no further efforts would be necessary. Max and I stood in shock as all attempts to save our son were stopped. The medical staff slowly backed away, leaving us alone with our son who was no longer ours.

I don't know how we had the strength in our legs to stand. Max nor I had any words, only guttural sobs, and gut-wrenching pain overcame us. Was it the pain that gripped our hearts that held us up, refusing to let us fall and forcing us to see?

I gazed down at my boy's long, beautiful eyelashes. I had prayed for those. I touched his ears which the natural color of flesh had drained from, leaving behind a sickening blue color where oxygen no longer flowed.

My hands touched his beautifully tanned chest that had been recently kissed by the golden sun. I felt the indentation left by the hands that tried to make his heart and lungs work again. I felt strange and far away.

I held Zach's large hands, the hands that used to fit perfectly in my own when he was a baby, but now my hands fit perfectly in his. His fingernails were softly rounded like always, but I could no longer see the little white half-moons. They were hidden behind ugly shades of cyan, another reminder that our son was beyond our reach.

I don't know how long we stayed with him. How do you walk away? How do you leave your baby there? How long is long enough? When do you say "Okay, you can call the funeral director now"?

I knew Zach was with Jesus; the way his body was so unnaturally still, his spirit had to be soaring high above in the heavens. I knew he was more alive now than he had ever been on this earth, but the fact he was alive in heaven, completely beyond our reach while Max and I stood there dying, was blaring into the silence, reducing us to dust.

While we were in with Zach, our precious Joshua had somehow gotten word his brother, his closest friend in the world, the one he had shared his childhood with, was badly hurt. He did not wait for us to return home to pick him up. When Josh heard, he ran into the night desperate to get to the hospital.

In sheer terror, his shaky wobbly legs carried him through the darkness of night to Zach. Heaving from running, Josh collapsed into our arms as his daddy looked into his tearful eyes to deliver the most devastating news of his life.

"Joshua, I'm so sorry. Honey, Zach is gone. You're the big brother now." Joshua, unable to stand on his own, embraces my husband. He buries his head in Max's shoulder and the two of them heave and sob as one. I hear Josh saying, "NO, NO, NO!"

I cannot protect my children from this. I want to spare them. I don't want this to be their reality. My focus has to bounce like a ping pong ball. I am sickened, heartbroken, and worried about all of us.

Just as the sun was coming up to announce a new day, we, a torn and irreparably broken family of five, walked out of the hospital into a new existence of heartbreak and loss. Our nightmare had followed us into a new day, and the day after that, and the day after that.

Nothing made sense. It felt like a terrible, horrible, awful nightmare we couldn't wake up from. I collapsed onto the oversized leather chair in the living room where Zach always sat. "I don't know how or if we can even survive this. What has happened to our family?" I said aloud but to no one, as I sat motionless, trying to figure out what to do next.

UFO's could have landed in our front yard and taken us all hostage, and I would not have been more shocked. There were calls to make and arrangements to be made, but I didn't think any of it was physically possible. I couldn't see through the tears, my head was pounding, my throat was parched, and I could not find words. I couldn't get my bearings, my lungs couldn't take in enough air, and I felt like I was suffocating in grief. My heart was so broken I didn't think it could continue beating to keep me alive. I didn't care if it did, anyway. I wanted to go to sleep and never wake up.

I felt like I was dying, and I welcomed it.

My mind reeled trying to fathom the unthinkable that has happened...to us. *Did it really happen? Is this real? Were we really that family now? The family that soon everyone in town would be talking about and feeling sad for? NO!!*

We cannot be going through this. Zach had never even had more than a scratch on him in his entire life. Never a broken bone, never any stitches, no major cuts, or bruises; how could his very first visit to an emergency room be his last?

Zach was healthy and strong. I just talked with him a few hours before. He was full of life! I had done my job well. I had kept him safe for nineteen years and now this! *Why, Zach??*

My mind flashed back to an hour ago while we were in the emergency room with him. His body was perfectly intact after the accident. He honestly didn't even look injured; he looked perfectly fine to me, like he was just sleeping. He wasn't cut or bruised or banged up or burned. The only evidence of the trauma was small circular exit wounds on his hand and the bottoms of his feet. The cyan color of his fingernails and ears were the only other indicators anything out of the ordinary had happened.

Is he really dead? I was there, and my husband was there when

Zach took his first breath, but he had taken his last breath on the side of a dark road, in the middle of nowhere, without his dad or me. I wasn't with him when the angels carried him away to a place I can't follow. Maybe it didn't really happen...*God, please tell me it didn't really happen*! I don't want death written into our story.

I continued to sit dazed and confused, afraid to move while my husband started making the difficult calls to inform our families. I could hear Max's words muffled by shock and sobs saying almost the same thing to each person he called, but I don't remember the words he said to them so early on a Sunday morning. I silently prayed God would give him the strength to keep making the calls. I knew I couldn't do it.

Word quickly spread throughout town, and within a half hour, neighbors and friends started showing up at our door. No one knocked or rang the doorbell; they just slipped in quietly to sit with us in our overwhelming, unthinkable grief.

The announcement was made in all the church services around town, so before noon our home was filled with food, flowers, and more love and compassion than we could contain. I have never experienced that kind of love demonstrated in my entire life. God was very present with us during this most difficult time. He so lovingly showed up through our family and friends. They swooped into action becoming His hands and feet. I will never ever forget the comfort we felt from the tremendous outpouring of love God sent to our home that day and many other days to come.

For many of Zach's friends, this is their first encounter with the unthinkable cruelness of death. They have lost one of their own, and now they wander around our home lost. We all huddle together, attempting to hold one another upright, our tears mingling. Faces are contorted with the various looks of shock, grief, and disbelief. Bewilderment seized us all.

I only remember bits and pieces about that day when everyone from near and far arrived to surround us, to hold us together, and to shower us with kindness. I know I was present and awake--I know I was sitting, sometimes motionless-zombie like, and sometimes rocking as if I was holding an imaginary baby.

But my arms were empty, and my heart was hollow. It felt surreal, like I was outside of my body, watching from a safe distance but still somehow nearby. I think God knew I couldn't take it in all at once--only little by little. The sudden unexpected onslaught of pain was killing me softly. I realized a part of me had died with Zachariah.

People moved mechanically around us, fixing food, taking care of our littles, answering the constant ringing phone, and managing the continuous flow of grievers. Late that night, the crowd dispersed leaving us alone in our sadness for the first time. It was just us five because one of us was missing; the absence of Zach's presence was as thick as fog.

Somehow, we made it through Sunday, the first day. The first day Zach's siblings had ever lived a day without him. My heart breaks over and over for them; for us, for his friends, and for our tight-knit community.

Late Sunday night, Max and I finally retreated to our bedroom, the first time we would be alone since the trajectory of our lives careened out of control. We were on an unpredictable, terrifying roller-coaster ride screaming through the night. We held on to each other with all our might; neither of us really sure we would make it through this ride intact. We could not speak, for the pain was too intense and the grief too raw. We are together, but so totally alone. We sob into the other, beyond broken...neither one of us is strong enough to bear this load. Only by the grace of God did we survive that night, and the next, and the next. There was only one set of footprints visible in the sand because Jesus had to carry us all.

Exhaustion finally wins that night, and we fall into fitful bouts of sleep. We don't care if the sun ever rises again, because even when it does, our world is still dark, cold, and empty.

Chapter 56

SHATTERED

I cry endlessly for you but I promise, I won't let the tears erase the smiles you have given me. I promise I won't waste this unrelenting pain. ~Lee

I didn't know it was possible to cry while doing almost anything, but now I know it is. I cried through my morning shower, while getting dressed, and while trying to drink a cup of coffee that's gone cold. I can't eat even though my sister tries to coax me to take a few bites. I just can't. I am a zombie, an outsider in my own home. The tears don't stop. I don't think they ever will. The world is foreign, huge, and scary now. We are not safe.

People are coming and going. Some stay for an extended time, but others can't stand this pain, so they offer what they can and leave. I don't blame them. Death is ugly and scary, and I want to leave, too.

Food, dishes, paper goods, ice chests, fans, sympathy cards, toys and stuffed animals for the littles, boxes of Kleenex, flowers, and plants are everywhere. I don't keep track of any of it. I know I should because I will want to thank them for their kindness later, but I can't move. One of my friends keeps track; she writes it all down for us.

My eyes see the people who love us moving around, doing tasks

I should be doing. They are guests in my home, but I am frozen in place with a million jagged ice daggers stabbed through my heart. I sit rocking and crying while others take care of everything.

Some tasks others can do for us, but there are the important dreaded things we must do ourselves. We are the parents. It is our son who needs a casket.

I shudder at the thought. All of it sickens me. I am wrapped in anguish. I collapse from the pain. I scream, "WHY GOD?? I thought you loved us!!"

I battle paralyzing thoughts that remind me of my past and tell me this is all my fault. I'm being punished for my sins. I begin to doubt and question the goodness of God. If He is REALLY good, then why did He let this happen to Zach? I don't want to spend my life being jealous of other parents whose kids survived that night. I don't want to resent them or hate God.

I don't understand how there were so many people at that scene, and it was OUR son who was killed! Why was Zach singled out? Why did he have to die? I don't want this to be my life.

I hate me. I hate everyone. I hate my life. I just hate.

The pendulum of emotions swings haphazardly back and forth. One minute, I see how God is with us: hovering, comforting us, providing for us, and carrying us. But the next minute, I am angry, raging against Him, mad He allowed this to happen, and pissed He didn't STOP it! *YOU COULD HAVE INTERVENED...oh God, why didn't you?!* I want to sit in His lap and be a little girl. I need Him to hold me close, but at the same time, I want to scream at Him, pounding his chest and running as far as I can get away from Him. I am an emotional train wreck.

Do we really have to go to the funeral home and make burial arrangements for our firstborn? How do parents who were planning to send their son to church camp that day find themselves sitting numb and dumb in the local funeral home? I had nine months to prepare for his birth; how is it even possible to plan for a burial in only a few days?

Caskets and obituaries are for old people who have lived out their days and are ready for this life to be over; not for nineteen year olds who were unfairly struck down by a random turn of events in the prime of their lives!

Later that day, when we arrive at the funeral home, we are not yet able to see our son's empty shell. They tell us he is not ready for "viewing" yet. Where is my son?? Did he spend the night on a cold, steel, silver gurney while we were warm in our beds?

Oh Jesus, help! I am failing miserably at keeping the morbid, incessant thoughts at bay. I need to clear my head...I want to tear my hair out and run screaming into the parking lot, but I don't. I sit quietly and try to think of the best way to honor and memorialize my precious son. Max and I are led to a conference room and seated at a large table to begin the preparations.

I don't like the word "funeral," so we decide to call it a Celebration of Life. It sounds better, even though I hate that, too.

I'm reeling. I'm lost in a foreign county, like we've just been dropped off, abandoned somewhere desolate, strange, and God-forsaken. I don't speak this language. I can't understand what I'm hearing. *WE ARE NOT SUPPOSED TO BE HERE,* I scream silently for no one to hear.

The funeral director is talking and speaking clearly, but my focus wanders. He sounds like Charlie Brown's teacher...blah blah blah...blahhhh. He is professional and patient with us; I know he has had many similar conversations with other families.

He gives us a list of belongings to gather at home. He says we should bring clothes back later today so he can get Zach dressed. How will we decide what Zach will wear? He was so particular about his clothes. What if we pick what he wouldn't want to wear? I decided to let Joshua and his friends help me.

Next, the funeral director advises us to select photos for a slideshow. Somehow, we are expected to condense a lifetime of love and joy into a slim column of facts for an obituary. How can his entire life of birthday parties, holidays, ball games, vacations, and everyday events of just over nineteen years possibly be reduced to a fifteen-minute slideshow?

Now Max and I have to pick a time and a date in the very near future to lay our boy to rest. We need to rush a bit, so we won't interfere too much with everyone's 4th of July plans. People will want to return to their normal lives and celebrate Independence Day with their families.

It feels like we will never celebrate anything EVER again! Why did Zach have to die so close to one of his favorite holidays? Why did he have to die at all?

Max and I chose the date. We settled on July the 3rd. I remember when this date used to be a happy day. That's the date three years ago when we brought Tylee home from her extended stay in the NICU. Now this July 3rd would represent grief, sadness, and loss--a day of goodbyes.

The day when we bury our oldest son.

Now the funeral director leads us to a large showroom floor where caskets of various types, colors, and sizes are on display. *Oh God...please help us. How is it even possible to choose one of these metal boxes for our son? I hate them all. I don't want any of them!! I don't want Zach anywhere near here! He had his whole life ahead of him--what the hell happened?! Please God, help me be strong...we cannot do this without You, Lord.*

When Max and I finished making the arrangements, we drove home in a confused daze. Our small home was even more crowded with loved ones. More people arrive to offer their sympathy, but no one knows what to say. What can they say? They want to be helpful, but we can see they are hurting, too. As I start down the hall, I hear one of Zach's classmates wailing uncontrollably from his bedroom. It's my responsibility to comfort him, but I don't know how. I don't know how to do any of this.

The absence of Zach's presence impacts us all. We are thankful for this mass of people who are here to grieve with us. How will we ever be able to show enough gratitude for all they are doing to help us navigate this darkness? I don't think we ever can.

The next day, we try to mentally prepare to go see our first born now that he is ready for viewing; except we don't know how to do this next hard thing either. *Do we take Micah and Tylee to see their brother? What about Josh... what will this do to him?*

I remember when Zach was born. We were so nervous to bring him home from the hospital. We were not confident in our ability to take care of a living infant. Now we are confident we DO NOT have the ability to care for him in death. How will we keep our composure when we see our son's body resting in a casket?

What if I lose my mind? What if I freak out and lose control? What if I start screaming and never stop? What if I can't leave him there? I'm lost...I don't know how to comfort my husband and my three other children. I can't do this.

OH God, I can't do this! How do we prepare our children, especially Joshua and Micah, to see their brother's deadness on display? How do you explain death to a five- year old?

We stumble around in the utter darkness of grief. Our beautiful son is now dressed in the clothes we've selected for him to wear. Zachariah looked so peaceful lying there. I fought the urge to shake him. I resisted begging him to wake up. Instead, I silently pleaded with God to raise him, all the while knowing in my heart the answer is still no.

I floated mindlessly between bewilderment, anger, denial, and confusion trying to make sense of an unbelievable tragic turn of events that has completely flattened us. I relate to my Lord and Savior

Jesus when He cried out in a loud voice as his physical body was close to death. "My God, my God, why have you forsaken me?"

Even though we resisted with all of our might, July 3rd arrived. The high school gymnasium was where we gathered with family and friends to say our goodbyes to Zach. None of our community churches were large enough to accommodate the crowd of mourners who came to honor our son.

We had been to this place where our son played basketball many times before. I would give anything to be gathered here to cheer for the home team again...instead we are gathered for our son's funeral.

In this same foyer, we stood only one month before with happy tears. With Zachariah proudly wearing his cap and gown, we posed for graduation photographs and celebrated his accomplishments. Now, I am looking at a casket--MY son's casket-- positioned in the exact place where Zach stood with us smiling broadly and beautifully. He was so alive only days ago.

There were no seats unfilled. People stood in the back and spilled out into the foyer. I am beyond grateful for all who showed up to honor our son. Once the service was concluded, we stayed seated while rows upon rows upon rows of people were escorted into the foyer where the casket was positioned for all to see Zach for the last time.

As his friends and family members leaned in to kiss him or to whisper one last secret Zachariah would literally take with him to his grave, I prayed for peace and comfort to surround them all. When the last of the mourners filed past to pay their respects, we were led into the very halls where he had walked and laughed with friends throughout his high school years.

Suddenly, I can hardly stand. I'm stunned and sickened to the core. I feel like I will pass out at any moment. My head is swirling. I'm lightheaded. I want to crawl into the casket and lay there with my baby boy.

We eased our way over to where Zach's body was beautifully displayed in front of the trophy case. I want to rewind time to about a month ago when we stood in this exact spot, smiling for the camera so a few of our precious moments could be frozen in time on senior college day.

Dear God, please hold us...Jesus, help! We need strength! We cannot do this without You.

As the crowd waited outside just beyond the glass doors, I leaned on my husband, our sixteen-year-old son Josh, a few dear friends, and Jesus to get through those moments. The walls seemed to sway. How I stayed upright, only God knows. I cling to Max and our three children who are living this nightmare, too.

I realize people have been standing for quite some time outside in the scorching sun. They are waiting for us to emerge from the gym. Out of consideration, I know we only have a few minutes left with Zach before they will close the lid for the final time.

Oh God, I don't know if I can let them close it!

I don't want to look away from Zach. I want to stay with my son forever; no, I want him to stay with us! I held his hands. I kissed his handsome face, leaving my lipstick prints behind and not wiping them away. I want my kisses to be sealed up with him.

My heart is shattered, and I can't understand why it's still beating. I brush my fingers across his long, beautiful eyelashes, and I thank God once again for answering my prayers about his eyelashes.

I am desperate to memorize his face. I want him to open his eyes! I want to hear him laugh...*Oh my God, how will I exist without his laughter?*

If I survive, Lord, you will have to make it so...I'm dying.

Zach's navy-blue Hollister t-shirt is now tear-stained. I circled the tear drops with my fingertips, knowing each one represented a story or memory from one of his family or friends who have loved him, too.

I leave his shirt and face covered with an ocean of my fresh, salty tears.

Suddenly, I know I want a few of his soft brown curls to be cut from his hair. I have some of his curls from his first haircut tucked safely away in his baby book. I want to add his last curls to his book. I go to the funeral director and ask him to please trim some curls before he closes him in. He says he will.

I want to stop time. I don't want the next part to happen. I don't want the lid on my son's life closed forever.

We finally walk away, knowing the next part must come. We step outside where friends and family from close by and those from far away wait in a line to grieve with us. It took several hours for everyone in the line to get to us, but they waited, while being scorched by the blazing sun, to offer their condolences. No one knew what to say or do. They just clung to us and cried knowing that their gift of standing with us in our grief would have to be enough...and it was.

Before we left for the cemetery, we watched as Zach's classmates released a huge bouquet of balloons with messages of love for him written on them. All eyes were fixed on the balloons as they floated away higher and higher. Soon everyone one of them disappeared into the heavens, leaving the sky as empty as our hearts were that day.

It's time to drive to the cemetery in a long procession. We are driving to the small plot of land we purchased a few days ago to lay our son to rest. I don't know if I can let them lower him into the dark hole that has been prepared to receive him. *Please make it stop! I don't want this to be real!! I can't breathe.*

I ask God why He took Zach back so soon. I used to think giving birth was painful, but now I know the twenty-eight-hour labor and delivery was easy... giving Zach back is excruciating.

We heaved and sobbed inside the car as we followed close behind the shiny black hearse leading the procession of mourners to the cemetery. I'm looking out the side window to avert my focus away from the black car slowly taking my son to his final resting place. I'm praying, pleading with God for strength and comfort.

I am worried sick about my husband and other children. *How will Joshua live without his brother and best friend?* I am trying to be present for them, but I really just want to be absent from all of this.

As I write this paragraph, I can still vividly picture a young girl's face streaked with tears, distorted in pain as she stood with us near the grave. She was one of Zach's best friends, and she was visibly shaken to her core. I wanted to go to her and wipe away her tears and pain. I wanted to reassure her everything was okay...but I couldn't because it wasn't.

I looked around in dismay but in awe of the depths of love this crowd represented for Zachariah. Hours and hours of hot sun before, after, and now as we closed the graveside portion of the service. I don't have words to express how thankful we are for those who endured the pain with us.

The service concluded, and I was escorted away from the grave and taken to our car. Someone brought Micah and Tylee to me. I was driven back to our home where people were gathered to comfort us.

Max and Joshua stayed at the grave with Zach's pall bearers who were also his closest friends They each lovingly took part in the burial. By the sweat of their brow, as their tears moistened the red clay beneath their feet, they shoveled dirt on the shiny navy-blue casket until it was completely covered. They stood with Zach until the last bit of earth was replaced.

Finally, at sunset, they could say in unison, "It is finished." The tent was torn down, the green turf was rolled up, and the chairs were hauled away. They cried until their eyes ran dry, and their parched throats begged for drink. A mound of brownish-red Texas dirt covered with colorful flowers was where they parted ways leaving behind a son, a brother, a cousin, a best friend...and a lifetime of memories.

From the moment Zachariah was born, a light entered our lives. When he was a toddler, I taught him the children's song "This Little Light of Mine." He would hold up his chubby pointer finger to represent "his light" and sing loud enough for all to hear: "This little light of mine, I'm going to let it shine, let it shine, let it shine, let it shine!"

And he did. Zach's light shined. It shined brightly enough to light the way for others. Just after midnight, on June 29th, that light was suddenly extinguished, and my oldest, beloved "sonshine" was taken away.

We found out later there was a party that night. There was drinking. There were intoxicated teenagers trying to make it home by curfew. There was a car wreck. There were fearful classmates too afraid to call proper authorities or parents. There was a frantic phone call made to Zach who had not been at the party, who had not been drinking, and who had not been in the car accident.

There was a fatality at the scene of the car wreck.

The victim was Zachariah.

When Zach got the call from two girls with whom he had just graduated, he did not hesitate to jump into the car and drive himself and one of his friends to the scene which was about twenty miles from town. He stopped the car on the side of a country road. Without even thinking of his own safety, he opened the door and stepped out of the car to help the girls.

Zach immediately encountered live electrical lines which had been brought down when the girl's car crashed into a power pole. There on that dark road, Zachariah lost his life. He willingly responded when he could have said, "Call someone else."

The Bible verse John 15:13 says, "Greater love has no man than this, that a man lay down his life for his friends."

Love for his friends took him out of the safety of home that night and into danger. Love drove him to that scene. Love Himself was waiting there to take Zach to his Heavenly home.

Zachariah taught us some unforgettable lessons. I would sum them up like this.

Zach lived life to the fullest every day, making the most of each moment he was given.

Zach lived on purpose without regret.

Zach never wasted a single day.

Zach put others before himself.

There's a difference between *purpose* and *potential*. Some would say Zachariah did not have a chance to fulfill his potential on this earth and unfortunately, they would be correct; he did not fulfill his *potential*. His potential was beyond measure.

But...I believe with all my heart Zach's *purpose* was fulfilled. The purpose he was predestined and created for by God was fulfilled. I don't begin to understand, but I know God doesn't take us to Heaven one second before He knows it's time.

Zach did fulfill his purpose...and in doing so...he changed mine.

You see, I only *thought* his light went out that night. Now, I've realized it didn't. Zachariah is shining brighter than he ever has before, just from further away. On a dark road that night, Zach didn't lose his life--he is more alive now than ever! He just crossed over and stepped into his shine! He lives among the angels in a place called Heaven, where there is no darkness, no tears, no pain, no sickness, and no sorrow. A place where LOVE dwells...and now Zach dwells there, also.

And HOPE holds us together while we wait.

Chapter 57

INTO THE LIGHT

"Within you is the light of a thousand suns."~Robert Adams

The haunting memories of that night are forever cemented in our minds. When Zach died, a part of each of us died, too. An irreplaceable member of our family ran ahead of us to go live with Jesus. Our family was forever changed in the blink of an eye.

We will always have an empty chair at our table, no matter how many loved ones are gathered around close. We will always be a family of six, but now we are a party of five. Our hearts are beyond broken. Zachariah Tyler is missing from our presence but etched on our hearts for all eternity.

My heart has never known such sorrow.

When our family was hurled into dark and unknown territory, we stumbled around in the darkness, getting all banged up and bruised on rocky terrain for many long months. We longed for normalcy, wanting just one day without the stabbing, throbbing pain of loss.

We were desperate to find level ground. Each of us was forced to carry our share of the heavy weight of grief; not even young Micah or Tylee were exempt. Even now, I break all over again every time I see one of them struggling to keep their head above the turbulent waters.

Our family was forced to totally abandon the ship of smooth sailing and plunged into the rough waters in the sea of grief; tossed to and fro on the unrelenting waves where sadness, sorrow, pain, and grief wrote themselves into our story.

But we found we are not alone in these murky waters. Our lifeguard, Jesus, walks on water. He knows how to swim, and He knows how to get us to shore.

In knowing "the One" who holds the universe in His hands is also holding on to us, we can withstand these waves another day. God gently reminds us we are not alone on this journey of life after grief. Our loving heavenly Father is right there in the midst of it with us. He never leaves us for a second. We know we are securely held. There is unexpected joy, unfathomable peace, and unending love in the midst of the storm. We are safe in His capable hands. We trust Him, even when we don't understand...even when the answer is no.

There is purpose in the pain; there is a greater plan.

The night Zachariah went to live with Jesus, I vowed before leaving the hospital that with God's help, I would not waste a moment of this pain. Somehow, someway...if God would show me how, I would use my story the good, bad, and ugly to help others and bring Him glory.

So, when feelings of despair and depression tried to overtake me, as they often did, I began to fight back against them. There were many days when I did not want to get out of bed--when I wanted to die because my heart hurt so badly. Every day, though, I made the decision to *not* let these horrible, unwanted circumstances dull my shine. Instead of succumbing to the pain and living in the grief, I have allowed this lonely road of sorrow and anguish to transform me into someone who was strong enough to speak the truth.

And in His faithfulness, God began a healing transformation in me that continues to this day. I soon realized the strength to do hard things does not lie within me. No, I could not do any of this on my own, but hand-in-hand with Jesus, I could and did weather the storms.

The tedious journey of inner healing has required me to reveal the dark secrets I had been protecting for over twenty years. I cried out to Jesus multiple times to give me the courage to tell Max. In the quiet hours I spent with Jesus, He assured me that He had been preparing Max for this reveal and that it would be okay. And when the timing was right, He did give me that courage. Many tears were shed the day I finally opened my closet full of skeletons and let them spill out for Max to see. But Jesus was right. He had prepared Max and reminded me once again that I could trust Him...and as He promised, it was okay.

The fact you are reading these very words is evidence God is using for good what the enemy meant for harm.

Grief has done its work in my heart and soul. It has helped me become more sensitive to the pain of others. I can easily recognize a broken heart, and that brokenness compels me to reach out. Tears of compassion and empathy overwhelm my heart when others are hurting. I can hear the silent anguish-filled cries, and that pain resonates deep within my soul. Finally, now, I am strong enough to help others and am determined to do so.

In this, I have found my purpose.

You see, for all these years, I have been too afraid and ashamed to tell anyone my past and my story. And that's the goal of our worst enemy, Satan, who wants to keep us isolated and quiet. He likes it best when we cower in fear and stay hidden under the weight of shame and guilt.

But during the months of learning to live "life after death," God started showing me the way out from the guilt that had kept my lips sealed until now. That's when the Lord asked me to write my story-- ALL of it--and freely share it with everyone. I had promised it the night Zach went to heaven, and now God was asking me to follow through. God is a gentleman, though, and He never forces us to do anything against our will. When He asked, I said "yes."

Some say time heals all wounds, but I disagree. Earlier in these pages, I mentioned time is a master of disguise and an illusion that makes a fool out of all. Time only puts distance between you and the tragedy which *lessens* the pain, but it never heals. Only Jesus alone can heal our brokenness.

In the first lines of this book, I told you hopelessness can creep up while we are making our best attempt at traveling this road called life. When you least expect it, despair has a cruel way of sneaking in to rob your peace and steal your joy, reminding you of all that has been lost. Those self-defeating whispers threaten to undo the progress you have made and knock you off course.

But thankfully, I have learned the secret, and I want to share it with you now. You *can* talk back; in fact, you can shout if you need to! Those whispers will stop mid-sentence every time if you interrupt them with the TRUTH of God's word!

Allow me to paraphrase one of my favorite scriptures, Rev 12:11. It says we overcome our enemy (and his taunting whispers) with the WORDS of our TESTIMONY! That's great news! You can talk back to the devil, and according to James 4:17, when we submit to God and resist the devil, he WILL FLEE from us!

I can trace the enemy's lies all the way back to my childhood as a young, innocent girl. My doll, Bananas, was flawed and ugly, but I loved her dearly, despite her appearance. And just like Bananas, God loves you and me no matter what we have been through or what we look like on the inside or outside. Maybe I could relate to her more than my other dolls because even at the age of four, I already felt ugly and broken. And that's when it "started with a whisper" --whispers of shame, doubt, fear, abandonment, and many others when I was just beginning life. And if I'm guessing, the same is true for you, too. I bet you can remember times you felt unworthy, ashamed, inadequate, helpless, or hopeless. You see, my friend I can fondly call you that now because you have walked with me through my most difficult times--you have an enemy, too. He's the same deceitful enemy as mine.

This enemy of your soul, the devil, wants you to believe his lies and they are lies because there is no truth in him. He wants you to quit and give up; his job is to *wear you out*. But you DO have a choice.

You do not have to believe those lies. You can escape from the weight of hopelessness, lift the veil of shame, break free from the torment of fear, calm the sea of despondency, and leave the desolate place of brokenness once and for all! Sister, you do not have to stay there for another minute. I can introduce you to the ONE who holds the keys to your freedom.

Our rescuer's name is Jesus...and He loves you and me unconditionally. There is nothing you have done or could ever do in the future that will make Him reject you. He wants to set you free from the pain of your past and the bondage of sin. He is the only one who can. Trust me, I know.

Now when those whispers--the ones that used to defeat me and render me helpless--try to sell me their lies, I simply don't buy them anymore! It took practice and diligence, but I can recognize them easily, no matter what disguises they wear. I've heard them all and believed them all, but now I KNOW the TRUTH, and He is the WAY out. He freely gives a new LIFE to all who ask.

Through it all, I have learned that-

FAITH trusts.

HOPE believes.

LOVE abides.

JOY awaits and these promises come in many forms.

There is joy in the laughter of children.

There is comfort in the arms of a loved one.

There is love and support from friends and family both near and far.

There is PEACE that passes all understanding, that guards our hearts and minds in Christ Jesus.

Wherever you find yourself at this very moment no matter the circumstances, whatever you are fighting for or fighting against always remember there is beauty in your ashes.

If you are like me, having loved and lost or faced great disappointment and heartache, I have a special word of encouragement for you...

You have what it takes.

You are stronger and more courageous than you think.

There is HOPE for your tomorrows because the best is yet to come!

Please give your broken heart to the Lord Jesus Christ. I promise, He will free you from the bondage that has anchored you for so long. You were made to soar like an eagle, high above the storms of life, and with Him...you, too, can "REIGN IN HOPE."

Letter In Closing

Dear Reader,

I hope that my story has touched your heart or maybe even inspired you to keep going when you feel like giving up. God has planted seeds of greatness in you that are getting ready to burst open with new life! Water them with the Word of God. Allow the "Son" to nurture them, and they will grow beyond anything you can think, hope, or imagine!

It would be my honor to connect with you beyond the confines of this book. You can visit www.reigninhope.com or www.leeannmonty.com to watch a short video message that I recorded especially for you! Additionally, you will find words of inspiration, encouragement, hope and life nuggets to help you thrive in the face of adversity! If you have a prayer request, a praise report or just need a place to share what's on your heart-I invite you to leave me a message. I'm a prayer warrior, I would love to pray for you.

I am here to support you. I look forward to hearing from you!

With love!

Lee Ann Monty

ABOUT THE AUTHOR

With over three decades of life and educational learning, Lee Ann Monty has a uniquely genuine voice that shines through in her newest tell all book on love and redemption. Lee Ann's life filled with hardships, overcoming difficult trials, and surviving significant loss inspired her to write this book to empower others through crises. She believes the heart of every person has seeds of greatness. Those seeds combined with optimism, courage, grace, and purpose can be cultivated into a personally fulfilling life and legacy for those to come.

Her sheer determination intermingled with a positive mindset and a strong Christian faith has shaped her into the woman of courage she is today. Lee Ann's personal life experiences have molded her into a caring, loving, and understanding mentor and life coach. She shares her powerful and inspirational story of triumph over trials at conferences and events. Lee Ann is a #1 international best selling author, speaker, and proudly co-owns a boutique with her daughter.

Lee Ann and her husband Max have been married for twenty-eight years and live in Texas. They have four amazing children: Zachariah - who lives in heaven, Joshua, Micah and Tylee.

You can connect with Lee Ann at reigninhope.com, leeannmonty.com or on Facebook at facebook.com/leeannmonty.

www.ingramcontent.com/pod-product-compliance
Lightning Source LLC
Chambersburg PA
CBHW060005100426
42740CB00010B/1399